Enforced Disarmament

From the Napoleonic Campaigns to the Gulf War

PHILIP TOWLE

CLARENDON PRESS · OXFORD

1997

Oxford University Press, Great Clarendon Street, Oxford OX2 6DP

Oxford New York

Athens Auckland Bangkok Bogota Bombay
Buenos Aires Calcutta Cape Town Dar es Salaam
Delhi Florence Hong Kong Istanbul Karachi
Kuala Lumpur Madras Madrid Melbourne
Mexico City Nairobi Paris Singapore
Taipei Tokyo Toronto
and associated companies in
Berlin Ibadan

Oxford is a trade mark of Oxford University Press

Published in the United States
by Oxford University Press Inc., New York

British Library Cataloguing in Publication Data
Data available

Library of Congress Cataloging in Publication Data
Data applied for

ISBN 0-19-820636-4

1 3 5 7 9 10 8 6 4 2

Typeset by Vera A. Keep, Cheltenham
Printed in Great Britain
on acid-free paper by
Bookcraft Ltd., Midsomer Norton
Nr. Bath, Somerset

Acknowledgements

This book has benefited greatly from a number of university departments and institutions which have invited me to discuss my ideas on enforced disarmament. I am particularly grateful to Professor Mark Zacher of the Institute of International Relations at the University of British Columbia, Professor Brian Bond and Dr Michael Dockrill of the Institute of Historical Research at London University, Dr Bruce Hoffman of the Department of International Relations at the University of St Andrews, Professors Derek Beales and Tim Blanning of the Modern History Seminar at Cambridge University, Dr Glyn Stone and Dr Ted Johnson for their arrangements at the Second Pan-European Conference on International Relations in Paris, the convenors of the British International History Seminar in Southampton in September 1995, and Mr Nigel de Lee of the Department of War Studies at the Royal Military Academy, Sandhurst. I would also like to thank Dr Zara Steiner of New Hall College, Cambridge, Professor Jeremey Black of Exeter University, Professor Richard Langhorne of Rutgers University, Mr David Fischer, formerly of the International Atomic Energy Agency, and various officials in the Foreign and Commonwealth Office for reading and commenting on individual chapters. I am most grateful to Tony Morris and the staff of Oxford University Press for their helpful guidance and encouragement. I am, of course, alone responsible for the errors which remain in the text. Without the assistance of the Public Record Office at Kew, the National Archives in Washington, and the University Library in Cambridge this work would have been impossible.

Contents

Tables

Abbreviations

ACDA	Arms Control and Disarmament Agency (US)
IAMCC	Inter-Allied Military Control Commission
IAEA	International Atomic Energy Agency
IISS	International Institute for Strategic Studies
NATO	North Atlantic Treaty Organization
NPT	Non-Proliferation Treaty
SIPRI	Stockholm International Peace Research Institute
UNIDIR	United Nations Institute for Disarmament Research
UNSCOM	United Nations Special Commission

Introduction

> When they say, as they said before and will say again, that
> collectively, as a nation, they must be equal with ourselves
> and that 'equality' implies an equality of arms, then a man
> who has renounced vengeance and is undeluded by ideologies,
> even by his own, will know what answer to give . . . It would
> be an expense of spirit to hate them meanwhile, but suicide to
> trust them.
>
> Charles Morgan, *Reflections in a Mirror*, 1946

Disarmament and arms control are firmly associated in the public
mind with efforts to maintain international peace through compromise and negotiation. However, there is a much older type of
disarmament, which is not the product of give and take but is
imposed upon a defeated enemy. Forced disarmament is the subject
of this book. It was used frequently in the ancient world as an
alternative to massacre or enslavement and it is the United Nations'
policy today in Iraq. It was part of every major peace settlement
from the Treaty of Utrecht in 1713, through the Paris negotiations
in 1815 and 1919, to the postwar agreements in 1945. Democracies
almost automatically have recourse to it when they are in a position
to impose peace upon their enemies, yet relatively little thought has
been given to its efficacy.

Can it maintain the imbalance of forces created by war and, if so,
for how long? Does it simply infuriate the defeated while bringing
few advantages to the victorious states? How can the vanquished
evade such measures and what can the victorious states do to
prevent evasion? What role does public opinion play in supporting
forced disarmament by the victors and backing its evasion in the
defeated state? Is there any difference between the disarmament
measures imposed after a limited and after a total war? Can states
be disarmed even without going to war and, if so, in what circumstances?

Unless such issues are widely ventilated, states will insist on disarming their enemies after future wars without properly weighing the advantages and disadvantages of their actions. This study is intended, at least, to raise the issues and to encourage a wider debate.

THE VICTOR'S CHOICES

In the ancient world victors frequently made their victory permanent by resorting to genocide, imperialism, enslavement, ethnic cleansing, hostage-taking, terrorism, and forced conversion. In the twentieth century too, Hitler and Stalin used even the most ferocious of these measures to deal with nations which became the object of their hatred. None could be used today by a victorious liberal democracy.

There are, in fact, surprisingly few ways in which a victorious liberal democracy can treat an enemy, whose forces have been totally defeated, to preserve the imbalance of power and the favourable political situation created by its triumph. The number has indeed been dramatically reduced as democratic systems and moral inhibitions have developed since the eighteenth century. Genocide and enslavement are inconceivable, and imperialism merely threatens to destabilize the state which tries to absorb alien peoples. The Western Powers agreed to ethnic cleansing by the Russians, Poles, and Czechs in 1945 but were horrified by the results.[1] Until medieval times, terrorism continued after the end of the fighting. The people living in cities which had refused to surrender were massacred or enslaved to warn other cities not to resist. But, as Churchill told Stalin at the Teheran conference, it was impossible for the democracies to carry out mass executions or to terrorize people who had laid down their arms. Thus hostage-taking is useless for a liberal Western state because the hostages cannot be harmed in retaliation for their country's behaviour.

In ancient and medieval times conquered people were often forced to convert to the victors' religion. After a few generations they might well forget the reasons for their ancestors' conversion and become genuinely attached to their new religion. Deliberate 're-education' of defeated peoples was tried by the democracies in Germany and

---

[1] See the description of the effects of this policy in A. M. de Zayas, *Nemesis at Potsdam* (Routledge & Kegan Paul, London, 1979).

Japan after the Second World War. However, it was their helplessness and the discredit into which their military and political leaders had fallen, rather than allied re-education, which encouraged the vanquished to accept both the democratic institutions imposed on them and their own disarmament.[2] Re-education will have an impact only if people want to believe what they are being taught and are convinced of its logic.

After every major victory since 1815 British governments have insisted that the vanquished change their government. Napoleon, Kaiser Wilhelm, and the Nazi leaders were either exiled or threatened with trials for war crimes. But changes of government will not necessarily transform the policy of a defeated state unless the people themselves alter their views and this is precisely what the victors find so hard to achieve. Vindictive peace terms may weaken the defeated but at the cost of fostering their hatred. On the other hand, there is no guarantee that magnanimous terms will overcome the resentment caused by defeat itself. The French rallied to Napoleon on his return from Elba in 1815, despite the generous peace terms negotiated the previous year.

Reparations and partition can still be imposed upon defeated enemies by liberal democracies, but their efficacy is limited. Modern warfare and economic progress have made indemnities and reparations less feasible. After a very prolonged war a defeated people is usually so impoverished that it is difficult to exact reparations on any scale; weakening the defeated is acceptable, starving them is not. Moreover, developed economies are now so interlocked that the damage done to a major state by imposing heavy reparations upon it will harm the economies of those it is intended to benefit. Partition of the territory of the defeated country runs counter to modern nationalism. It will be accepted by the conquered people only if there are already deep fissures in the state. Because of its divisions, Austria–Hungary fell to pieces at the end of the First World War, while Germany and Italy remained intact. In the case of homogeneous states partition will almost certainly need to be permanently enforced; the two Germanies reunited in October 1990, as soon as the Soviets ceased to stand in their way.

[2] For an optimistic view of the efficacy of re-education see N. Pronay and K. Wilson (eds), *The Political Reeducation of Germany and her Allies after World War Two* (Croom Helm, London, 1985).

ENFORCED DISARMAMENT

Given that there is no way of insuring against revanchism, it is not surprising that Western democracies have also insisted on disarming their enemies after every major victory since 1815. Even if their government has changed, left to themselves, the defeated people will eventually rebuild their armies so that they can try to reverse the verdict of battle. A combination of forced disarmament and magnanimity may thus be the most attractive option for a victorious democracy. Unfortunately, they have often been regarded by the vanquished as inherently incompatible because the limitation of their forces has been seen as a humiliating restriction on their sovereignty and a mark of distrust. In many cases this faced the victors with a stark choice between the political advantages of reconciliation and the security which forced disarmament provided. Admittedly, the Germans and Japanese accepted their disarmament in 1945, so it could go hand in hand with a policy of reconciliation. However, in time this would probably have changed and the vanquished people would have resented the disarmament measures imposed on them. In the event, before resentment built up the victors had reversed their positions and had themselves pushed their former enemies into rearmament.

Unlike some of the alternatives discussed above, such as partition or reparations, forced disarmament addresses only one aspect of the power of nations. A nation might be disarmed but its economic and demographic strength may steadily increase. If the allies had carried out the 'Byrnes Plan' in 1946, Germany and Japan would have been totally demilitarized until 1986. The contrast between their economic strength at that time and their lack of military power would have been even more glaring than it actually became. Many victors have rightly feared that the vanquished would turn economic into military power and widened, or considered widening, the scope of disarmament to encompass the civilian economy. The obvious problem is that, to be effective, restrictions on the economy have to be so far-reaching as to threaten the population with poverty, if not with outright starvation. If they cannot ignore such suffering, victors have simply to accept the limited efficacy of enforced disarmament and to watch for signs of efforts by the defeated power to break the treaties and begin to rearm.

Forced disarmament is itself divided into two types which follow different sorts of war. Limited wars are sometimes succeeded by limited measures of enforced disarmament and total wars by more far-reaching measures. The more limited type is not expected or intended to keep the vanquished wholly at the mercy of the victorious power but simply to alter the balance of forces between them. If the defeated state begins to break the agreement, this may also be a warning that it plans to go to war again. Thus the demilitarization of Eyemouth in the sixteenth century, of Dunkirk and Azov in the eighteenth, and of the Black Sea in the nineteenth, were examples of this restricted 'strategic' sort of measure. On the other hand, the destruction of the Long Walls of Athens after the Peloponnesian War; the demilitarization of Carthage before the Third Punic War, and the measures imposed on the defeated powers in 1919 and 1945 were designed to leave them completely at the mercy of the victors.

Such far-reaching disarmament measures perform a very important psychological function. During a total war the citizens of the victorious powers will have lost relatives and friends. They will have been frightened by the military success of the enemy. Fear will produce hatred and may encourage the citizens to demand the destruction of the enemy, thereby threatening the inhibitions which have grown up against mistreating the vanquished. Any residual enemy strength will keep fear and anxiety alive; only by placing themselves completely at the mercy of the victors can such fears be quieted. In this situation there are close parallels with the animal kingdom where duals between males of the same species are followed by the submission of the vanquished and his acknowledgement that he is absolutely within the power of the victor.[3]

ORIGINS AND DEVELOPMENT

It is not surprising that forced disarmament has a very ancient history. It was indeed the first type of disarmament, practised for millennia before nations began to negotiate mutual reductions in their weaponry. The Greeks and Romans had both religious and strategic reasons for destroying the weaponry of conquered peoples. Demolishing enemy ships or forts was a way of trying to maintain enemy weakness. Burning ships and other combustible weapons was a sacrifice to the gods who had presided over the victory.

[3] K. Lorenz, *On Aggression* (Methuen, London, 1967).

6 *Introduction*

Unfortunately, the destruction of equipment did not replace genocide or enslavement because these disarmed an enemy for good by
obliterating his manpower. Destroying equipment was another
option when the conqueror wished to show his humanity or to
produce a less than final solution. This was often good strategy as it
left him the option of rebuilding the vanquished armies should he
need them as allies in future wars.

Thus forced disarmament played a considerable part in two of
the greatest struggles in antiquity, the Peloponnesian War between
Athens and Sparta and the Punic Wars between Rome and Carthage. At the end of the Peloponnesian War in 404 BC, when the
Athenian fleet had been defeated and the city was besieged, the
Spartans and their allies seriously considered destroying Athens
completely. Instead the Athenians' envoy persuaded the Spartan
commander that, if the city were disarmed, the Spartans could
afford to allow it to survive. The Long Walls which connected
Athens with its port of Piraeus were knocked down, and the
remainder of the Athenian fleet was destroyed. For about a decade
the Athenians remained compliant and then, with Persian help,
they began in 393 to rebuild the walls and turned on the enemy
who had chosen to spare them. Thus were the limitations of
magnanimity exposed.[4]

After the first two Punic Wars the Romans imposed some measures of forced disarmament on the Carthaginians. At the end of the
first war the Carthaginians had to pay massive reparations, stop
recruiting mercenaries in Italy, and keep their fleets out of Italian
waters. After the second war 500 of the Carthaginian warships
were taken out to sea and burnt, their war elephants had to be
surrendered, and they had to promise to train no more.[5] Even so the
city gradually recovered its strength and, as it did so, the urge to
destroy it completely began to spread among the Romans. When

[4] For a modern history of the end of the war see D. Kagan, *The Fall of the
Athenian Empire* (Cornell University Press, Ithaca and London, 1987), pp. 396 ff.
See also C. D. Hamilton, *Sparta's Bitter Victories* (Cornell University Press, Ithaca
and London, 1979), chapter 5; W. K. Pritchett, *The Greek State at War* (University
of California Press, Berkeley, 1991). For the importance of fortifications in Greek
warfare see A. W. Lawrence, *Greek Aims in Fortification* (Clarendon Press,
Oxford, 1979).
[5] B. Caven, *The Punic Wars* (Weidenfeld and Nicolson, London, 1980); S. L.
Dyson, *The Creation of the Roman Frontier* (Princeton University Press, 1985),
pp. 238 ff.; N. Bagnall, *The Punic Wars* (Hutchinson, London, 1990). For the
second Punic War see Livy, *The War with Hannibal* (Penguin, London, 1974).

fighting broke out between Carthage and one of Rome's North African allies, the Romans raised armies to impose their will. The Carthaginians were so alarmed that they agreed to hand over hostages and the weaponry of their army, but the Romans were not appeased. Once they felt their enemy was at their mercy, they told them that the city was to be destroyed. The Carthaginians still had their extensive fortifications and they decided to resist with what weapons they could manufacture. The outcome was inevitable; in the end the Roman army broke through the defences. Many were killed but 50,000 Carthaginians were captured and sold into slavery, while their city ceased to exist.[6]

Rome's destruction of Carthage paved the way for its domination of most of Europe and North Africa. Forced disarmament of the type considered in this book is used in multipolar international systems. Neither the Roman Empire at its zenith, nor the Dark Ages which followed fitted into this category. But the forced disarmament of one country or city by another again became important in the early modern period. Very often it was used by a state which was strategically on the defensive but had secured what it feared was only a temporary victory over its expansionist neighbours. As in the ancient world, it was fortifications and ships which were the most frequent victims of these measures because these were the most complex and sophisticated weapons, and it would take time to rebuild or replace them. Such preparations would give other states warning of the intention of the defeated states to avenge their humiliation.

Thus, when the French allied with the Scots during the sixteenth century, the English repeatedly insisted that the fortifications held by the French in Scotland should be destroyed before there could be any lasting peace between them. They were particularly afraid of the fortification of Eyemouth just to the north of their own fortified town of Berwick on the east coast. In a series of agreements, beginning with the Treaty of Boulogne in 1549, the French promised to destroy the Eyemouth fortifications. However, such agreements were not always fulfilled and the fortifications were relatively easy to rebuild. It was not until the severance of the Scottish–French links that the Treaty of Edinburgh in 1560 ended

---

[6] Caven, *The Punic Wars*, pp. 273 ff.

the threat to England's northern borders and led to the final destruction of Eyemouth's fortifications.[7]

In the eighteenth century the English brought similar pressure to bear on the French to prevent them fortifying Dunkirk. Louis XIV had employed his tireless engineer Vauban to turn Dunkirk into his most modern port. But in 1713, after France's defeats in the War of the Spanish Succession, Article IX of the Treaty of Utrecht laid down 'that all the fortifications of the city of Dunkirk be razed, that the harbour be filled up, and that the sluices of moles which serve to cleanse the harbour be levelled'.[8] What the British demanded was not just demilitarization but the complete wrecking of the port for civilian as well as military purposes. It was not surprising that the French resisted by every means at their disposal, while the British introduced on-site verification, posting officers to Dunkirk to see that the agreement was observed. Each war between the two countries saw the French feverishly trying to restore the port and intending to use it in their plans to invade the British Isles.[9] Each peace treaty down to the American War of Independence saw the British insisting on the demilitarization of Dunkirk. What they gained from their insistence was some warning when the French were expecting conflict to occur. Demilitarization also hindered French efforts to use it as a naval base in wartime. But these strategic advantages were bought at the price of constant friction with the French government. Ironically, disarmament also encouraged the seamen of Dunkirk to turn to smuggling goods into Britain

[7] On the Treaties of Cateau Cambresis see J. G. Russell, *Peacemaking in the Renaissance* (Duckworth, London, 1986). For English policy see J. Stevenson (ed.), *Calendar of State Papers, Foreign Series of the Reign of Elizabeth* (HMSO, London, 1863, reprinted 1966 by Kraus Reprints, Liechenstein). On Eyemouth see E. Layhe, *The History of Berwickshire's Towns and Villages* (Entire Productions, Berwickshire, 1994), p. 42 and D. J. Withrington and I. R. Grant, *Statistical Account of Scotland* (E.P. Publishing, Wakefield, 1979), vol. 3, p. 169.

[8] C. Parry, *Consolidated Treaty Series* (Oceana, Dobbs Ferry, 1969), vol. 27, pp. 483 ff., vol. 30, pp. 65 ff., and vol. 42, p. 291. On Dunkirk see A. Cabantous, *Histoire de Dunkerque* (Editions Privat, Toulouse, 1983) and F. J. Herbert, *Soldier of France; Sebastien le Prestre Vauban* (Peter Lang, New York, 1989), pp. 32, 38 ff. and B. Pujo, *Vaubin* (Albin Michel, Paris, 1991).

[9] See particularly J. Corbett, *England in the Seven Years War* (Longmans, London, 1907), vol. 1, pp. 88, 99, and vol. 2, pp. 19, 21, 40, 305–6, 315. See also W. Michael, *England under George I* (Macmillan, London, 1939), p. 86; J. Black, *The Rise of the European Powers 1679–1793* (Edward Arnold, London, 1990), p. 104; G. G. Butler, *Colonel St Paul of Ewart, Soldier and Diplomat* (St Catherine Press, London, 1911).

in peacetime and to piracy against British ships in wartime to balance their loss of naval employment.[10]

While the British and French were locked in conflict on one side of Europe, the Ottoman Empire was trying to defend itself against Russian expansion. The struggle between the two Eastern Empires began with Peter the Great's decision to mount an expedition against the Turks and Tartars in 1695. Whenever he and his successors were victorious, they captured and strengthened the town of Azov so that they could build a fleet on the inland seas. Whenever the Ottomans reversed this process, they insisted that Azov and the fortifications in the surrounding area should be destroyed.[11] They believed that a demilitarized zone would prevent friction between the two empires and so it might have done, had the Russians not been bent on expansion. In the 1770s the Russians achieved their ambition. Azov and its vicinity were now securely in their grasp and the Treaty of Kucuk Kaynarca laid down that it should remain 'in perpetuity' in Russian hands.

British and Ottoman demands for restricted measures of disarmament had protected them for a time against the power of their neighbours, but these were essentially defensive measures imposed after limited wars and they could not long reduce the strength of the French and Russians. Only if these states had abandoned their political objectives, as the French abandoned their Scottish ambitions after the Treaty of Edinburgh, would such forced disarmament measures have endured. In the meantime, nothing except on-site verification, persistence in demanding that the treaties be fulfilled, and threats to use force if this were not the case ensured that disarmament actually took place. Each defeated party hid behind its local agents, pretending that it was not responsible for their attempts to evade the treaties and, in the French case at least, this was sometimes true. On their side, British governments found that they were not free agents; once the French had agreed to destroy Dunkirk, Members of Parliament were always ready to criticize the government if it failed to keep Dunkirk unfortified.

[10] Cabantous, *Histoire de Dunkerque*; H. M. Scott, *British Foreign Policy in the Age of American Revolution* (Clarendon Press, Oxford, 1990), pp. 21, 51, 76.
[11] R. K. Massie, *Peter the Great: His Life and World* (Gollancz, London, 1981); S. Shaw, *History of the Ottoman Empire and Modern Turkey* (Cambridge University Press, 1976); *Treaties &c between Turkey and Foreign Powers 1535–1855*, compiled by the Librarian and Keeper of the Records, Foreign Office (Harrison, London, 1855).

The targets of these various measures were the traditional ones of fortifications, but each target brought innovations. The demilitarization of Dunkirk introduced on-site verification while the Ottomans experimented, however ineffectively, with demilitarized zones.

In contrast to these limited measures, at the end of the eighteenth century the French Revolution ushered in a new era of warfare and of peacemaking. As we shall see in the next chapter, Napoleon imposed much more far-reaching measures on his enemies and particularly insisted on drastic limitations on the numbers in their armed forces. His enemies were given no chance of pleading that it was their subjects who had evaded the disarmament measures imposed on them, while France's extensive espionage system made formal verification unnecessary. Napoleon's forced disarmament measures were designed to place the vanquished completely at the mercy of the French Empire, and he would perhaps have succeeded if he had not overreached himself by invading Spain and Russia.

NEGLECT OF FORCED DISARMAMENT

Despite this rich and extensive past, historians have often been blind to the emphasis which statesmen placed on forced disarmament. Interest in Napoleon's disarmament measures has been so limited that many historians erroneously ascribe the disarmament of Prussia to the Treaty of Tilsit. In 1815 allied governments looked on the occupation of French fortifications and the use of French reparations to pay for new ones in the Netherlands and Germany as among the most important ways of preventing future French aggression, yet no one would think this from reading the standard historical accounts of the negotiations. Lorna Jaffe, the historian of British policy on German disarmament after the First World War, has commented on the paucity of references to it in the standard histories. Similarly, a recent study of the Treaty of Trianon, which was imposed on Hungary after the First World War, virtually ignores the way the country was forced to reduce its armed forces.

Winston Churchill spoke of the forced disarmament of Germany as the primary allied war aim in the Second World War, but few historians emphasize this point. The treaties which the US Secretary of State, James Byrnes, drew up for this purpose in 1946 have been almost completely forgotten and occupy only a few lines in the most extensive study of his policies.[12] Military historians have been more interested in wartime strategy than in peacemaking; diplomatic historians have concentrated on political measures rather than on the military aspects of the great peace conferences. This is not to deny that there have been excellent monographs on past cases of forced disarmament, but hardly any of the thousands of general books on arms control and disarmament mention this type of measure.

Until the Iraqi defeat in the Gulf War and the decision by the UN Security Council to demand the partial disarmament of the defeated state, forced disarmament evoked very little interest among academics and experts on strategy. Neither the collections of documents produced by the US State Department and the Arms Control and Disarmament Agency (ACDA) nor those produced by the Stockholm International Peace Research Institute (SIPRI) listed forced disarmament measures. The situation started to change only with the path-breaking work on forced disarmament published by the United Nations Institute for Disarmament Research (UNIDIR) in 1992.[13]

The neglect of the study of forced disarmament measures cannot be ascribed to the greater success of disarmament and arms control agreements freely negotiated between equal powers. Many arms control and disarmament negotiations have been unsuccessful. The

---

[12] For one treatment of the 1815 negotiations which virtually ignores the question of enforced disarmament see H. Kissinger, *A World Restored* (Victor Gollancz, London, 1973). For Jaffe's views on the Paris Peace Conference see L. S. Jaffe, *The Decision to Disarm Germany* (Allen and Unwin, London, 1985), p. xi. For the Treaty of Trianon see B. K. Kiraly, P. Pastor, and I. Sanders, *War and Society in East Central Europe: A Case Study on Trianon* (Brooklyn College Press, New York, 1982). For Churchill's views see W. S. Churchill, *The Second World War: The Hinge of Fate* (Reprint Society, London, 1953), p. 552. For Byrnes's period as Secretary of State see P. D. Ward, *The Threat of Peace: James F. Byrnes and the Council of Foreign Ministers 1945–6* (Kent State University Press, 1979), p. 93.

[13] Among the various monographs see, for example, Jaffe, *The Decision to Disarm Germany*; W. E. Mosse, *The Rise and Fall of the Crimean System 1855–1871* (Macmillan, London, 1963); D. G. Williamson, *The British in Germany 1918–1930: The Reluctant Occupiers* (Berg, New York, 1991); R. O. Paxton, *Parades and Politics at Vichy* (Princeton University Press, 1966). For the absence of references to forced disarmament in modern collections of arms control treaties see *Documents on Disarmament 1945–1959*, vol. 1 (Department of State, Washington, 1960); SIPRI, *Arms Control: A Survey and Appraisal of Multilateral Agreements* (Taylor and Francis, London, 1978). For the UNIDIR study see F. Tanner (ed.), *From Versailles to Baghdad: Post-War Armament Control of Defeated States* (United Nations, New York, 1992).

treaties produced by such negotiations frequently had relatively little military impact.[14] The majority have concentrated on weapons which are not of central importance to the armed forces concerned. In contrast, particularly after total wars, forced disarmament measures usually limit or destroy the enemies' most effective weapons: the Athenians' Long Walls and warships, the castles and fortified towns of medieval Europe, the aircraft, tanks, and warships of the Kaiser's Germany, Iraq's missiles and nuclear and chemical weapons.

Moreover, however complex and drastic they are, forced disarmament measures are often decided very quickly. The victorious allies determined the permitted size of the Bulgarian, Austrian, and Hungarian armed forces within a few days in 1919. Such limitations would have taken years to negotiate between the Central European states, if they could have been achieved at all. Czechoslovakia, Romania, Yugoslavia, and Poland refused to limit their forces in any way, despite the limits imposed on their neighbours. Admittedly, forced disarmament measures are often ephemeral; the demilitarization of the Black Sea after the Crimean War only endured until 1871; Germany cheated on the Treaty of Versailles from the beginning, and when Adolf Hitler came to power in Germany in 1933 he immediately sought ways of overturning the Treaty altogether. Yet agreed disarmament measures may also collapse when they are no longer in the interest of the parties. Forced disarmament differs in that, except by forestalling some worse 'punishment', it is very rarely in the interests of the vanquished.[15] Equally, it is far more favourable to the interests of the victors than any agreed measure is likely to be. Given the hostility of the vanquished, it survives for as long as the victors are willing to threaten the use of force to maintain it.

Many of those who write about arms control suffer from the delusion that a balance of power and military equality between potential enemies is the best way to maintain peace. If that were the case, then necessarily the imbalance preserved in forced disarmament measures would be destabilizing. In fact, near equality in military strength constantly tempts revisionist powers to go to war

[14] See particularly the list of the post-World War II agreements in SIPRI *Arms Control*, pp. 151 ff.
[15] Some would argue that nations can benefit economically from being disarmed, but see the comments in the conclusion of this book.

in order to upset the status quo.[16] If the victorious powers establish a political system to their liking and bolster it with an imbalance of power in their favour, this is by far the most stable type of international system. Such stability is usually threatened by the inability of victorious powers to maintain their alliance. Then one or more members of the victorious coalition will be tempted to rearm the defeated, a balance of power will be recreated, and the system will again become unstable.

The final reason for the general indifference to enforced disarmament is that, during the Cold War, East–West tensions generally prevented the Great Powers from co-operating to compel smaller ones to disarm. At the same time, Germany and Japan played a major part in Western alliances. It was considered undiplomatic, even embarrassing, to mention the fact that they had recently been regarded with such fear that allied leaders wanted to keep them totally demilitarized for forty years. Thus forced disarmament was ignored or regarded as of merely historic interest.

DEFINITIONS AND DISTINCTIONS

Some commentators would argue that the subject of enforced disarmament is too diffuse because all war is about disarming the enemy; each aeroplane, each tank destroyed in the fighting is an act of disarmament which makes the enemy more amenable to the will of the victors. As the Prussian strategist, Carl von Clausewitz, put it, 'the aim [of war] is to disarm the enemy. . . . this is bound to be so. If the enemy is to be coerced you must put him in a situation that is even more unpleasant than the sacrifice you call on him to make.'[17] However, this book is not concerned with the disarmament which is an intrinsic part of battle but with the treatment of the enemy's armed forces and armaments after the fighting has stopped.

Some analysts would say that disarmament is the wrong term to use since the destruction of fortifications or the reduction in the numbers of a vanquished army are partial measures or, in modern terminology, 'arms control'. On the other hand, forced disarma-

---

[16] The best exposition of this view of the causes of war is G. Blainey, *The Causes of War* (Sun Books, Melbourne, 1973).

[17] M. E. Howard and P. Paret (eds), *Clausewitz: On War* (Princeton University Press, 1984), p. 77.

ment can be total, as the demilitarization of Germany and Japan was supposed to be after 1945. In UN terminology, disarmament is the comprehensive term incorporating more limited measures of arms control; thus it is the most appropriate one for the range of measures being studied.

Forced disarmament usually occurs after wars and, more rarely, when a state believes that it has no chance of resisting a threatening power and gives way even before the war has been fought. The Carthaginians, for example, temporarily abandoned their weapons because they felt resistance to Rome was useless before the Third Punic War. But the most famous or infamous example of this form of disarmament took place in 1938, when the Czech government was compelled to abandon its defences in the Sudetenland, not after a war but after the Munich 'agreement'. In the 1980s Libya was apparently prevented from building a chemical weapons factory by US threats. In these three cases one nation or group of nations achieved the advantages which are usually derived from war without actually having to fight. But they had to be prepared to do so if the weaker state resisted.

Coercion plays some part in the 'freely' negotiated arms control agreements which are not covered by this study. The Washington Treaty of 1922, which settled the affairs of the Pacific region and also dramatically limited the US, British, and Japanese fleets, was negotiated freely by the US and British governments, but it was bitterly resented by many Japanese, particularly in the armed forces.[18] It was seen by them as just as much an example of forced disarmament as those which take place after defeat in war. Sectional opinions of this sort are quite common; what was unusual in Japan was the intensity of the feelings and the consequent determination to breach the treaties. Some of the parties to the Nuclear Non-Proliferation Treaty (NPT) signed purely because they were pressed to do so by the superpowers. But North Korea and Iraq are exceptional because military pressure was brought to bear to make them observe the NPT. The degree of coercion in other cases was thus much less than in the examples studied here, where war or the threat of war was ever present.

---

[18] S. Asada in D. Borg and S. Okamoto (eds), *Pearl Harbor as History* (Columbia University Press, New York and London, 1973).

Partly because the history of forced disarmament measures has not been written, commentators have mistakenly claimed that allied policy towards Iraq in the 1990s was unique rather than typical of the behaviour of democratic nations towards their defeated enemies. One of the allied inspectors in Iraq suggested that the Iraqi experience was unique because Iraq was compelled to accept inspection, because of the level of deception and resistance practised by the Iraqis, because inspection was so intrusive, and because a special commission had been set up to carry out the inspection. In fact, every one of these aspects of the Iraqi situation applied equally to Germany in the 1920s.[19]

As they were unfamiliar with the history of forced disarmament, statesmen have often drawn false conclusions from the past. The disarmament measures imposed on Germany in 1919 were deliberately designed to avoid the mistakes made by Napoleon in 1808 when he restricted the size of the Prussian army. But Lloyd George, Balfour, and others misunderstood the Prussian response to Napoleon's measures. They exaggerated the importance of limiting the number of German troops and underestimated the significance of the cadre of officers and NCOs.[20] In 1945 the US Secretary of State, James Byrnes, was apparently unaware of the difficulty of persuading an allied coalition to continue enforcing disarmament measures unless the coalition had forces actually stationed within the defeated country.

The importance of forced disarmament has recently been highlighted by US efforts to prevent North Korea and Iraq from developing nuclear weapons. But forced disarmament is a recurring aspect of international relations and has had a much greater historical impact than measures negotiated between equal powers. It takes place when states are independent but unequal in their power, and the more potent state is determined to perpetuate the imbalance without destroying the weaker state completely. It produces common patterns of evasion and coercion which have implications both for weak powers and for strong ones. There are tactics of forced disarmament just as there are tactics of war-making or peace-

[19] D. Kay, 'Arms inspection in Iraq: Lessons for arms control', *Bulletin of Arms Control*, no. 7, August 1992; see also F. Halliday, 'The Gulf War of 1990–1991 and the study of international relations', *Review of International Studies*, April 1994, p. 118.
[20] W. O. Shanahan, *Prussian Military Reforms 1786–1813* (Columbia University Press, New York, 1945), p. 14.

making. The significance of the issue, its neglect in studies of strategy and arms control, and the ignorance of statesmen and diplomats are the justifications for writing this narrative history of forced disarmament.

I

Napoleonic Disarmament

Dunkirk and the fortresses on the Russo-Ottoman border were demilitarized in eighteenth-century peace treaties because of the dominating part such fortifications played in the warfare of the period. Victorious powers tried to restrict the most powerful and complex weapons systems available to their vanquished enemies. With the outbreak of the French Revolution and Napoleon's subsequent seizure of power, the international scene and the nature of warfare were transformed. French expansion was based on mass armies raised by conscription; Napoleon's military successes turned very largely on good intelligence, rapid manoeuvres, and the concentration of his armies on the battlefield. Fortifications remained important but played a less central role than they had in eighteenth-century warfare. Because the size of armies was now so crucial, it was not surprising that Napoleon tried to limit the number of men under arms maintained by his defeated enemies.

Napoleon's armies conquered Italy, the Low Countries, and the smaller German states. They overwhelmed the Austrians and threatened Russia and Turkey. In 1806 they defeated the Prussians at the battles of Jena and Auerstadt. Two years later the upstart emperor restricted the size of the Prussian army to 42,000 men. In 1809 he defeated the Austrians once again, seized many of their territories, and limited their armed forces to 150,000 men. Successive peace treaties very often provided for the occupation of conquered fortresses, though some, such as Breslau, were to be destroyed as soon as they were taken.[1] All newspapers mildly

---

[1] There are several collections of Napoleon's letters and orders which give some idea of his attitudes towards forced disarmament. Napoleon III ordered the publication of a 32-volume series which was published by Henri Plon between 1858 and 1870. Subsequently Leon Lecestre edited a collection under the title *Lettres inédites de Napoléon I*, which was also published by Plon in 1897, and Leonce de Brotonne edited another volume with the same title the following year, which was published in Paris by Honoré Champion. There is also the multi-

critical of the French were suppressed, priests who criticized French actions were arrested, and partisans were crushed.[2] Both Austria and Prussia were impoverished by savage reparations which paid for their own conquest and occupation. These were neither the limited, strategically defensive measures favoured by the British and Turks during the previous century nor the result of demands by vengeful and fearful publics after total victories. They were rather the consequence of a deliberate and coherent policy of imperial expansion. Europe was saved from the oppression of forced disarmament and the payment of tribute only by the brutal and heroic resistance of the Spanish guerrillas, by British subsidies, and by the death of so many of Napoleon's veterans during the invasion of Russia in 1812.

THE GENESIS OF NAPOLEON'S DISARMAMENT MEASURES

The imposition of numerical limitations on a defeated army was unusual before the Napoleonic Wars but not unique. It normally occurred when a conqueror planned subsequently to absorb the lands of the defeated people into his own empire. Thus, as the once mighty kingdom of Poland became gradually weaker in the eighteenth century, its three neighbours, Prussia, Russia, and Austria, began to absorb its territories. The first partition took place in 1772, with the predators seizing more than a quarter of the kingdom. The remainder, though nominally independent under King Stanislaw-August, was actually dominated by Russia. In 1787 the king had to ask the Russian empress for permission to expand the

volume series of the *Correspondance militaire de Napoléon Ier* which was published by Plon in the 1870s under the orders of the War Ministry. The most extensive account in English of the impact of forced disarmament on the Prussian army is W. O. Shanahan, *Prussian Military Reforms 1786–1813* (Columbia University Press, New York, 1945). See also W. M. Simon, *The Failure of the Prussian Reform Movement, 1807–1819* (Cornell University Press, Ithaca, NY, 1955); E. F. Henderson, *Blucher and the Uprising of Prussia against Napoleon, 1806–1815* (Putnam, New York and London, 1911); H. Rosinski, *The German Army* (Pall Mall Press, London, 1966); G. A. Craig, *The Politics of the Prussian Army, 1640–1945* (Clarendon Press, Oxford, 1955). On Breslau and its fortifications see 'Ordre de faire démolir les fortifications de Breslau', 5 December 1806, *Correspondance militaire*, vol. 4, no. 821, p. 288.

[2] Lecestre, *Letters inédites*, vol. 1, no. 120, p. 72, no. 138, p. 87. One of the most notorious incidents occurred in 1807 when Napoleon ordered the execution of two Prussian comedians who lampooned French soldiers from the stage; Lecestre, *Lettres inédites*, vol. 1, no. 172, p. 108.

tiny Polish army in return for helping her to fight the Turks.[3] Catherine refused the offer of help but, while she was dealing with the Ottomans, the Poles tried to free themselves by reforming and democratizing their country and voting to raise an army of 100,000 men. In March 1790 they made the mistake of trusting the Prussians and allying with them to offset Russian influence. Provoked by these assertions of independence, in 1792 the Russians used an appeal by a renegade group of Poles and allegations of Polish 'Jacobinism' as excuses for an invasion.

The Prussians not only failed to come to the help of their ally, as they had contracted to do, but actually joined in the second partition which further reduced Polish lands.[4] The Russians assembled a Polish Diet at Grodno in July 1792 and forced it to accept the terms demanded, including not only the surrender of territory but the forced disarmament of the army. It was the implementation of this second demand which sparked Poland's final desperate resistance. In March 1794 General Madalinski refused to disband the cavalry garrison at Ostroleka and advanced on Cracow. The following month, led by the nationalist hero, Tadeusz Kosciuszko, the Poles defeated the Russians at the battle of Kilinski. But the Prussians once more joined in the attack and helped the Russians defeat the Poles at the decisive battle of Maciejowice. When the Poles tried to negotiate with the victorious Russian commander, General Suvorov, he replied, 'Treaties are not necessary. The soldiers must be disarmed, and all weapons handed over to the Russians.'[5] Warsaw capitulated on 5 November 1794. This time Austria joined in the partition which removed Poland from the map of Europe until 1918.

The French were often sympathetic towards Poland in its troubles but helpless to defend it. Poland's ruthless despoilers, the conservative monarchies, were also France's enemies and there was both ideological and national sympathy between the two peoples. Napoleon's own attitude towards Poland was, no doubt, opportunistic.[6]

---

[3] N. Davies, *God's Playground: A History of Poland*, vol. 1 (Clarendon Press, Oxford, 1981), p. 528. See also O. Halecki, *A History of Poland* (Routledge, London, 1978).

[4] For the terms imposed on Poland in 1792 see C. Parry, *The Consolidated Treaty Series*, vol. 52 (Oceana, Dobbs Ferry, NY, 1969), pp. 85 ff.

[5] W. R. Morfill, *Poland* (T. Fisher Unwin, London, 1893), p. 248.

[6] D. McKay and H. M. Scott, *The Rise of the Great Powers, 1648–1815* (Longman, London, 1983), p. 313. In June 1810 Napoleon ordered the newspapers not to use the word 'Poland'. See Brotonne, *Lettres inédites*, order to General Savary, 16 June 1810, no. 607, p. 251.

In 1797 he authorized the recruitment of émigré Poles into his army
and, at his instigation, the Treaty of Tilsit in 1807 led to the
establishment of a small Duchy of Warsaw. His treatment of
Prussia in the various negotiations closely resembled Prussia's prior
treatment of Poland, and his partition of Prussian territory, his
threats to dismember the country completely, and his disarmament
of the Prussian army were therefore all particularly ominous to
Prussian patriots. Apart from taking a malicious satisfaction in
emulating Prussian and Russian behaviour towards their weaker
neighbour, Napoleon's decision to reduce the size of the Prussian
army reflected both the nature of revolutionary warfare and the
difficulty of restricting the key elements in contemporary power.

LIMITATIONS ON PRUSSIA

King Frederick William and his advisers had brought this fate upon
their country by their vacillation and incompetence. As Napoleon's
power expanded, Prussia had failed to join the various alliances
which opposed him and had thus become increasingly isolated. The
Prussians alienated Britain, the paymaster of the anti-French coalition, by accepting Hanover, the ancestral home of the British kings,
from Napoleon's hands. Austria was still recovering from its defeat
at the battle of Austerlitz and was in no position to reinforce
the Prussians. In mid-September 1806 Napoleon told his Foreign
Minister, Talleyrand, that the idea of Prussia challenging him on its
own was ridiculous but that the Prussians had been arming heavily
out of fear. His aim was to reassure the Prussians and, at the same
time, to reinforce his armies in Germany to be ready for all eventu-
alities. 'Au lieu de dire: Désarmez ou la guerre! qui est encore trop
effrayante pour la Prusse, je dirais: Désarmez si vous voulez que je
n'arme pas davantage.'[7] Thus, when the Prussians went to war with
France shortly afterwards, Napoleon saw the reduction in Prussian
military power as a central war aim. Only the Russians came to
Prussia's assistance, but the Prussians had suffered two major
defeats and lost the main part of their country before the Russian
armies arrived.

    The military incompetence displayed by the Prussian officer
corps equalled Frederick William's political incompetence. The

[7] Lecestre, *Lettres inédites*, vol. 1, no. 124, letter to M. de Talleyrand, 12
September 1806, p. 73.

army, which had held the whole of Europe in check under Frederick the Great, was now fifty years behind the times. Ironically, its recruiting system had been disorganized by the absorption of the ill-gotten Polish lands. By 15 October Napoleon was able to announce that 30 to 40,000 prisoners of war had been taken, including 20 generals, and 25 to 30 flags, and 300 guns. A month later Magdeburg fell, together with another 22,000 prisoners, 6 flags, and 800 guns.[8] Berlin itself was taken a mere eighteen days after the beginning of the war, though the struggle continued into 1807, with the Russian army operating alongside the remains of the Prussian forces in East Prussia. At Eylau the allied armies inflicted heavy losses on the French, but Königsberg fell after the French victory of Friedland, and on 25 June Napoleon began peace talks with Tsar Alexander at Tilsit.

Prussia was saved from total destruction only by the tsar's loyalty. Brandenburg, Silesia, and East Prussia alone remained to Frederick William, who lost about half of his territory and people. Napoleon also imposed massive reparations. Originally set at 73 million francs, he increased them the following year to 140 million. The 4.5 million Prussians had to struggle to raise the money, despite the ruination of their economy by Napoleon's 'Continental' economic system, which banned trade with Britain. When Prussian plenipotentiaries complained, they were told that their arguments were absurd, that no concessions would be made, and that it was not for the victors to justify themselves to the vanquished.[9] The bulk of the French army of occupation was withdrawn from July 1807, but Marshal Soult remained in Berlin and French troops continued to occupy key fortresses. Napoleon amused himself with the thought that the Prussians had to pay for the upkeep of one of his corps.[10]

During the negotiations at Tilsit in 1807 Napoleon was at the apogee of his power. He controlled the whole of Europe from Gibraltar to Berlin. Russia and Austria were cowed but independent; there were rumblings of discontent from the oppressed peoples, which burst into the open the following year. Spanish opposition to the French presence grew with Napoleon's deposition of the

[8] *Correspondance militaire*, vol. 4, nos 804 and 814, pp. 236, 268.
[9] Lecestre, *Lettres inédites*, vol. 1, letter to M. Daru, 12 October 1807, no. 181, p. 113.
[10] *Correspondence de Napoléon Ier publiée par Ordre de l'Empereur Napoléon III*, vol. 17, letter to M. Daru, 10 October 1808, no. 14369, p. 542.

Spanish royal family in May 1808, and two months later 20,000
French soldiers capitulated to the Spaniards at Baylen in the southern mountains. The following month the British general, Arthur
Wellesley, defeated another French army at Vimiero and the French
fell back behind the Ebro. Napoleon estimated that he would need
200,000 men to crush the Spanish, the Portuguese, and their British
allies. He would also have to strip the Prussian and German
garrisons of his most experienced soldiers.

The summer of 1808 was thus the moment when Napoleon's
apparently unstoppable progress at last began to meet effective
resistance. Since the Treaty of Tilsit in 1807, the Franco-Russian
alliance had been the dominant political factor in European politics.
Napoleon wanted to strengthen and renew this agreement to protect his hinterland before leaving for Spain. He also had to finalize
the peace terms with Prussia. Prussian ministers advised their king
to hide their anti-French plans behind the veil of co-operation.
They should even offer to lend Napoleon an army corps, but it
should be ready at any moment to change sides and join the
Austrians and the rest of Germany in an anti-French uprising. The
king instructed Prince William of Prussia, who was negotiating
with the French, to act accordingly. William offered an offensive
and defensive alliance in exchange for the withdrawal of the
occupying French forces. Prussian troops would also assist the
French in Germany.[11]

Prussian thinking was reflected in a letter Frederick's chief minister, Baron von Stein, sent to the Grand Master of the Prussian
court. Stein reasoned that, if Napoleon refused the French offer, it
would show that he had decided to destroy Prussia completely.
German determination was growing daily and should be encouraged. Spanish resistance had given men hope, and a war between
France and Austria was inevitable.[12] Stein's letter was given to the
Prussian agent, Koppe, who was subsequently arrested by the
French as a spy. Then it was sent to Napoleon, who raged against
the Prussian delegates, threatened to tear up the Treaty of Tilsit,

[11] A. Sorel, *L'Europe et la Révolution française* (septième partie; Plon, Paris,
1903), p. 291; L. Madelin, *Histoire du Consulate et de l'Empire; l'affaire d'Es-
pagne, 1807–1809* (Hachette, Paris, 1945), p. 190; G. Lefebvre, *Napoleon from
Tilsit to Waterloo 1807–1815* (Routledge and Kegan Paul, London, 1969), p. 28.
[12] Sorel, *L'Europe et la Révolution*, p. 292. For the war in Spain see W. F. P.
Napier, *History of the War in the Peninsula and in the South of France* (Constable,
London, 1992).

and insisted that Stein must be dismissed. Marshal Soult was told
that the Prussian king should not be allowed to return to his palace
until Stein was sacked.[13]

In Paris, Prince William wanted to resist Napoleon's terms,
but he was intimidated by the threats made by Napoleon and
his ministers. The prince was told that any delay in agreeing
would jeopardize the whole settlement. He was also surrounded by
frenetic activity as the empire prepared for war in Spain and
Napoleon sent emissaries rushing across the Continent to mobilize
his forces and overawe potential enemies.[14] The prince signed the
oppressive Treaty of Paris on 17 September 1808 and accordingly
the Emperor confirmed his Foreign Minister, Comte de Champagny, in office for a further period.[15] Having secured his rear,
Napoleon prepared to move his forces from Germany. He made a
personal appeal to their loyalty on the following day. On the one
hand, he told them that he needed them to put Europe's peace on a
secure footing by crushing the Spaniards and English; on the other
hand, he assured them that their achievements already equalled
those of the Roman legions.[16]

Ten thousand troops were nevertheless to be left in Prussian
cities until an indemnity of 140 million francs was paid. The
Prussians had to go against their monarchical and constitutional
principles by recognizing Napoleon's brothers—Joseph as king of
Spain and Joachim as king of the two Sicilies. Menacingly, the
Emperor guaranteed the integrity of Prussia only while the Prussians remained his loyal allies.[17] The Paris Treaty was followed
by a separate series of negotiations, which took place in Berlin in
November, laying down the ways favourable to France in which
military roads were to be kept open for their convenience, and the
garrisons of Glogau, Kustrin, and other cities were to be fed and
paid for.[18] The poverty-stricken Prussians had to supply a ration for
each French soldier of 12 ounces of fresh meat and 8 of bacon,

---

[13] *Correspondance de Napoléon Ier*, vol. 17, letter to Marshal Soult, 10
September 1808, no. 14309, p. 503. See also Lecestre, *Lettres inédites*, vol. 1, no.
345, p. 238.
[14] *Correspondance de Napoléon Ier*, vol. 17, p. 491.
[15] Brotonne, *Lettres inédites*, no. 344, p. 145.
[16] *Correspondance de Napoléon Ier*, vol. 17, no. 14338, p. 521.
[17] The text of the various treaties signed in Paris can be found in Parry,
Consolidated Treaty Series, vol. 60, p. 143.
[18] G. F. de Martens, *Supplément au Recueil des principaux traités*, vol. 5,
1808–1814 Dieterich, Gottingue, 1817, p. 106.

while the 'Army of the Rhine' as a whole was to receive 69,000 litres of wine and 138,500 litres of beer. The fortifications of a number of German cities, including Danzig, Stralsund, and Düsseldorf, were demolished.

The limitations on the Prussian army were negotiated secretly in Paris and listed in 'Separate Articles'. Napoleon wanted to humiliate and weaken the Prussians without angering the tsar, who still regarded himself as Berlin's protector. The French Foreign Minister, Champagny, pretended to the Russian ambassador in Paris that the negotiations were only about finance and that Russia would consequently be little interested. He also told the Austrian ambassador, Prince Metternich, that the negotiations would 'terminate all the differences which still exist with' Prussia.[19] In an interview with Metternich on 25 August, Napoleon himself said that 'Prussia will become the strongest Power of the second order.'[20]

Article I of the Separate Articles began, 'Son Majesté le Roi de Prusse, voulant éviter tout ce qui pourrait donner l'ombrage à la France, prend l'engagement de n'entretenir pendant 10 ans, à compter du 1er Janvier 1809, que le nombre de troupes ci-dessous spécifié.' There could hardly have been a more abject humiliation of the once proud Prussian state and army. The Treaty went on to specify that the Prussian army would be composed of 10 regiments of infantry comprising 22,000 men; 8 regiments of cavalry amounting to 8,000 men; 6,000 artillery and engineers, and a Royal Guard of the same number. In ten years the Prussians would be freed from these limitations, but in the meantime they were not to raise any auxiliary forces and they were to assist the French emperor with 16,000 men in any war which broke out against Austria.[21]

That Napoleon felt the need both to limit the Prussian army and, ironically, to provide for its assistance, reflected the extent of the demands made on him in the autumn of 1808. He always showed total contempt for Frederick William and his country,[22] but he knew that the Austrians were reforming their armed forces as quickly as possible and that they were led by the bitterly

---

[19] R. Metternich (ed.), *The Memoirs of Prince Metternich*, vol. 2 (Charles Scribner's Sons, New York, 1880), p. 248.

[20] Metternich, *Memoirs*, vol. 2, p. 256.

[21] Parry, *Consolidated Treaty Series*, vol. 60, pp. 147 ff. Simon mistakenly attributes these limitations to the Treaty of Tilsit; see Simon, *The Failure*, p. 160.

[22] Metternich, *Memoirs*, vol. 2, p. 390.

Francophobe Count Stadion. Austria was to bide its time until it could wreak its revenge.[23] When Napoleon met the tsar at Erfurt, immediately after forcing the Paris Treaties on the Prussians, the Russians also proved less malleable than expected. Alexander realized that Napoleon's position had dramatically weakened because of his Spanish difficulties, and that the French now needed his support. Moreover, Alexander was secretly advised throughout the Erfurt Conference by Prince Talleyrand, the Vice Grand Counsellor and former Foreign Minister of the French Empire, who knew all the strengths and weaknesses of the French position. The tsar persuaded Napoleon to reduce the reparations imposed on Prussia by 20 million francs, and he refused the most exacting French demands. The Franco-Russian alliance was renewed in October 1808, laying down the terms for negotiations with Britain, but the relationship between the two emperors did not become stronger.[24]

PRUSSIAN RESISTANCE

The period from 1807 to 1813 is both one of the most wretched and the most inspiring in Prussian history. Although the country was utterly humiliated by French victories and oppressed by the exactions of the French army, a small coterie of reformers struggled to transform the Prussian state and enable it to contribute effectively to the resistance against France.[25] The political reform movement was originally led by Baron von Stein, who persuaded the king in October 1807 to end serfdom and free the Prussian peasants. New systems of finance, education, and urban government were also to be introduced so that Prussia would be turned into a 'modern' kingdom and the people would be motivated to defend the country in any future war.[26] However, the interception of Stein's

[23] C. A. Macartney, *The Habsburg Empire, 1790–1918* (Weidenfeld and Nicolson, London, 1968), p. 184; R. A. Karn, *A History of the Habsburg Empire, 1526–1918* (University of California Press, Berkeley, 1974), p. 222.
[24] J. Orieux, *Talleyrand: The Art of Survival* (Secker and Warburg, London, 1974), pp. 356 ff.; D. Chandler, *The Campaigns of Napoleon* (Weidenfeld and Nicolson, London, 1967). The treaty text of 12 October 1808 is in *Correspondance de Napoléon Ier*, vol. 17, no. 14372, p. 544.
[25] See particularly the account in Simon, *The Failure*, pp. 145 ff. For reparations imposed on Prussia see Henderson, *Blucher*, p. 29; Martens, *Principaux traités*, p. 102, 'Conventions between France and Prussia for Payment of War Contributions, Evacuation of the Country and Provisioning', 17 September 1808.
[26] Craig, *The Prussian Army*, pp. 38 ff.

letter brought his part in the Prussian reforms to an end. On 16 December 1808 Napoleon declared him an outlaw and the statesman had to flee to Austria.

This was not the only time that the emperor interfered in Prussian politics to weaken the patriotic party; the military reformer, General Scharnhorst, was forced from office in 1810. Such interference was as important as the formal arms control measures in weakening Prussian power.[27] On 25 July 1807 Frederick William had entrusted Scharnhorst with the direction of the Military Reorganization Commission, which was to introduce the changes that defeat had shown were necessary. The king picked Scharnhorst because of his powers of analysis and because he was one of the few officers who had distinguished themselves in the recent campaign. But, true to his cautious nature, the king also balanced the Commission with conservatives who would try to ensure that nothing too radical was attempted. It took some months before Stein and Scharnhorst managed to have these men replaced with members of their own party.[28]

Frederick the Great had been able to defeat his enemies by iron discipline, but armies trained on these lines could not fight on equal terms with the national forces unleashed by the French Revolution. The Prussian people needed to want to defeat the French in a way they had not demonstrated in 1806. They also had to want to join the army. In theory, Prussia had had national service since 1701, but in practice, most Prussians served only in the reserve, which had a few weeks' training a year. The nobility, middle classes, and skilled workers were in any case exempt. The standing army was made up of Prussian peasants and volunteers from other countries, who were frequently tricked into serving. The reformers sought a dramatic improvement in army conditions and abolished many of the most vicious punishments, such as running the gauntlet. They hoped that military service would no longer be looked on with fear and desertion would be reduced.[29]

According to the conventional view, the Prussian reformers evaded the restrictions in the Separate Articles by the 'Krumper' system, under which soldiers served for a brief period then passed

---

[27] Henderson, *Blucher*, p. 31; Craig, *The Prussian Army*, p. 55; Shanahan, *Military Reforms*, p. 158.
[28] Shanahan, *Military Reforms*, pp. 100–2.
[29] Shanahan, *Military Reforms*, pp. 39, 135 ff.

into an ever growing reserve that tripled the manpower available. This view was challenged by the American historian, William Shanahan, in 1945. Shanahan argued that, far from wanting to use the Reserve or Krumper system to evade Napoleon's restrictions, the reformers hoped to introduce a genuine form of conscription so that all Prussians would serve in the army. They also began their schemes long before the Paris Treaty was signed. In 1807 they proposed that everyone should serve in a militia, and in March of the following year Stein and the Military Reorganization Commission itself backed a plan for a national militia to be called the Provincial Troops.[30] But the king and many members of the government were hostile. The upper classes would also have objected to any proposals which meant that their sons would be forced to serve alongside members of the lower classes. While the small body of reformers saw conscription as a means of reforming the state and increasing national power, most educated Prussians saw national service as a threatening innovation borrowed from the French Revolution.[31]

The Separate Articles of the Paris Treaty were designed to prevent the measures which Scharnhorst had envisaged and which the Austrians were actually introducing. Article III laid down, 'il ne sera fait . . . aucune levée de milice ou de garde bourgeoises, ni aucun rassemblement tendant à augmenter la force ci-dessus spécifié.' The Military Reorganization Commission tried to evade these limitations by establishing a National Watch in every city. Napoleon himself had approved a civil guard to maintain order in Berlin; the reformers wished to build on this by giving the National Watch equal status with the army and making everyone serve in its ranks. It seems most unlikely that Napoleon would ever have allowed such a transparent evasion of the peace treaty. His spies kept him well enough informed of what was going on in Prussia. Indeed, Napoleon himself sent out orders as to who was to be arrested or executed for opposition to his regime.[32] But Napoleon had no need to block the reformers' scheme since Frederick William did so instead. The king was motivated by social conservatism and fear of provoking the French, although the costs would also have presented a formidable obstacle, given Prussian poverty and French exactions.

[30] Shanahan, *Military Reforms*, p. 152.
[31] Shanahan, *Military Reforms*, p. 156.
[32] Brotonne, *Lettres inédites*, no. 210, p. 88; no. 242, p. 100; no. 260, p. 109.

Prevented from establishing a militia under whatever name, the Military Reorganization Commission urged reforms of the existing canton system of recruitment. Under this system, each area was responsible for raising a specified number of men for the armed forces.[33] The Commission proposed that everyone should be liable to service, but those actually joining would be selected by lot rather than by social class. Not surprisingly, this too was rejected by the king. However, the struggle did not end there. When Austria went to war with France in 1809, Frederick William set up a new commission to study conscription. Since this was filled by Scharnhorst and other reformers, the outcome of their deliberations was easily foreseen. But the defeat of Austria at Wagram in July meant that it was most unlikely that Frederick William would risk French wrath by introducing national service. The Prussians were fortunate not to have been forced to send troops to help Napoleon defeat the Austrians, as they were committed to do under the fifth of the Separate Articles.[34]

Meanwhile the reformers continued to prepare their case. On 5 February 1810 one of their number, Boyen, detailed the way universal service might operate. His proposals were so clearly formulated that they became the basis of the law which was actually passed on 3 September 1814, when Prussia could finally throw off its French shackles. But in 1810 such plans were impractical, not least because Europe was suffering from recession exacerbated by the Continental system.[35] Frederick William tried to persuade Napoleon to postpone payment of the Prussian indemnity. The emperor replied that Prussia could find the money by dissolving the whole army except for the Royal Guard, which was itself limited by the Separate Articles to 6,000 men. The Prussians had to continue paying and the army's budget had to be reduced still further to find the funds.[36]

While the reformers were struggling to introduce conscription, they continued with the traditional Krumper system. Under this scheme, trained men were placed in reserve and their places were taken by recruits. However, Shanahan argued that the objective

[33] Shanahan, *Military Reforms*, pp. 159 ff.
[34] Parry, *Consolidated Treaty Series*, vol. 60, p. 147, Article V.
[35] Shanahan, *Military Reforms*, p. 155.
[36] Henderson, *Blucher*, p. 157.

was not to build a massive reserve to evade the Separate Articles but simply to provide replacements for casualties in wartime. In any case, from 1808 onwards the tendency was to recruit soldiers into the army who had been members of regiments dissolved after the defeat in 1807.[37] Such a system plainly made use of the existing skills of old soldiers, but it meant that between the Peace of Tilsit until the middle of 1809 only 863 reservists without any military training were recruited into the armed forces. The new War Department sent out a stream of orders trying to reverse this process and encourage training of a wider contingent, but it had to contend with the natural tendency of the regiments to prefer experienced soldiers.[38]

Economic factors also kept the army small. In June 1808 there were some 50,000 officers and men in the Prussian army, but nearly 24,000 of these were on leave to reduce costs. According to Shanahan's figures, the following year the army had 'grown' to 52,000 but only 22,000 were actually serving. Figures for 1810 show nearly 34,000 with the colours, 10,781 on leave, 1,300 garrison troops, and 3,300 sick. There were also 22,380 soldiers from disbanded regiments, of whom 11,218 could still bear arms.[39] Thus Shanahan argued that the king's caution, the conservatism of the Prussian elite, and Prussian poverty all combined with Napoleon's measures to keep the country weak and oppressed. Moreover, the reformers were not pursuing a carefully thought out plan of evasion through the Krumper system.

The danger in the Shanahan thesis is that it might encourage historians to ignore the extent to which contemporaries believed Prussia was deliberately evading the peace treaty. The Separate Articles were consciously designed to make evasion more difficult. Napoleon himself was perpetually suspicious of Prussian actions. In August 1810 he told Champagny, 'si les compagnies [of Prussian soldiers] sont de 100 hommes, il est clair qu'on peut les doubler en deux mois de préparatifs et que au lieu de 40,000 hommes la Prusse pourraient en avoir 80,000.' The emperor asked for more information on Prussian actions and demanded a monthly report on the power of all his neighbours.

Napoleon's fears help to explain the origins of the Krumper

---

[37] Shanahan, *Military Reforms*, p. 162.
[38] Ibid., p. 166; Craig, *The Prussian Army*, p. 55.
[39] Shanahan, *Military Reforms*, p. 176.

'myth'.[40] Yet they were exaggerated and it was not until after Napoleon's defeat in Russia that, with financial assistance from Britain, Prussia could introduce the bulk of the reforms which Scharnhorst and others had advocated for so long.

THE DISARMAMENT OF AUSTRIA

While Napoleon was forcing the Prussians to sign the Separate Articles, the Austrian government was preparing to defend itself by reforming and expanding its armies. Austria's pre-eminent soldier, the Archduke Charles, began to reform instructions and drill, dismissed twenty-five of the most incompetent generals, and tried to popularize the army by reducing the ferocity of military discipline. For the first time Austria now had a reserve system, with two battalions of reserves attached to each regiment. The severity of the French threat even persuaded the court to set aside their political suspicions of such a force and established a *landwehr* or militia which had grown to 150,000 men by 1809. Reforms were, however, limited by opposition to the government in the Austrian Diet, by Hungarian recalcitrance, by the conservatism of the army itself, and by the empire's economic problems. Previous wars had been partly paid for by printing money and inflation was worsening.[41]

From the beginning Napoleon regarded Charles's reforms with acute and justified suspicion and periodically he taxed Metternich about their nature and purpose. He claimed that Austrian military reforms made it difficult for him to withdraw troops from Prussia.[42] Even before the Erfurt Conference with Tsar Alexander, there was a danger that Napoleon would use the Austrian reforms as an excuse to attack Vienna. The emperor was further incensed by the Austrians' reluctance to recognize his brothers, Joseph as king of Spain and Joachim as king of the two Sicilies.[43] On their side, the Austrians deluded themselves about the strength of their position.

---

[40] *Correspondance de Napoléon Ier*, vol. 21, letter to Champagny, no. 16744, p. 2. Madelin's account in particular is at variance with Shanahan's. After wrongly ascribing the arms limitation clauses to the Treaty of Tilsit, he estimated that Prussia trained 120,000 men a year for two months and then sent them home to continue training in secret; Madelin, *Histoire du Consulate*, vol. 2, p. 62.

[41] Macartney, *The Habsburg Empire*, p. 183. See also G. E. Rothenberg, *Napoleon's Great Adversaries: The Archduke Charles and the Austrian Army 1792–1814* (Batsford, London, 1982), pp. 103 ff.

[42] Metternich, *Memoirs*, vol. 2, pp. 236.

[43] Ibid., pp. 252, 275.

With singularly bad judgement, Metternich argued that war was no longer popular in France and that the best troops were bogged down in Spain. He claimed that, as Austrian military efficiency was increasing, so French weakness and Austrian strength made its position twice as strong as it had been in 1805. Some of the emperor's advisers had their doubts and the Archduke Charles himself wavered, but the empress and most of the imperial entourage confidently pushed the country into war.[44]

Within one month of the outbreak of war on 9 April 1809, the delusions of Metternich and the war party were utterly exposed. Charles failed to attack before the French had concentrated their troops, and few Germans answered Austrian appeals to rise against the French. On the contrary, many fought on Napoleon's side, while the Russian forces in Galicia fulfilled the Erfurt agreement by menacing Austria from the east. The French army advanced rapidly on Vienna, which surrendered on 12 May. The Habsburg armies won one victory at Aspern the same month, but Charles was too cautious to exploit it. The Austrians' defeat at Wagram in July was decisive and they were compelled to sign an armistice which Napoleon insisted was effectively a capitulation.[45]

Despite his disastrous earlier miscalculations, Metternich now became Francis's adviser on foreign affairs. He warned the emperor that Napoleon would demand reparations and annex Austrian territory. He might also force the Austrians to disarm, but Metternich pointed out that the country's weakened economy would make some disarmament essential in any case. The vital considerations were to keep the cadres and the *landwehr* system intact. In the meantime, 'we must confine our system to tacking and turning and flattering. Thus alone may we possibly preserve our existence.'[46]

Peace was finally made at Schönbrunn on 14 October 1809. As usual, Napoleon waged a 'war of nerves' during the negotiations. On 19 August he told his Foreign Minister to threaten to divide the Austrian empire into three and to introduce the French legal code into the occupied territories. Champagny was to tell the Austrians that peace could not be made until their army was reduced and all

---

[44] Metternich, *Memoirs*, vol. 2, pp. 301 ff., 346; Maccartney, *The Habsburg Empire*, p. 187; Rothenberg, *Napoleon's Great Adversaries*, pp. 123–4.

[45] *Correspondance de Napoléon Ier*, vol. 19, instructions to Champagny, 19 August 1909, no. 15683, p. 364; Rothenberg, *Napoleon's Great Adversaries*, p. 170.

[46] Metternich, *Memoirs*, vol. 2, pp. 360 ff.

French, Belgians, and Italians serving in its ranks were handed over. As a result of Napoleon's negotiating tactics, when the terms became known the Austrians were pleased that Francis, at least, had not been forced to abdicate and see his lands partitioned. However, Metternich considered the Treaty so bad that he claimed to have had no part in the final negotiations.[47] The French seized the area round Salzburg, Upper Austria, and parts of Italy, including the Austrian outlet to the sea at Trieste. The Austrians also had to cede territories to Russia and Saxony. Napoleon promised to grant a free pardon to the Bavarian rebels, but this did not stop him executing their leader.

As with the Prussian treaties, the open agreements were accompanied by 'Separate Articles'. These laid down that the Austrian forces should be limited to 150,000 men and they also included provisions for reparations. But there were subtle differences between the two sets of Separate Articles, which reflected the fact that Austria remained a much more effective power than Prussia had been in 1807. The limitation on the size of the Austrian army was justified by the reduction in the size of the empire and by the need to avoid tension between the two states, rather than by the suggestion that it was to avoid annoying Napoleon. Limitations were also to last only until the maritime war against Britain ended, rather than for a fixed period, and there were no sub-limits on the numbers of artillery, cavalry, and other arms.[48]

Article V of the Separate Articles made clear that Napoleon had demanded 200 million francs from the occupied territories but had agreed to reduce this to 85 million. Thirty million was to be paid before Vienna was evacuated and the rest was to be raised in Amsterdam, Leipzig, and other financial centres. The various bills were to be paid off at the rate of 5 million a month from January 1810 for the first five months and then at the rate of 6 million a month. As in the Prussian case, reparations alone would have been enough to limit Habsburg power without the provisions for forced disarmament. Long after formal disarmament had been abandoned, Vienna remained in such a weakened economic state that its forces were notoriously badly equipped and poorly protected against the

---

[47] Metternich, *Memoirs*, vol. 1, pp. 110 ff.

[48] The Separate Articles are not included in most Treaty series. The text of the rest of the Treaty is in F. Israel, *Major Peace Treaties of World History, 1648–1967*, vol. 1 (McGraw-Hill, New York, 1967), pp. 487 ff. For the Separate Articles see Parry, *Consolidated Treaty Series*, vol. 60.

weather. Army expenditure was reduced from 253 million florins in 1809 to 175 million in 1810 and 30 million the following year. Pay and allowances were frozen, no new weapons were produced, and stocks of equipment were run down.[49] In the meantime, the Austrians had to 'tack and turn' in Metternich's phrase. Within a year of the peace treaty with France, his appeasement policy led to the marriage of Marie Louise, the daughter of the Austrian Emperor, to the French usurper. Metternich told Francis that this greatly strengthened Austria's position but that 'in spite of the marriage periods may occur when we shall have to summon all our energies to avert or resist the threatened danger of subjection.'[50] In the meantime, Metternich worked to improve Austria's position by negotiation. He acted as intermediary in an abortive attempt to mediate between Napoleon and Pope Pius VII, though he also worked to undermine the Franco-Russian alliance.

On 24 September 1810 Metternich brought a visit to Paris to a close by an interview with the French Emperor. He had warned Napoleon that he would try to have the disarmament clause cancelled. 'Your Majesty acknowledged that, should we resolve to make war on you, we should not be stopped by that stipulation; while during peace it is equally useless and humiliating.' Apparently Napoleon was disappointed that the Treaty had not given him a more effective means of controlling Austrian power. Metternich was able to argue that it humiliated Austria without providing any real strategic advantage. Accordingly, Napoleon agreed to its annulment to please his father-in-law.[51] Within a week he was writing to the Austrian Emperor, 'J'ai vu plusieurs fois le comte de Metternich. Je lui ai parlé du sentiment que je port a votre majesté imperials.' Despite the importance which Napoleon said he ascribed to the Separate Articles limiting the Austrian army, he was willing to set them aside to please his father-in-law

---

[49] On Austrian military expenditure see Rothenberg, *Napoleon's Great Adversaries*, p. 74. For the Austrian army's achievements in the final years of the Napoleonic wars see D. G. Chandler, *The Campaigns of Napoleon* (Weidenfeld and Nicolson, London, 1967), pp. 945 ff. See also D. Hamilton-Williams, *The Fall of Napoleon* (Arms and Armour Press, London, 1994), pp. 35-6.
[50] Metternich, *Memoirs*, vol. 2, pp. 38 ff. For another view of Metternich's policy see G. Mann, *Secretary of Europe: The Life of Friedrich Gentz, Enemy of Napoleon* (Archon, 1970), p. 173.
[51] Metternich, *Memoirs*, vol. 2, p. 466.

'et de lui donner de nouvelle preuve de mon estime et de ma haute considération'.[52]

The effects of this change were primarily moral rather than physical. Metternich warned Francis at the time, 'we are on the point of a complete financial collapse, of a reduction of the army caused by this, of a thorough prostration of strength constraining us.' Gunther Rothenberg, the historian of the Austrian army, calculated that there were, in theory, 259,918 men under arms in 1810, though only 171,066 were actually available for service. He also quoted the British agent in Vienna, John Harcourt King, who claimed that, in fact, only some 60,000 could really be put in the field.[53]

Events from September 1808 to September 1810 demonstrated that limiting the manpower of defeated armies was an integral part of the Napoleonic system; that such stipulations were kept 'separate' or secret, presumably because they were regarded as particularly humiliating; that, even when they were secret, these provisions became widely known and they were still regarded as degrading by the defeated power; that they were unnecessary and ineffective, and that Napoleon's most decisive tactic for weakening his enemies was either seizing their territories or imposing reparations.

The arms limitation measures imposed by Napoleon on Prussia in 1808 and on Austria the following year were certainly of a type unusual before the twentieth century, except where the conqueror intended to absorb the conquered territory into his own empire—as in Poland in the 1790s. Verification of compliance with limitations on manpower requires a very high degree of control by the dominant power, the sort of domination which Napoleon had over Prussia and Austria, or Hitler had over France between 1940 and 1942. Even then, the conquerors were always suspicious that the vanquished were not obeying their orders. Where full occupation or brutal reprisals are not possible, the defeated will circumvent their obligations, as the German army did in the 1920s.

Napoleon's restrictions did make it more difficult for the Prussian reformers to establish conscription or an effective militia

[52] *Correspondance de Napoléon Ier*, vol. 21, letter to Francis II, no. 16968, p. 159.
[53] Metternich, *Memoirs*, vol. 2, p. 483; Rothenberg, *Napoleon's Great Adversaries*, pp. 174-5. Rothenberg ignored the fact that Napoleon had abandoned the formal disarmament of Austria in September 1810.

system. But Prussian military power was effectively checked by more traditional methods such as the reduction in the size of the country, the indemnity imposed by the French, and Napoleon's spasmodic persecution of the reformers. The conservatism of the king and most of the aristocratic and middle-class Prussians, and the intrinsic poverty of the country, acted as a further brake on progress. In the circumstances, the reformers did all they could to increase Prussian power by improvements in training and in the technical wings of the army. However, they did not invent a sophisticated system of evasion which enabled them to train 150,000 reserves, as Napoleon suspected and many later historians believed. In the Austrian case, disarmament was only imposed for a year but Austrian power, like Prussian, was mainly restricted by its financial problems and the conservatism of vested interests. There is always a trade-off in enforced disarmament between the strategic advantages achieved by such measures and the political disadvantage of further embittering defeated enemies. In Napoleon's case the disadvantages outweighed the advantages. Before his defeat they made Austria and Prussia more determined to join his enemies. After the battle of Waterloo, as the next chapter will show, they encouraged the Prussians to press for a harsh and repressive peace treaty.

One of the most important effects of Napoleon's measures occurred nearly a century after his death. The 'Krumper myth' propagated by nineteenth-century historians had a major impact on the statesmen who negotiated the Treaty of Versailles after the First World War. Lloyd George, Balfour, and others believed that they had to stop Germany again evading forced disarmament through a Krumper system, and the provisions of the Treaty of Versailles were designed to meet this contingency.[54] In this they failed because of the innate strength of the German state. Napoleon's efforts were largely unnecessary because of Prussian and Austrian economic weakness; conversely, Allied attempts to impose forced disarmament on Germany in the 1920s were ineffective in the long run because of Germany's demographic and industrial power, and the unwillingness of the British and French to fight to preserve the Treaty of Versailles.

[54] Shanahan, *Military Reforms*, pp. 13 ff.

2

The Demilitarization of French Fortresses in 1815

By 1814 the whole of Europe from Gibraltar to Moscow had suffered for two decades from the ravages of French armies in wars which were almost unlimited by conventional restraints. Allied statesmen, who gathered in Vienna in 1814 and in Paris a year later, had thought long and hard about ways of preventing a recurrence of French aggression. Their solutions were comprehensive— political, strategic, and military. After some hesitation in 1815, the political solution they favoured was the restoration of a reformed Bourbon monarchy which, they hoped, would prevent future revolutions and the aggression that went with them. Their strategic answer was to keep the alliance together and to isolate France if it again showed signs of wanting to upset the international status quo. Their military answer was to revert to the pre-Napoleonic policy of demolishing existing French fortifications or constructing new ones in friendly territories. This, they believed, would end the imbalance of power which had encouraged French aggression ever since Vauban surrounded France with lines of fortifications during the reign of Louis XIV.

Historians have seriously underestimated the importance attached to these fortifications in the negotiations between allied leaders in 1815.[1] The negotiators clutched at almost anything which would reduce further threats. However, they eschewed the Napoleonic system of limiting enemy force levels, partly because

[1] H. A. Kissinger, *A World Restored* (Gollancz, London, 1973); C. K. Webster, *The Congress of Vienna, 1814–1815* (Thames and Hudson, London, 1963), p. 25; H. Nicolson, *The Congress of Vienna: A Study in Allied Unity: 1812–1822* (Constable, London, 1946), p. 235; G. Ferrero, *The Reconstruction of Europe: Talleyrand and the Congress of Vienna 1814–1815* (Putnam, New York, 1941), pp. 93 ff.; D. Cooper, *Talleyrand* (Jonathan Cape, London, 1964); P. W. Schroeder, *The Transformation of European Politics, 1763–1848* (Clarendon Press, Oxford, 1994), pp. 517 ff.

these had been unsuccessful and partly because they did not want to increase the numbers of unemployed and embittered French veterans. Furthermore, allied leaders naturally grasped at familiar and time-hallowed measures in contrast to Napoleon's revolutionary and imperialistic techniques. Thus the focus on fortifications was a consequence of both the rejection of alternatives and the natural conservatism of the allies.[2]

Initially, they hoped to achieve a lasting peace by winning over the French with their magnanimity. The Peace of Paris, which the allies negotiated with Louis XVIII in May 1814, was a model of restraint and conciliation. Despite the immensity of the upheaval and suffering which the French had inflicted on Europe for two decades, France was not forced to pay reparations; nor was it partitioned, nor were its armies disarmed or its fortresses demolished. Indeed, the Treaty laid down that the Powers had 'the complete right to fortify any point in their respective States which they may judge necessary for their security'. France kept the frontiers which it had held in 1792 while, at the same time, some of the other states around its borders were strengthened to discourage further French aggression. The British were determined to bolster the Netherlands by uniting it under the House of Orange and building frontier works. The German states were to be linked in a federation, while Germany's western frontier was to be guarded by Prussia and Bavaria.[3]

The Congress of Vienna was still in session when news reached it that this conciliatory policy had failed. Napoleon had escaped from exile in Elba on 26 February 1815 and the French army and people had rallied to his cause. It took the battle of Waterloo on 18 June and the loss of 12,000 British and Hanoverians, 7,000 Prussians, and 25,000 French before Napoleon could be neutralized once more and exiled to St Helena off the coast of Africa.[4] Once

[2] Editeur des Archives Diplomatiques, *Le Congrès de Vienne et les traités de 1815 avec une introduction historique par M. Capefigue* (Amyot, Paris, n.d.), pp. 1470 ff. See also T. D. Veve, *The Duke of Wellington and the British Army of Occupation in France 1815–1818* (Greenwood Press, Westport, Conn., 1992), pp. 93 ff.

[3] M. Hurst (ed.), *Key Treaties for the Great Powers 1814–1914*, vol. 1 (David and Charles, Newton Abbot, 1972), p. 1; G. J. Renier, *Great Britain and the Kingdom of the Netherlands, 1813–1815* (Allen and Unwin, London, 1930), pp. 266 ff.

[4] E. Longford, *Wellington: The Years of the Sword* (Weidenfeld and Nicolson, London, 1992), p. 329.

their armies had taken Paris, allied statesmen continued their deliberations in the French capital. Now they were inclined to take a more jaundiced view of the benefits of magnanimity. They believed that they were justified in forcing a measure of disarmament on the defeated enemy. Historians have minimized this decisive change which took place after Waterloo, but contemporary documents show that forced changes in the fortifications on the French frontiers became the panacea for the problems facing the negotiators.

THE POST-WATERLOO NEGOTIATIONS

The Allied statesmen were never clear in their own minds about whether they held the nature of the previous French regime or the correlation of forces responsible for French expansionism. But, as practical men, they were more concerned about how they could reduce the threats in future than about resolving conceptual dilemmas. Frequently they blamed what the Austrian negotiator, Prince Metternich, called 'armed Jacobinism' for the upheaval but, after Napoleon's escape from Elba, none was confident that the Bourbons would be sufficiently competent to secure their throne and prevent a fresh outbreak of such 'Jacobinism'.[5] Thus, if their political solution failed, they would rely on the strategy of keeping their alliance intact in case of a Bonapartist or Jacobin revival.

At the same time, all the chief negotiators also blamed French aggression on the excessive strength which Vauban's fortifications had given them. Metternich pointed out that France had lost its main army and all its equipment in 1812, but it had still managed to hold the rest of Europe in check for two years. In fact, modern historians of the final campaigns stress Napoleon's leadership and the mobility of his armies as the main factors which enabled France to resist, rather than its fortifications. Nevertheless, fortifications in Germany and Spain as well as France did considerably delay the allied advance. Wellington said afterwards that his army could not advance until he had taken Pamplona and Sebastian.[6] Thus, in July and August 1815, there grew up a consensus among the allied

[5] *Le Congrès de Vienne*, p. 1482.
[6] Philip Henry, fifth Earl Stanhope, *Notes of Conversations with the Duke of Wellington, 1831–1851* (John Murray, London, 1888), p. 4. For a modern view see D. G. Chandler, *The Campaigns of Napoleon* (Weidenfeld and Nicolson, London, 1967), pp. 945 ff.

negotiators that French frontier fortifications should be either destroyed or occupied while neighbouring states built up their own. Together with the exaction of an indemnity and the temporary occupation of France, this attempt to change the balance of military power was the most significant difference between the peace terms laid down in 1814 and those finally imposed.[7]

Lord Liverpool, the British Prime Minister, Capo d'Istria of Russia, Hardenberg, the Prussian Chancellor, and Metternich all produced extensive memoranda on how French aggression could be prevented in future. Liverpool gave the British delegate, Viscount Castlereagh, the Cabinet's instructions on 30 June. He argued that, if Napoleon remained at large, the allies were justified in demanding more security than they had been given in 1814. In particular they should annex some of France's frontier fortresses, including Lille. Alternatively, these could be taken over temporarily during Napoleon's lifetime or for a set period. Liverpool also wanted 'a severe example' to be made of those French officers who changed sides and joined Napoleon in 1815.[8] Castlereagh informed the British Prime Minister that his immediate concerns in Paris were to limit the rapacity of the Prussian army and, in particular, to stop it blowing up the bridges across the Seine. He also said that Britain's allies would never withdraw their armies from France without receiving an indemnity and that the French government was not strong enough to go against public opinion and execute those who had changed sides.[9]

After a long sitting of the Cabinet, Liverpool responded on 15 July. The government saw Louis's inability to punish those who had changed sides as a sign of a fundamental weakness which was irremediable. In particular, the king would never be able to rely on the loyalty of the French army. The British public believed that magnanimity had failed, that the French would never forgive the humiliation of defeat, and thus the allies would be unwise to worry about upsetting French sensibilities. Liverpool presented the Cabinet's views as moderate in comparison, yet it is difficult to believe that public opinion really limited government options. After such a ferocious and protracted war one would expect cries for vengeance,

[7] Hurst, *Key Treaties*, pp. 99 ff.

[8] Webster, *The Congress of Vienna*, p. 159. See also C. K. Webster, *British Diplomacy 1813–1815: Select Documents Dealing with the Reconstruction of Europe* (Bell, London, 1921), p. 340.

[9] Webster, *British Diplomacy*, p. 342.

and there was some pressure for Napoleon's execution. But the British people had not suffered as the Prussians and Spanish had from French occupation. The government felt able to ignore the public over Napoleon's fate, while he would certainly have been shot had he fallen into the hands of the Prussian army. If public opinion could be ignored over such an emotional issue, then it was not likely to influence the fine points of the peace settlement.

Nevertheless, Liverpool used the alleged attitudes of the public to strengthen his proposals. He suggested that the allies could either take back the 'principal conquests of Louis XIV' or occupy the key fortresses for five to seven years. In a clever move to reconcile forced disarmament with efforts to strengthen monarchical government in France, the allies would promise to hand the fortresses back to the Bourbons but to no other French government. In a similar move to create synergy between reparations and forced disarmament, the Netherlands and Germany could build up their own fortifications with the help of French indemnities. Liverpool maintained that this was perfectly just, since the French had broken their 'most sacred treaties' and the allies could have been far more rapacious, as indeed the French had been when they were victorious.[10]

Political leaders thus looked for security to military measures, while some of the more far-sighted military men sought safety in politics. The Duke of Wellington, commanding the allied occupation forces, emerged alongside Castlereagh and Tsar Alexander as one of the leading 'doves'.[11] He denied that the French people had been united behind Napoleon in 1815 or that the allies would have conquered the country so easily if they had resisted. Thus a distinction had to be made between people and government. Like his colleagues, Wellington was torn between the view that the wars had been caused by excessive French power and the view that they were a result of revolutionary doctrines. However, unlike many of the civilian statesmen, he saw no legitimate or lasting way of making substantial reductions in French strength. If the allies tried to force France to cede territory, Louis XVIII might simply refuse and embarrass the allies. In any case, 'if we take the cession, war

---

[10] C. W. Vane (ed.), *Correspondence, Despatches and Other Papers of Viscount Castlereagh* (John Murray, London, 1853), p. 431; Webster, *British Diplomacy*, p. 345.
[11] Webster, *British Diplomacy*, p. 357.

must be considered as only deferred, until France shall find a way of endeavouring to regain what she has lost.' Thus the political causes of war could alone be adequately addressed with any chance of making a lasting peace. This meant a temporary occupation of French fortresses and a lenient peace to strengthen the French king.[12]

At the opposite extreme from Wellington's lenient views were those of the Prussians. Their contribution to the debate was dated 4 August. The Prussians based their argument on the premise that France had betrayed the confidence placed in it by the allies the year before. Thus it would be unforgivable to show excessive leniency a second time. To weaken France, the allies could impose a massive indemnity, but a nation with more egotism than patriotism (like the French) would find the loss of territories less galling. Such a loss would hit only a few while an indemnity would hurt the whole population. Accordingly, it was appropriate to seize French territory and give it to France's neighbours, thus securing them against aggression. Temporary guarantees, such as the French occupation of Prussian fortresses during the late war, merely aggravated the conquered nation. In any case they did not address the principal problem, which was produced by long-term alterations in the balance of power. 'Lorsqu'une nation a surpassé sa défensive marquée par la nature ou par l'art, elle devient offensive et menaçante par ce pas même . . . et elle conservera cet esprit aussi longtemps que sa situation géographique restera la même.' From Louis XIV's time onwards this had been the case with France because it had been surrounded by weak countries while its own fortresses and frontiers offered it protection against its enemies. Unless France were pushed back towards a more defensive line, the situation and the threat to stability would persist. Such a line would be created if the French had to cede their part of Flanders to the Netherlands, Alsace and Lorraine to Germany, and other territory to the Kingdom of Sardinia.[13]

On 22 July Castlereagh had had a long conversation with the tsar, who was against seizing large areas of French territory but favoured dismantling French fortifications in the traditional

[12] Webster, *British Diplomacy*, p. 351.
[13] *Le Congrès de Vienne*, p. 1479, 'Memorandum du prince de Hardenberg, 4 août 1815'. I am indebted to Michael Juricic of King's College, London, for the suggestion that the Prussian memorandum was by Knesebeck, not Hardenberg, as this collection of documents suggests.

fashion rather than occupying them temporarily.[14] At the end
of July his Minister, Capo d'Istria, produced an extensive and
thoughtful memorandum on the subject. His ideas were very similar to those of the British representatives in Paris. He argued that,
above all, France must be saved from revolution and provide moral
and physical guarantees against future aggression. Among the
obstacles to expansion which he considered were alterations in
French frontiers, seizure or demolition of French fortifications on
the frontiers, confiscation of all military equipment, destruction of
the arsenals which produced it, and imposition of a heavy indemnity.[15]

In Capo d'Istria's view most of these courses had been ruled out
by the Treaty of Paris of 30 May 1814, which had been based on
the principle that France should not be treated as a defeated enemy.
If this principle were abandoned, then all allied engagements
up to that time would have to be rethought. Furthermore, Louis
XVIII would be undermined by a vindictive peace while conversely
a reformed French monarchy would provide the best guarantee
against the sort of revolution which brought Napoleon to power.
At the same time, Capo d'Istria proposed that the allies should
renew the Treaty of Chaumont, which bound them to co-operate
against Napoleon, and occupy France with the concurrence of the
French government until stability had been ensured there. Furthermore, he proposed that France should pay for the occupation and
for the construction of fortresses along its frontiers, which would
protect neighbouring states 'contre l'immense et menaçante ligne
des places fortes que la France présente le long de ses frontières du
côté de la Belgique et du Rhine'.[16] Thus the Russians sought to
avoid victimizing the French people, while building up fortifications in neighbouring countries to prevent future aggression.

Metternich's memorandum also took a middle course between
Prussian views and those expressed by the Duke of Wellington.
Like Capo d'Istria, he argued that the previous struggle by the
allies had not been a war of conquest but one against armed
Jacobinism. Then, in a clear reference to Prussian ambitions,
Metternich dismissed all sudden territorial changes inflicted for

---

[14] Webster, *British Diplomacy*, p. 350.
[15] *Le Congrès de Vienne*, 'Memorandum de M. Capo d'Istria, ministre de
Russia, 28 July 1815', pp. 1470 ff. For British criticism of the Russian paper see
Vane, *Castlereagh*, p. 454.
[16] *Le Congrès de Vienne*, p. 1471.

their own sake. On the other hand, he argued that the allies had the right to demand an indemnity for the costs of the war, a real and permanent guarantee that France had changed from an offensive to a defensive posture and the adoption of a form of government which was acceptable to the other Powers.[17]

Metternich too then argued that war had been encouraged by an imbalance of power. He reiterated the Prussian paper's argument that, since Louis XIV's time, France's frontier fortresses had tempted it into aggression. Its fortifications in Flanders, Alsace, and Franche-Comté were out of proportion to those of the surrounding countries and had been immensely strengthened by the introduction of 'the national guard' during the Revolution and the destruction of fortifications in other countries. Because of these advantages, the French people could feel confident that, though they might lose men and money in their wars, they would not have to suffer themselves. Coming from the Rhineland, Metternich knew that French governments had also destroyed all the fortifications in the Netherlands and Germany which offered resistance to their forces: 'Ehrenbreitstein, Philipsbourg, Ingolstadt et plusieurs autres places de la plus grande importance ont été demolies en entier.' Towns had been deprived of their ramparts and Savoy had had to promise not to fortify its passes.[18]

Thus, although the tone of the Russian and Austrian memoranda was different from the Prussian, and although they rejected partition for its own sake, all three addressed the problem of fortifications, Metternich wanted to see France deprived of the first line of its defensive works. In Flanders this meant giving the fortresses to the Netherlands; in Alsace the fortresses should be destroyed, except for Landau which should go to Germany to compensate for the loss of Philipsbourg, Strasbourg should cease to be a vast and menacing camp, while Brançon and other fortified places should be demolished. Finally France should be temporarily occupied by an army of at least 100,000 to 150,000 men.[19]

Liverpool's government was not as 'dovish' as the Duke of Wellington or even the Russians. On 28 July Liverpool argued that Russia was protected by distance, while Britain's position meant that it had more in common strategically with Austria and Prussia.

---

[17] *Le Congrès de Vienne*, 'Memorandum du prince de Metternich, août 1815', p. 1482.
[18] Ibid.
[19] *Le Congrès de Vienne*, p. 1486.

He also dismissed the tsar's proposal for demolition of French fortifications on the grounds that 'the dismantling of fortresses has rarely ever been completely effected. The works are partially destroyed, and may be restored for a small part of the expense at which they had been originally constructed.' Even if French fortifications were demolished and allied countries had not produced their own, victory would go to France, the state with the largest army while, if the Netherlands and other allies built fortresses, this would offer much greater security.[20] Against the Duke of Wellington, Liverpool argued on 11 August that nothing the allies could do would be likely to increase Louis XVIII's popularity. In a crucial phrase, which went to the heart of the issue, he said that 'the security of the neighbouring countries against France may be much more easily attained than the rendering of France orderly and pacific.'[21]

Talleyrand, who was serving as President of Louis's Council and Minister of Foreign Affairs, protested against the return of the art looted by Napoleon and complained constantly about the rapacity of the allied armies. When the allies sent him their ultimatum on 20 September, outlining their proposed changes in French frontiers, he argued that all annexations of French territory were unfair and sent the allies a long philosophical discourse on the rights of conquest and the types of war which made such conquests appropriate. He also argued that it was unnecessary to alter the European balance of power to France's disadvantage because there were already two countries which were larger than France in terms of population and geographical extent. But the allies expressed astonishment at receiving a list of observations on the rights of conquest and denied that this was the basis of their ultimatum. It was not conquest which was their objective but altering the balance of power and ensuring the peace of Europe. Thus Talleyrand's protests were ignored.[22]

By rejecting Talleyrand's arguments, the allies weakened his

---

[20] Webster, *British Diplomacy*, p. 351.
[21] Ibid., p. 359.
[22] *Le Congrès de Vienne*, 'Ultimatum sous forme de projet de Traité présenté le 20 septembre 1815 aux Plénipotentiaires français par ceux des quatre Cours alliées', p. 1523. See also 'Réponse des Plénipotentiaires français à l'Ultimatum des quatre Cours alliées, du 20 septembre, en date du 21 septembre 1815', p. 1531. 'Note des Plénipotentiaires des Cours alliées en réponse à la note des Plénipotentiaires français du 21 septembre, en date du 22 septembre 1815', p. 1535.

position in France. He had alienated the tsar by his opposition to Alexander's plans for Poland in 1814, and he had become more of a liability than an asset to the Bourbons and the French people. He was replaced on 26 September by the Duc de Richelieu, who was well acquainted with the Russians, having lived in exile in their country and served in the Russian army and as governor of Odessa. The duke saw the tsar and explaining that, as a long-term exile, he needed to be able to render some important service for his country if his position were to be secure. Alexander said that he was not absolute master of the four-power negotiations and the fears of the Netherlands would have to be taken into account, but he hoped to be able to modify the terms laid down by the allies. According to French historians, the tsar was as good as his word; the occupation was reduced from seven to five years and fewer territorial concessions were demanded, though Richelieu and his countrymen continued to complain.[23]

As befits a conservative coalition, unwilling to consider radical innovations in peace-making or other activities, the allies made no attempt to restrict the French army in the way that Napoleon had limited the Prussian and Austrian ones. Such an idea was considered from time only to be rejected, partly on the grounds that undisciplined mobs of ex-soldiers were likely to undermine the French government. Formally unrestricted by the allies, the French law of 1818 planned an army of 240,000 men and this was raised to 400,000 six years later.[24] Very soon the French were able to consider themselves second in military strength only to the Russians and second in naval power to Britain.

The final allied 'solution' to the problem presented by excessive French power had been laid down in the Protocol of the Four-Power Conference on the Territorial Arrangements and Defensive System of the Germanic Confederation of 3 November 1815 and the other Treaties signed in Paris on the 20th and 21st of the same month. The French had to cede a number of towns to the Netherlands, including Philippeville and Marienburg, and the King of the Netherlands received 60 million francs to help him fortify

[23] *Le Congrès de Vienne*, introduction, p. C. The interview between Alexander and Richelieu is on p. CV. For alterations in the territorial conditions imposed on France after Richelieu's appointment compare Capefigue, *Le Congrès de Vienne*, p. 1524 and Hurst, *Key Treaties*, vol. 1, pp. 129–30.
[24] R. Bullen, in A. Sked (ed.), *Europe's Balance of Power 1815–1848* (Barnes and Noble, New York, 1979), p. 131.

his eastern frontier.[25] The composition of the allied garrisons of Luxembourg, Mainz, and Landau was carefully stipulated and the French were to destroy their fortifications at Huninguen, which had 'been constantly an object of uneasiness to the town of Bâle'. They were to promise not to restore the fortifications or to build any others in the vicinity.[26] Thus the allies rejected the more drastic Prussian proposals for annexing Alsace, Lorraine, and French Flanders, not least because, if they had been followed, the other allies believed the French would seek revenge within a few years and the British and Russians would then be drawn into the war to preserve the status quo. Nevertheless, France was driven back to where its frontiers had been in 1790. The Saar and the fortress of Sarre-Louis went to Prussia, part of Savoy to the kingdom of Sardinia, and some French frontier districts were transferred to Switzerland.

The German Confederation received 60 million francs in French indemnities for its defences. A third of this went to Prussia for fortifications on the Lower Rhine, a third was to be spent on fortifications on the Upper Rhine, and much of the rest went to the kingdom of Bavaria. None of the recipients was given complete freedom of action. Britain was to work with the King of the Netherlands to ensure that his fortifications proceeded satisfactorily. Austria and Prussia were to determine with the rest of the German Confederation how the fortifications were to be improved on the Rhine frontier, and Austria was to work with the kingdom of Savoy on the improvement of its northern fortifications.[27]

As Metternich had suggested, France was to be occupied by 150,000 allied troops. This was deeply resented, not least because so many of the troops who originally occupied France had behaved so badly. The French were to supply the occupation forces with food, clothing, tobacco, and other necessities. The occupation was to last for a maximum of five years but the allies were to re-

[25] Hurst, *Key Treaties*, p. 99, 'Protocol of Conference between Great Britain, Austria, Prussia and Russia respecting the Territorial Arrangements, and Defensive System of the Germanic Confederation, Paris'. The Prussians and Austrians fought hard against using the French indemnity to pay for fortifications as, no doubt, they wished to use the funds for their own purposes; see Vane, *Castlereagh*, pp. 484, 500.

[26] Hurst, *Key Treaties*, p. 134, 'Protocol of Conference between Great Britain, Austria, Prussia, and Russia, respecting the Fortification of the Netherlands, Germany and Savoy, Vienna 21 November 1815'.

[27] Ibid.

evaluate it after three to assess 'the progress which shall have been made in France in the re-establishment of order and tranquillity'. In fact the allies met French delegates at Aix-la-Chapelle in October 1818. They agreed to withdraw their forces by the end of November as the French government 'had fulfilled with the most scrupulous and honourable punctuality all clauses of the Treaties and Conventions'.[28]

The French were never reconciled to the 1815 treaties,[29] yet the political agreements which brought the Napoleonic Wars to an end were a model of restraint, and some of the allied delegates from Austria and elsewhere had to defend themselves against bitter attacks from their own people because of their leniency.[30] Allied statesmen had acted as if they were dealing with the end of a limited war, although they knew how total the conflict had been. Only the Prussians and some of the smaller German states wanted to set aside this fiction. The French indemnity was set at 700 million francs. However, with the help of allied bankers, the indemnity was paid off by 1820. Some strategically important points were removed from French control, yet the allies made no attempt to destroy or divide the country. Allied statesmen generally wanted to avoid alienating the French people. They realized that they might need to co-opt France against one of their allies, as Castlereagh and Metternich had done when they called on Talleyrand to resist Russo-Prussian ambitions in Eastern Europe in 1814.

Most of the allies also made a theoretical distinction between the French people and Napoleon. Once Napoleon had been exiled, they saw that it was in their interests to win over the people and support Louis XVIII. They knew that he would be undermined if the terms imposed were too harsh. All were aware that the distinction between people and leader was artificial. There must have been some sardonic smiles among the allied negotiators when Talleyrand told them, in September 1815, that France ought to be treated as leniently then as in the previous year, because in 1814

---

[28] Hurst, *Key Treaties*, p. 140, 'Convention between Great Britain (Austria, Prussia, Russia) and France for the Evacuation of the French Territory by the Allied Troops, Aix-la-Chapelle, 9th October 1818'.

[29] D. Porch, *Army and Revolution, France 1815–1848* (Routledge and Kegan Paul, London, 1974).

[30] G. Mann, *Secretary of Europe: The Life of Friedrich Gentz Enemy of Napoleon* (Archon, Hamden, Conn., 1970), p. 247.

Napoleon was the clear and legal leader of the French people, whereas in 1815 he was simply a usurper.[31] Everyone knew how the emperor had been welcomed on his return from Elba by joyous crowds and carried on their backs into his palace. The distinction between people and ruler was one of convenience rather than logic, but it is the basis of all lenient peace treaties.

Historians have rightly commended the statesmanship employed in the treaties of 1814 and 1815 but have generally remained silent on the military logic behind allied policies. This can be explained in part by the general indifference of diplomatic historians to military questions. The subsequent fate of the military terms laid down in the treaties must also have encouraged historians to disregard their contemporary importance, yet fortifications occupied more space in allied memoranda in the summer of 1815 than political issues.

Following the 1815 treaties, the allies continued to work on their defences. However, the Prussians and Austrians were half-hearted in their efforts, and plans for a German federal army were hampered by their quarrels and initially by the lack of a threat from France.[32] In the Netherlands, British and French money was used for fortifications and the construction was overseen by the Duke of Wellington. The Duke would not accept the withdrawal of the army of occupation from France until the fortifications were well advanced. By 1818 Wellington was sufficiently pleased to report that the Dutch king 'will have some of the finest fortresses in Europe' and thus the occupying forces could leave.[33] In the long run, however, allied plans were undermined by Dutch–Belgian tensions. In 1830 the union between the two peoples fell apart. The Great Powers now became worried that France might be able to capture the barrier forts and use them to strengthen its own defences. Ironically, in December 1831 they agreed that the fortresses at Menin, Ath, Mons, Philippeville, and Marienburg were to be demolished before the end of December 1833. The remaining fortifications, which the Belgians were considered able to hold, were to be strengthened. But, although the Belgians were party to the agreement, it was not until 1859 that they began

---

[31] Capefigue, *Le Congrès de Vienne*, p. 1533.
[32] L. J. Baack, *Christian Bernstorff and Prussia: Diplomacy and Reform Conservatism* (Rutgers University Press, New Brunswick, 1980), ch. 9.
[33] Veve, *The Duke of Wellington*, p. 98.

to strengthen their defences when they built a new fortified camp near Antwerp.[34]

The military logic behind the 1815 arrangements was weak. France had not expanded primarily because of the strength of its fortifications but both because the French Revolutionaries had tapped the whole power of the nation through conscription and because Napoleon had known how to make the best use of this energy on the battlefield. Fortifications had strengthened French resistance at the end of the Empire, but Napoleon's military genius had still been the most important factor. Even if allied logic had been right in believing that Vauban had made French defences too strong, in practice neither French reparations nor allied assistance would ever be sufficient to erect a similar barrier in Germany and the Netherlands. The Dutch had failed to build such a barrier in the eighteenth century and the allies would do so again in the 1820s.[35]

Rightly doubtful whether they could secure the Bourbon monarchy, allied statesmen concentrated on maintaining allied cohesion and changing the balance of power. Ironically, we now know that France was ceasing to dominate European politics for reasons quite out of the control of French or allied governments. The French population was not growing as fast as the population in Germany, Britain, and elsewhere. Its economy was also falling behind Britain's as the Industrial Revolution began to change the face of the world. Both these tendencies were accentuated by the French Revolution. Thus the alteration in the balance of power, which Liverpool, Tsar Alexander, Metternich, and Hardenberg sought through fortifications, was achieved by the textile manufacturers of Manchester and the family planning of the French peasants.

Half a century later, when German industrial and demographic power was allied to the Prussian military system developed in opposition to Napoleon, it was the French who relied upon their

---

[34] D. H. Thomas, *The Guarantee of Belgian Independence and Neutrality in European Diplomacy, 1830s–1930s* (D. H. Thomas, Kingston, RI, 1983), particularly pp. 28–9, 120, 413; Hurst, *Key Treaties*, p. 214, 'Convention between Great Britain, Austria, Prussia, and Russia and Belgium relative to the Belgic Fortresses, 14 December, 1831'.

[35] R. Geike and I. Montgomery, *The Dutch Barrier 1705–1719* (Cambridge University Press, 1930), p. 368; P. J. Block, *History of the People of the Netherlands*, Part V (Putnam, London, 1912), pp. 30 ff.; A. C. Carter, *The Dutch Republic in the Seven Years War* (Macmillan, London, 1971). Arguments about who should pay for the new barrier began immediately after the Treaty of Paris in 1815; see Vane, *Castlereagh*, vol. 3, pp. 65, 428.

remaining fortifications to defend their country and the European
status quo. The Franco-Prussian War in 1870 became very largely
a war of sieges: the envelopment of Metz, Sedan, and Paris itself.[36]
Indeed, one important effect of the treaties of 1815 had been to
make the French concentrate on fortifying their capital.[37] The sieges
of 1871 provided an ironic footnote to the efforts by allied statesmen in 1815 to weaken Vauban's handiwork.

[36] M. E. Howard, *The Franco-Prussian War* (Dorset Press, New York, 1990).
[37] P. Griffith, *Military Thought in the French Army, 1815–1851* (Manchester
University Press, 1989), pp. 150, 159 ff.

3

The Crimean War and the Demilitarization of the Black Sea

The Crimean War of 1854–6 was prolonged for almost a year by the British government's determination to banish Russian naval power from the Black Sea. For Palmerston's government, this became the most important objective in the war. Like most forced disarmament measures after limited wars, it was tactically offensive and strategically defensive, since it was designed to separate the expansionist Russians from the decaying Ottoman Empire. The Russian government accepted the banishment of its fleet only after its naval forces in the Black Sea had been destroyed and it had been isolated diplomatically. Like the demilitarization of Dunkirk in the eighteenth century, neutralization of the Black Sea was a limited measure, which did not reduce the totality of Russian power, but it was still deeply resented as a national humiliation. Consequently, as soon as his enemies were weakened in 1870, the tsar denounced the neutralization of the Black Sea, thereby provoking an international crisis which might easily have led to a second war. Thus, despite its limited scope, forced disarmament occupied a central role in the diplomacy of the period, a position which it was not to occupy again until the 1920s.

BACKGROUND

After the peace settlement of 1815 French opinion remained revisionist, but the French lacked the power to change the status quo and none of the Great Powers was willing to support any French move to upset the settlement. Serious threats arose, not so much from the Great Powers but from revolutionary forces, which produced the massive political upheavals of 1848, and also from the continuing decay of the Ottoman Empire in the east. The first direct conflict between the Great Powers since 1815, the Crimean

War of 1854, was the result of the continuing struggle between the
Russian and Ottoman Empires to dominate the Black and Azov
Seas. It was also part of the growing worldwide struggle between
the British and Russian Empires and impinged on the confrontation
between Austria and Russia for the domination of the Balkans.
In June 1853 Russian troops invaded the Turks' Danubian prin-
cipalities of Wallachia and Moldavia, and in response the British
and French sent their fleets through the Dardanelles as a gesture of
support for the Ottoman Empire. The British were anxious to
protect Turkey in order to keep the Russians as far away from the
vulnerable routes to their Indian Empire as possible.[1] Napoleon III,
proclaimed French Emperor in 1852, was determined to assert his
presence on the European stage and to give what support he could
to the forces of nationalism in Poland and elsewhere. Anglo-French
sympathy encouraged the Ottomans to take a belligerent line and
this led to the destruction of their fleet by the Russians at the battle
of Sinope in November 1853.[2] In turn this Turkish defeat persuaded the British and French to declare war on St Petersburg in
March 1854.

Most of the Crimean War revolved around Anglo-French efforts
to seize and destroy the Russians' Black Sea port of Sevastopol.
They managed to achieve this in September 1855 after months of
bitter fighting. The allied victory was, however, counterbalanced
by the Russian capture of Kars from the Turkish forces in November 1855. The British wanted to send forces to help the Turks
regain the Kars region to the east of the Black Sea. By that stage,
however, the French forces were suffering heavy losses from illness
and the French people were increasingly war-weary. The Russians'
victory at Kars also made it easier for the tsar to accept peace terms
because it restored his army's pride.[3] Thus, in the spring of 1856,

---

[1] The main accounts of the demilitarization of the Black Sea are W. E. Mosse,
The Rise and Fall of the Crimean System 1855–71 (Macmillan, London, 1963),
and V. J. Puryear, *England, Russia and the Straits Question, 1844–1856* (University of California Press, Berkeley, 1931). Lord Palmerston wanted to see the
Crimea and Georgia given to the Turks, Poland re-established and Finland given
to Sweden. See G. P. Gooch (ed.), *The Later Correspondence of Lord John Russell*
(Longman Green, London, 1925), vol. 2, p. 160, memorandum of 19 March
1854.
[2] The British Cabinet suspected that their Ambassador at Constantinople,
Stratfield Canning, was going against their wishes and encouraging Turkish
intransigence; H. Maxwell (ed.), *The Life and Letters of George William
Frederick Earl of Clarendon* (Edward Arnold, London, 1913), vol. 2, pp. 17, 29.
[3] Mosse, *Rise and Fall*, pp. 22 ff.

under pressure from the major neutral powers, the Russians grudg-
ingly conceded the terms demanded by the victors, particularly the
neutralization of the Black Sea, together with withdrawal from
Kars and from the Ottomans' Balkan provinces.[4]

NEUTRALIZATION OF THE BLACK SEA

The British and French had four main objectives in the war: that
Russia should end its occupation of Moldavia and Wallachia, that
the Danube should be opened for merchant ships, that Russian
naval power in the Black Sea should be curtailed, and that Russia
should abandon its claim to interfere in the Ottoman Empire as the
protector of the Christians. From the British point of view, the
third of these was by far the most important and, in December
1854, when the French proposed that they should simply ask the
Russians to limit their naval dominance in the Black Sea, London
insisted that this was imprecise and inadequate. The British wanted
the aim to be 'de faire cesser (mettre fin) la prépotence de la Russie
dans la Mer Noire'. In practice, the British wanted the destruction
of Sevastopol and other fortifications on the littoral and the reduction of the Russian fleet to four warships.[5]

It was precisely these aims which seemed most likely to hinder
the negotiations in Vienna, where the belligerents met in March
1855 to find a way of ending the war. Gorchakov, the Russian
representative, said that his country would not accept them even
after six years of war, as any limitation on Russian ships would
forfeit his country's honour. Russia had no desire to destroy the
Ottoman Empire but believed it was bound to collapse. When it
did so, the Russian government was determined to be in a position
to stop a hostile power capturing Constantinople.[6] Seen from St
Petersburg, the Russian position was thus defensive, a response to
the problems presented by Ottoman weakness. Seen from London,
the Russians were acting according to a long-term offensive plan to
expand at Ottoman expense and capture a warm-water port in the
Mediterranean or elsewhere.

The Austrians acted, to some extent, as mediators. On most issues
they leant to the allied side and had actually signed a secret treaty

[4] Puryear, *England, Russia*, pp. 427 ff.
[5] Puryear, *England, Russia*, p. 358.
[6] Puryear, *England, Russia*, p. 378.

promising to join the allies if the Russians refused to come to terms. However, they sympathized with the Russian position on naval forces. Austria proposed that, rather than trying to limit Russian naval power, the negotiators should allow warships from non-littoral states into the Black Sea as a counterbalance, something which was banned under the 1841 Convention governing the Straits of the Dardanelles. The Russian negotiators were authorized to accept this as a lesser evil, rather than limitations on their forces, but the Turks disliked it because it took away their control over warships passing the Straits. The British opposed it because they had no intention of stationing large forces in the Black Sea, and they believed that Russian forces would capture Constantinople before any other power had time to send warships to the area.[7] In public they put forward the more altruistic argument that limitations would reduce naval rivalry between the powers, whereas attempting to achieve a balance within the Black Sea would encourage it.

It was the French Foreign Minister, Drouyn de Lhuys, who suggested that 'neutralization', or what today would be called demilitarization, of the Black Sea might be an acceptable compromise. Drouyn's plan would have eliminated all warships from the sea; he did not propose to demilitarize Russian ports because he believed they would be useless if there were no fleet to fill them. Unfortunately, his proposal reached Vienna just as the issue was going to be discussed at the conference, and Gorchakov instantly dismissed it as an 'absurd conception even to the Austrians'. He argued that neutralization would leave Russia defenceless before Turkey, which could build up its naval forces in the Dardanelles. The Russians would also be powerless before Anglo-French forces, which would only be kept from the Black Sea by a paper agreement. However, if the Russians remained hostile to the proposal, the British became enthusiasts for the French plan and wanted to extend it to the Sea of Azov. Indeed, it is surprising that they had not thought of it themselves, given how well it suited their interests and how similar it was to the agreement they had negotiated with the United States over the Great Lakes between Canada and the United States of America.[8]

---

[7] Puryear, *England, Russia*, p. 387.

[8] For the initial demilitarization plan see Puryear, *England, Russia*, p. 381. For the agreement on the Great Lakes see P. A. Towle, *Arms Control and East-West Relations* (Croom Helm, London, 1983), pp. 164 ff.

The British negotiator, Lord John Russell, encouraged the Russians to be more flexible by pointing out that even the Sun King, Louis XIV, had accepted the demilitarization of Dunkirk, a parallel which may not have evoked much enthusiasm among Britain's French allies. However, Gorchakov replied, quite rightly and equally tactlessly, that the French complied only because of the extent of their military defeats.[9] The British, French, and Austrians also tried to produce alternative proposals which might be acceptable, such as limiting Russian warships in the Black Sea to six, the number still seaworthy in the area. But none of these ideas proved negotiable. The Austrians refused to support the terms the allies were demanding or to become belligerent when the Russians rejected them. Consequently, the first round of peace talks broke down. They were only to be resumed in 1856 when the military situation had changed.

In the meantime, however, bilateral discussions continued. In November 1855 Russia and France again discussed the neutralization of the Black Sea, as both were suffering the economic effects of war. Prussia was putting pressure on the Russians to make peace and the tsar feared that Sweden and Austria might join his enemies. By then, for St Petersburg to accept the neutralization of the Black Sea was only to accept the status quo, since their main port and fleet had been destroyed. On the other hand, once Kars was captured the Russians became less sensitive about their honour. If this made them more tractable, the French government increasingly looked for a compromise. Napoleon III refused to back British pressure on Russia for the neutralization of the Sea of Azov and the port of Nikolaev, which lay 16 miles north of the Black Sea on the river Bug.[10]

The British were thus initially the most disappointed with the peace terms which emerged when formal negotiations recommenced in Paris in February 1856. Palmerston, the British Prime Minister, had hoped that the war would continue. He was apparently pessimistic about the duration of the new agreement on the Black Sea and expected Britain, Turkey, and Russia to be at war again within a decade. Many others agreed that the neutralization

---

[9] Puryear, *England, Russia*, p. 397.
[10] For the Franco-Russian negotiations see W. Baumgart, *The Peace of Paris 1856* (ABC-Clio, Santa Barbara, Calif., 1981), p. 63. For Napoleon's disagreements with Britain see Puryear, *England, Russia*, pp. 423 ff.

would not last. Count Beust, who was then a Saxon minister and later Austrian Foreign Minister, tried to persuade the Russians to accept allied terms precisely because they would be temporary: 'it was a demand so utterly untenable that it would die a natural death, it being against the nature of things to forbid an empire of eighty millions to have ships of war in its own waters.'[11] Nevertheless, the Treaty of Paris and associated agreements did achieve much of what the British hoped for. Article XI laid down that the Black Sea's 'waters and ports . . . are formally and in perpetuity interdicted to the Flag of War, either of the Powers possessing its Coasts, or of any other Power'. The only exception was that the Russians and Turks were allowed to keep six ships of 800 tons and four of 200 for inshore work. They were specifically banned from building 'Military–Maritime Arsenals' of the Sevastopol type, and in this respect the terms went beyond the original neutralization proposal put forward by Drouyn de Lhuys.

Of course, this did not give complete protection to the Turkish Empire, as the Russian army could still advance through the Balkans to the Straits of the Dardanelles or on Turkey's eastern frontiers via Kars (which they recaptured in 1877). On the other hand, such a course would leave their southern coasts vulnerable to attack from Turkish or allied warships which might, in those circumstances, ignore the Treaty of Paris and enter the Black Sea. Thus, from the Ottoman point of view, the treaty seemed a reasonable compromise and certainly provided all the protection which enforced disarmament could give. From the Russian point of view, the perspective was naturally very different. They had two ways of evading the treaty; one was to wait and then simply start building up their forces in the Black Sea without informing the other signatories of the Treaty of Paris. However, this was unlikely to go unobserved because the allies had met the contingency by insisting that their consuls should be stationed in the Black Sea ports, and the British Admiralty certainly kept close watch on Russian naval activities.[12] Moreover, such incremental methods would not be public enough to

---

[11] *Memoirs of Count Beust* (Remington, London, 1887), vol. 1, pp. 142, 384 ff.
[12] See Article XII of the Treaty of Paris; Hurst, *Key Treaties*, vol. 1, p. 321. For Admiralty observation of Russian naval activities see ADM/1/6198, letter from the Admiralty to Admiral in command Malta, 10 January 1870. The Austrian correspondent of *The Times* argued in 1870 that Russia could secretly have built a whole fleet of ironclads in the area, but this is incredible; see Mosse, *Rise and Fall*, frontispiece.

undo the humiliation the Russians felt they had suffered, and yet they could still provoke an allied military response. The other alternative was simply to wait until the hostile coalition weakened, as inevitably it would eventually, and then denounce the treaty. This was the course they followed.

THE END OF NEUTRALIZATION

Russia's opportunity came in 1870, when French forces were defeated by Prussia and Napoleon III was driven from power. Gorchakov was now Chancellor and he must have had some satisfaction from telling the Powers in November 1870 that Russia no longer felt bound by the Treaty of Paris because the agreement had been infringed by the other parties. The Moldavians and Wallachians had changed the status quo by uniting to form Romania and electing a foreign king. But they were not parties to the treaty and, as the Austrians retorted, the other alleged breach, involving the entry of foreign warships into the Black Sea, was equally unsubstantiated, unless this was a reference to the unarmed foreign warships which had accompanied sovereigns on their journeys.[13] It was clear to all that these were only excuses for Gorchakov's announcement.

In theory Britain, France, and Austria were bound by the tripartite treaty of April 1856 to go to war if there were any threat to the treaty or to the integrity of the Ottoman Empire. But the Turkish Ministers realized that, with the French helpless, the other parties were likely to ignore their obligations. The sultan told the Russian ambassador that, if he was to lose the protection given by neutralization, he wanted some quid pro quo, such as a guarantee by Russia not to support Christian insurrections against his Empire.[14] Austria had been defeated by Prussia in 1866 and felt threatened by both Prussia and Russia. Beust, who had originally been so sceptical of the neutralization proposal, had now become the Austrian Foreign Minister. He still regarded neutralization as a 'complete mistake' and had proposed a revision of the Treaty of Paris in 1867. But he was totally opposed to allowing Russia

[13] Beust to Count Chotek, 16 November 1870 in *Memoirs of Count Beust*, vol. 2, Appendix E, pp. 367–72.
[14] B. Jelavich, *The Ottoman Empire, the Great Powers and the Straits Question 1870–1887* (Indiana University Press, Bloomington and London, 1973), p. 31. For Austrian views see *The Memoirs of Count Beust*, vol. 2, pp. 221 ff.

to denounce the treaty unilaterally. The Austro-Hungarian State Council decided that they would follow the British lead and Beust instructed the Austrian ambassador in London to act accordingly, even if that meant war.

Thus everything turned on the British response. But Palmerston was dead and, although some members of the government including Granville, the Foreign Minister, had served under Palmerston, the new Prime Minister, W. E. Gladstone, took a very different position. He deeply disliked the Ottoman Empire and, to the satisfaction of the *Journal de St Pétersbourg*, he had also announced that he clung to his previous opinions about the futility of the neutralization clauses.[15] Thus the Russians had chosen their moment well, although they overlooked Gladstone's belief in the sanctity of treaties. As with Beust, it was not the ending of the neutralization of the Black Sea which rankled with the Prime Minister. Indeed, Gladstone was particularly irritated when the British ambassador in Constantinople described neutralization as by far the best way of protecting the Ottomans from Russian attack. What antagonized Gladstone was the fact that the Russians had denounced the Treaty of Paris without waiting for the agreement of the other parties. He was determined that Russia's fault should be rectified by negotiation and diplomacy rather than war.[16]

Gladstone's opinions were typical of British radicals. The Crimean war had been bitterly denounced at the time by leading British radicals, such as John Bright, who saw it as a war for territory and imperial advantage. Bright was also appalled at the idea of helping the Muslim Turks to dominate the Balkan Christians, at what he saw as Palmerston's unscrupulous ambition, and at the bellicosity of the press and people.[17] In 1870 the radicals' legacy was still strong within the ruling Liberal Party. The philosopher John Stuart Mill wrote to his younger colleague, the essayist and politician John Morley, encouraging him to use his pen to combat the pro-treaty belligerence of the Conservative press. 'As for the rights of the question,' Mill wrote,

---

[15] A. Ramm, *The Political Correspondence of Mr Gladstone and Lord Granville, 1868–1876* (Royal Historical Society, London, 1952), vol. 1. See also Mosse, *Rise and Fall*, p. 179 n. 2 and Sir Charles Dilke's quotation from the *Journal de St Pétersbourg*, reprinted in *The Times*, 31 March 1871.

[16] Jelavich, *The Ottoman Empire*, p. 34.

[17] *The Diaries of John Bright* (Cassell, London, 1930) particularly pp. 159, 160, 184, 189.

it is doubtful whether they are not substantially on the side of Russia. At all events we are not bound in honour to carry out the treaty when our most important co-signatory can give no help . . . As for the argument that Russia is simply casting off all treaty obligations, that simply points to the fact that all such obligations always have been disowned directly the party unwillingly bound by them perceives a relaxation of force in the powers which attempt to bind it. This will always happen so long as treaties are made in perpetuity.[18]

Both Gladstone and Granville were shocked at the tone of the British press. Gladstone refused to allow any reinforcements to be sent to the Mediterranean fleet in case this exacerbated tensions, while Granville repeatedly emphasized that no Cabinet was less likely than theirs to allow itself to slide unawares into war.[19] Yet, ironically, it was the threat of war which eventually offered a solution. Odo Russell, an under-secretary at the Foreign Office, was sent to the Prussian camp outside Paris to persuade Bismarck to support the British protest against Russian behaviour. Going beyond his instructions, Russell gambled that the Prussian Prime Minister would be most impressed if he warned that the crisis might lead to war. In the event his bluff worked and Bismarck, who did not want another war breaking out to complicate his quarrel with the French, suggested that a conference should be convened in St Petersburg to discuss the issue. The British jibbed at St Petersburg but agreed to convene a conference in London in January 1871.[20]

If the British had expected the Prussians to back them against Russia, the continental Powers would have smiled at their naïvety. Both Beust and his French colleagues believed that Gorchakov and Bismarck had reached agreement before the Franco-Prussian War broke out. The Russians would prevent interference in the dispute between Berlin and Paris by the neutrals and, in recompense, they would be able to denounce the Black Sea clauses.[21] The

---

[18] F. W. Hirst (ed.), *Early Life and Letters of John Morley* (Macmillan, London, 1927), pp. 169 ff.

[19] On the Mediterranean Fleet see Gladstone to Granville, 19 November 1970, in Ramm, *The Political Correspondence*, p. 161. For Gladstone's views on the press see p. 166, Gladstone to Granville, 22 November 1870, paragraph 5.

[20] According to W. E. Mosse, *Rise and Fall*, p. 170, Bismarck had already decided that a conference was needed before Russell arrived. For the British government's attitude to Odo Russell's comments see Ramm, *The Political Correspondence*, pp. 176, 179, 181.

[21] Beust, vol. 2, p. 222; C.-R. Franous, *Alexander II, Gortchakoff et Napoléon III* (Plon, Paris, 1913), pp. 521, 533.

reverberations of the Crimean War were continuing to affect European politics. Whether or not Beust was right, Prussian and Russian interests dovetailed neatly at the expense of the forced disarmament measures won at such cost in 1856.

When the London conference met, the British hoped that the Russians could be made to withdraw their denunciation of the Treaty of Paris, but in the event it was simply put to one side. The conference spent the first few days waiting for the French Foreign Minister, Favre. But Bismarck was well aware that the French hoped to use the conference to appeal for neutral support in their current struggle. Accordingly, the conference had to proceed without the French Minister. The British insisted that its first task was to agree that treaties could not be unilaterally denounced. The Declaration of London accordingly laid down that 'it is an essential principle of the Law of Nations that no Power can liberate itself from the engagements of a Treaty, nor modify the stipulations thereof, unless with the consent of the Contracting Parties by means of an amicable agreement.' Thus a general principle of international law was enunciated as a direct result of the abrogation of the forced disarmament clauses imposed on Russia.

The Russians reluctantly accepted the implicit reprimand in the expectation that they would achieve their main objective with regard to the Black Sea. The Treaty of London of 13 March 1871 ended the neutralization of the sea and Britain's primary war aim in the Crimean War was thus undone. However, to achieve this the Russians had to accept a Straits regime which was unsatisfactory from their point of view, because the Turks insisted on compensation for the loss of their protection given by neutralization. Turkey wanted complete control over the passage of warships through the Straits but, when this was rejected, it accepted a compromise proposal. Article II of the new treaty laid down that in peacetime the sultan could open the Straits to friendly warships 'in case the Sublime Porte should judge it necessary in order to secure the execution of the stipulations of the Treaty of Paris of the 30th March 1856'. The Turks had insisted they should be able to allow the entry of 'friendly' rather than 'non-riverain' warships. The British objected, but the Turks even threatened to leave the conference over the issue. They maintained that the phrase 'non-riverain' was so obviously aimed against Russia—the only major riverain naval power—that, at some time or another, St Petersburg would denounce it just as it had denounced neutralization. Indeed, the Russian press had already started to complain. In the end, Turkish freedom to admit or deny the entry of warships into the Black Sea was effectively restricted only by reference to the Treaty of Paris.[22]

The Russians did not want foreign warships in the Black Sea at all, nor did they want the sultan to have control of the Straits of the Dardanelles so that their warships could not pass freely into the Mediterranean. The *Moscow Gazette* complained, 'the object in view was not to assure the power of the Sultan but to bind and enchain Russia . . . our Black Sea fleet cannot become really important, for it is condemned for ever to remain shut up. And yet we may any day find that we have the English as our close neighbours in the Black Sea.'[23] Such was the price for abrogating the hated neutralization agreement.

The Russian press may have been dissatisfied but so was the British. The government had to defend itself against scathing criticism of its appeasement from the Conservative leader, Benjamin Disraeli, Sir Charles Dilke, and others. The Foreign Minister, Lord Granville, asserted, quite reasonably, that the Treaty of Paris had given Turkey a breathing space which it had used to build up its naval forces. Indeed, Granville argued that Russia did not have a single warship which could take on the Turkish ironclads.[24] Whether or not this last claim was true, it is fair to say that the regional naval imbalance in Turkey's favour continued for some years. Even when Russia attacked Turkey again in April 1877, the war was confined to the Balkans and the Caucasus because the Tsar's forces could not then challenge the Turkish navy.

Granville was on much weaker ground when he claimed that the Ottoman Empire was now treating its Christian subjects with greater sensitivity and thus that there was less danger of interference in its affairs and less need to protect the empire by treaty.[25] Only four years later the European Powers again demanded that the

[22] For Russian views see the *Moscow Gazette*, 6 March 1871, reproduced in 'A Russian View of the Treaty of London', *The Times*, 30 March 1871. For the negotiations see Jelavich, *The Ottoman Empire*, p. 55.
[23] 'A Russian View of the Treaty of London', *The Times*, 30 March 1871.
[24] FO 65 830, pp. 49–60. The Admiralty was receiving information that the Russians were already rebuilding their Black Sea forces, but this proved unfounded. See ADM 1 6198 Admiralty to the Foreign Office, 10 January 1871.
[25] For Disraeli's views see Ramm, *The Political Correspondence*, p. 22, Gladstone to Granville, 15 February 1871. See also Sir Charles Dilke's attack in *The Times*, 31 March 1871.

Porte should improve its treatment of the Christians, and it was partly the massacres of Bulgarians by the Turks in 1876 which led to the Russo-Turkish War the following year. The really powerful argument which the government deployed in 1871 against standing by the letter of the 1856 settlement was that Russia could only be made to uphold the neutralization of the Black Sea by force. The government also claimed that it would be Britain almost alone which would have to wield this force. Both Ministers and Members of Parliament knew this was not true as Turkey, Austria, and Italy would have backed a strong British stance and Beust, in particular, was contemptuous of Gladstone's claims.[26]

The Crimean War influenced the military balance in the Black Sea throughout the second half of the nineteenth century. For the first fifteen years the position was particularly advantageous for the Turks because Sevastopol was destroyed, and the Russians were prevented from rebuilding either the port or their Black Sea fleet. Even after the Treaty of London liberated St Petersburg from the neutralization clauses of the earlier treaty, it took many more years before the Russians had recaptured their local naval dominance. Furthermore, the rules governing the passage of warships through the Straits remained less favourable to them than those drawn up at the London conference in 1841 because the 1841 rules absolutely prohibited 'foreign' warships from passing through the Straits in peacetime. From 1871 the sultan could decide what 'friendly' warships should pass to uphold the Paris Treaty.[27]

Against this success for the Western Powers must be set the fact that neutralization as such lasted only until 1871, yet to achieve it the allies had continued the Crimean War for almost another year after April 1855. Neutralization also caused constant friction with the Russians as they regarded it, not as a reasonable compromise securing both Turkish interests and their own, but as the hated symbol of their humiliation, the sort of measure which they could and did from time to time impose upon Turks and Bulgarians.[28]

[26] Jelavich, *The Ottoman Empire*, p. 28; Mosse, *Rise and Fall*, p. 179, and *The Memoirs of Count Beust*, vol. 2, p. 225.

[27] M. Hurst, *Key Treaties of the Great Powers*, vol. 2 (David and Charles, Newton Abbott, 1972), p. 468.

[28] Hurst, *Key Treaties*, vol. 2, p. 534, 'Preliminary Treaty of San Stefano', Articles VIII and XII. The Ottoman army was to leave Bulgaria and all the local fortresses were to be destroyed. The smaller Balkan states were also banned from having warships on the Danube.

One historian of the Paris Treaty, W. E. Mosse, dismissed it altogether because 'it did not stand the test of time' and because Palmerston himself had not expected that it would do so. But this reflected Palmerston's view that the war should have been continued. Important aspects of the settlement did in any case endure for several decades. Furthermore, no settlement could last in its entirety if Turkey was weak and Russia expansionist. Palmerston's point was that in such circumstances the settlement would have to be defended within a decade or so. This was a realistic appraisal. Indeed, virtually all measures of forced disarmament have to be protected in this way because they are intended to shore up the status quo against a revisionist power. Palmerston can be criticized, not for backing an ephemeral settlement but for leaving his successors with the apparent options of accepting Russia's denunciation of the treaty or making war once again. Seen in this light, Gladstone neatly side-stepped the dilemma by producing a compromise which avoided humiliating the former victors and left even the Turks reasonably content.

The negotiators in 1856 could, of course, have recognized the temporary nature of the settlement by explicitly limiting its duration, as John Stuart Mill suggested in 1870. This would have been unpopular at the time because it would have appeared to render the sacrifices made in the war less worthwhile. Moreover, it is not unreasonable for statesmen to leave open the possibility that a treaty will last, even if they regard this as inherently unlikely.

Thus one limited demilitarization clause of the Treaty of Paris has survived. During the Crimean War the fighting spread from the Black Sea to northern waters. The British insisted that this should be reflected in the peace terms and that the Aland Islands at the entrance to the Gulf of Bothnia should be demilitarized. The Russian fortress there had been destroyed by British warships and London did not want to see it rebuilt. The Russians reluctantly agreed. When Finland became independent after the First World War, it accepted the terms of the agreement annexed to the Treaty of Paris in 1856. The Ahvenanmaa Islands, as they are called by the Finns, were to harbour 'no military or naval establishment'. In wartime the islands were to remain neutralized, though the Finns were allowed to mine the islands' waters in order to protect them.[29]

[29] *League of Nations Armaments Yearbook* (Geneva, 1932), p. 419.

Thus the arrangements reached in 1856 continued in completely different circumstances when the British were no longer coercing the Russians and ownership of the islands had changed. But the Alands were hardly of comparable strategic importance to the Black Sea, and neither the Russians nor the Finns had much incentive to reverse the islands' demilitarization.

The neutralization of the Black Sea and of the Aland Islands established no strong tradition which was copied in other nineteenth-century agreements. The treaties which concluded later major wars either contained no provisions for enforced disarmament or reverted to the historic preoccupation with fortresses. This was true of the Franco-Prussian War of 1870, which opened the way to the Russian overthrow of the 1856 settlement. After most of the French armies had been defeated and Paris was besieged, the chief of the Prussian General Staff, Count Moltke, wanted to disarm the Paris garrison and imprison the troops in Germany. He would then have fought on until all French forces were destroyed.[30] Significantly, given the emphasis placed on French fortresses in 1815, the war had turned into a succession of sieges of such fortified positions as Belfort, but it had also become a national war for the French, waged by guerrilla as well as conventional forces.

During the armistice, before the final Peace of Frankfurt was negotiated, the Parisians had to give up their outer forts, dismount the guns from the city walls, and hand over all arms beyond those needed for the 12,000 men who were to keep order. In other parts of France both sides were to withdraw 10 kilometres to prevent the continuation of the conflict.[31] Much more important, in the Treaty of Frankfurt the French had to cede Alsace and much of Lorraine, including the fortifications of Metz, which Moltke insisted were worth 120,000 men to Germany in a war.[32]

Germany now had a massive predominance over France, reinforced by the imposition of an indemnity of 5,000 million francs.

[30] M. E. Howard, *The Franco-Prussian War* (Dorset Press, New York, 1990), p. 436.
[31] Howard, *The Franco-Prussian War*, pp. 441–2.
[32] Howard, *The Franco-Prussian War*, p. 448. For the Treaty of Frankfurt see Hurst, *Key Treaties*, vol. 2, p. 496. For the impact on Metz see F.-Y. Le Moigne, *Histoire de Metz* (Editions Privat, Toulouse, 1986). For later French efforts to fortify the frontier see A. Mitchell, *Victors and Vanquished: The German Influence on Army and Church in France after 1870* (University of North Carolina Press, Chapel Hill and London, 1984), pp. 53 ff.

Unlike the attempt to demilitarize Azov in the eighteenth century or the Black Sea after 1856, the Peace of Frankfurt did not strengthen the weak against the strong but the strong against the weak. It could be overthrown only through a European war in which France had acquired sufficient allies to counterbalance German superiority.

4

The Disarmament of Germany
after the First World War

After the First World War, the democratic nations tried for the first time in the modern period to impose far-reaching disarmament measures on their enemies. These were not the limited defensive measures imposed on France in 1815 or Russia in 1856 but the continuation of the allied offensive to break the power of Germany and its former allies, Austria, Bulgaria, and Hungary. Turkey escaped the same fate only because it stood up to allied forces. Germany resisted with all the means at its disposal, including propaganda designed to divide the victors, through deceit and evasion to threats against allied inspectors. Austria, Bulgaria, and Hungary protested against the measures imposed on them and Hungary, in particular, did attempt to resist but was too weak to do so effectively or to make its opposition of much importance except to its immediate neighbours. Germany's opposition had more serious political implications, though this was not what undermined the settlement. Rather it was the survival of Germany's latent power and the unwillingness of the allies to fight in defence of the treaties.

The disarmament provisions of the Armistice in November 1918 and of the Treaty of Versailles fourteen months later were as far-reaching as the allies could make them. Most of the German high seas fleet scuttled itself in Scapa Flow and the German air force was abolished. The army was to be reduced to 100,000 and, to prevent the build-up of reserves, officers were to serve for twenty-five years and men for twelve. Only armaments sufficient for such a small army were to be retained and the rest of the German arsenal was to be destroyed under allied supervision. Certain types of weapon, such as submarines, tanks, and poison gases, were considered so threatening that they were prohibited altogether.

Factories producing weapons beyond the needs of the remaining armed forces were to be destroyed. The whole process was to be verified on the spot by separate Inter-Allied Commissions of Control for the army, air force, and navy.

THE GENESIS OF THE PROGRAMME

Just as the Paris agreement of 1808 limiting the Prussian army had been preceded sixteen years before by the forced disarmament of Poland, so, coincidentally, the disarmament of Germany after 1919 was preceded by German attempts to disarm Russia and other neighbouring states. When the Russian armies collapsed in revolution and civil war, the new communist government first sought a halt to the fighting by signing an armistice at Brest-Litovsk on 15 December 1917. This was followed by the peace imposed by Germany at the same venue on 3 March 1918. The agreements removed a vast area of Russia from Soviet control, though some of this was to be restored when their armies were completely demobilized. Article V of the Treaty specified that 'units recently organized by the present government' were to be included in this general demobilization.[1] The Tsarist army had already disintegrated and the Soviet delegates to the Brest-Litovsk negotiations discovered that their country's trenches were empty. It was the development of the forces of the revolutionary Soviet state which the Germans wished to control.

Brest-Litovsk reflected German plans for the rest of Europe. In the event of their victory, Germany was to take control of all approaches to its territory. To the west this meant dominating or absorbing Luxemburg, the Briey area of France, and Belgium; to the east it meant taking control of Poland. In secret peace negoti-

[1] On the forced disarmament of the Soviet Union see J. W. Wheeler-Bennett, *Brest Litovsk: The Forgotten Peace, March 1918* (Macmillan, London, 1938), pp. 403 ff. The best analysis of the background to the forced disarmament of Germany is by L. S. Jaffe, *The Decision to Disarm Germany: British Policy towards Postwar German Disarmament, 1914–1919* (Allen and Unwin, London, 1985); on the disarmament process itself see D. G. Williamson, *The British in Germany 1919–1930; The Reluctant Occupiers* (Berg, New York, 1991) and J. H. Morgan, *Assize of Arms, being the Story of Germany and Her Rearmament, 1919–1939* (Methuen, London, 1945) and Morgan's article, 'The disarmament of Germany and after', *Quarterly Review* 481 (October 1924); (hereafter *Quarterly Review*). On Weimar see G. A. Craig, *Germany 1866–1945* (Clarendon Press, Oxford, 1955). See also F. L. Carsten, *The Reichswehr and Politics, 1918–1933* (Clarendon Press, Oxford, 1966).

ations with Belgium in 1915, the German government insisted that the Belgians would have to abandon their neutrality and hand over their railways and fortifications. Belgian forces would simply be used to maintain internal order. Poland was to be reunited under German control and Polish armed forces raised to help the Central Powers had to swear allegiance to Germany. The disarmament clauses in the Treaty of Brest-Litovsk have to be placed within this general context. Russian forces could offer no threat to Germany in 1918, but German hegemony had to be assured for the future; as the German Chancellor, Bethmann Hollweg, had put it earlier, 'if Europe is ever to achieve peace, this can only come through Germany occupying a strong and unassailable position . . . the English policy of the balance of power must disappear.'[2]

Lenin, the leader of the new Soviet state, never intended to abide by the Treaty of Brest-Litovsk, though he saw that, given the state of his armies and allied unwillingness to assist them against Germany, there was no alternative but to sign. 'I don't mean to read it [the treaty] and I don't mean to fulfil it, except in so far as I'm forced,' Lenin declared. He also told the British representative in Russia, Bruce Lockhart, that Germany would not be able to exploit the conquered territories because of the passive resistance of the inhabitants. Lenin was very conscious of the Prussian analogy at this time, arguing that the Treaty of Tilsit was 'ten times more humiliating than the one we have just made with Germany . . . We have signed a Tilsit Peace just as the Germans did, and just as the Germans freed themselves from Napoleon, so will we get our freedom.'[3] Such freedom came more quickly than Lenin expected with the defeat of the Central Powers in 1918.

The forced disarmament of Russia was motivated entirely by German strategic aims. The forced disarmament of Germany reflected more varied motives. For French politicians it was indeed an obvious way of enhancing their country's security. At the same time, disarmament of the vanquished fitted well with the widespread beliefs in Britain and America that weapons were the main cause of warfare and that this particular war had been a struggle against Prussian militarism. President Wilson reflected such a view

[2] For Bethmann Holweg see F. Fischer, *Germany's Aims in the First World War* (Chatto and Windus, London, 1967), p. 199. On German plans for Belgium and Poland see Fischer, *Germany's Aims*, pp. 217, 237.
[3] Wheeler-Bennett, *Brest Litovsk*, pp. 276 ff.

in the fourth of his fourteen points enunciated on 8 January 1918. This envisaged all countries disarming down to 'the lowest point consistent with national safety'. The British Prime Minister, Lloyd George, was also determined to avoid keeping British troops in Europe and to moderate French demands for a strategic buffer in the Rhineland. This he saw as more likely to alienate Germany than forced disarmament. But, whatever their initial motives, the allied statesmen could agree on the objective. Indeed, they became enthusiasts for the policy of forced disarmament which they wanted to apply to all the defeated nations.[4]

Neither the British nor the American government had studied the problem of disarmament in depth or fully understood the implications of what they were doing. What examination of disarmament had been carried out in the Foreign Office during the war had simply underlined the inherent difficulties,[5] but the full extent of the verification problems only gradually became apparent. There were few precedents to show what was involved. As we have seen, British officials had been stationed in Dunkirk in the eighteenth century and allied consuls in the Black Sea ports after the Crimean War. However, it was relatively easy for them to discover whether or not the treaties were being infringed; the disarmament planned for Germany was vastly more extensive and complicated. Not only was manpower to be limited—as it had been in Prussia and Austria under Napoleon—but this was the first attempt to hobble an industrial power's ability to produce weaponry; Capo d'Istria had raised the possibility in 1815 only to dismiss it immediately as conflicting with the magnanimous terms previously agreed.

Just as ominously, the allied governments had not worked out how the disarmament of Germany would end and apparently they expected it to last indefinitely. Lloyd George is said to have believed that, once the Germans had been freed from militarism and conscription for five years, they would never accept it again. On such wild hunches and ill-formulated surmises can the fate of nations depend. No wonder that the head of the Foreign Office said Lloyd George's 'knowledge of many of the problems involved

[4] Jaffe, *The Decision*, pp. 165, 215. On Wilson's fourteen points see H. W. V. Temperley (ed.), *A History of the Peace Conference of Paris*, vol. 2 (Hodder and Stoughton, London, 1920), p. 302.
[5] Jaffe, *The Decision*, p. 65.

(in the peace process) was non-existent'.[6] Allied statesmen apparently had little knowledge of the history of forced disarmament and what they thought they knew was wrong. They had little consciousness of the examples of Dunkirk in the eighteenth century or the Black Sea after the Crimean War. If they had focused on these cases, then they might have seen that, unless the measures of disarmament imposed were loose enough to have some chance of acceptance by Germany, either Berlin would eventually throw off its 'shackles' or such a liberation would have to be covered by a thin veneer of legitimacy, as the remilitarization of the Black Sea was after 1871. The third possibility was to fight a series of wars and reiterate the disarmament provisions in each peace treaty, as had happened with the demilitarization of Dunkirk.

The extensive forced disarmament measures imposed on Germany were conceived by civilian politicians, not by their senior military advisers. The commander of the allied armies, Marshal Foch, had been reluctant to limit German weaponry under the original Armistice terms.

Nothing is easier than to propose and even to impose conditions on paper. It is simple and logical to demand the disarmament of the German Armies in the field. But how will you make sure of it? Will you pass through the German Armies and occupy before them the Rhine crossings? Demobilization? I am willing. But do you intend to occupy the whole of Germany? For if we do not occupy the whole of Germany, we shall never be certain that demobilization has been carried out.

Foch vacillated when he saw that the Germans would agree to massive disarmament without further fighting, and the Armistice did contain such demands. However, when the final peace terms were under discussion, the allied commander restated his doubts: 'it will be very difficult to verify and the results are more than doubtful. The only means of pressure is first of all for us to keep strong forces mobilized and as a second and additional means there is the blockade.'[7]

Because of these and other justified concerns it was difficult to

[6] For Lloyd George's views on conscription see Williamson, *The Reluctant Occupiers*, p. 23; Jaffe, *The Decision*, p. 188. For Foreign Office views of Lloyd George see Lord Hardinge of Penshurst, *Old Diplomacy* (John Murray, London, 1947), p. 229.

[7] A. Tardieu, *The Truth about the Treaty* (Hodder and Stoughton, London, 1921), pp. 66 ff.

reach agreement. No less than three commissions were appointed successively to decide the issue at the beginning of 1919. Finally, on 6 March the report of the military commission presided over by Marshal Foch was presented to the allied statesmen. Allied commanders proposed to limit the German army to 200,000 officers and men, with the men serving for not more than one year. Lloyd George objected that this would give the Germans 2 million trained men in ten years. Foch replied that it was not the ordinary soldier but the NCOs who were important and their numbers would be severely limited, while conscripts trained for only one year would soon lose their military efficiency. Robert Lansing, the US Secretary of State, backed up Lloyd George and the French Premier, Georges Clemenceau, also insisted that the issue should be decided by the politicians. And so it was; Germany was limited to a professional army, though Marshal Foch then insisted that it should be restricted to 100,000 not 200,000 men. According to Lloyd George's account of the conference, it was when these proposals were made that he said he thought it 'an obligation of honour' to link German disarmament to the idea of universal arms reductions foreseen in Wilson's fourteen points.[8]

Subsequently this gave the Germans grounds for complaints that the allies had not disarmed and eventually justified their denunciation of the Treaty of Versailles. In retrospect, the original scheme proposed by the allied commanders would have been far preferable. It would have been more satisfactory to the Germans themselves and made them less determined to evade the treaty. It would have been better not to link German limitations with chiliastic notions of general disarmament, which were to lead nowhere and cause constant irritation. Allied statesmen were also overimpressed by Prussian evasion of Napoleon's measures to disarm German after 1808. According to the Conservative elder statesman, Arthur Balfour, 'one of the few recorded attempts to crush militarism in a defeated state was Napoleon's attempt to destroy the Prussian Army after Jena. No attempt was ever less successful. As everybody knows, Napoleon's policy compelled Prussia to contrive the military system which has created modern Germany.'[9] Thus the

[8] D. Lloyd George, *The Truth about the Peace Treaties*, vol. I (Gollancz, London, 1938), pp. 591 ff.

[9] For subsequent French fears of the short-service German army see FO/371/14366, Folio C 8924, pp. 245 ff., interview with General Groener. For Balfour's

long-service army was imposed on Germany in 1919 to prevent the build-up of a 'Krumper' reserve and because the British and American associated conscription with militarism.

Despite the initial scepticism of Marshal Foch, French politicians took to the proposal for the disarmament of Germany because they assumed that the best way to maintain the imbalance of power created by the war was to multiply the methods of weakening the enemy. If a general dissolution of the German state was impractical, it should be weakened by reparations, by losing provinces peopled for the most part by Poles or other nationalities, by disarmament, and by the secession of the Rhineland. Not all of these measures were accepted by the other allies, but many were, and no one played the moderating role as effectively as Wellington, Castlereagh, and Alexander had done in Paris in 1815.[10] Furthermore, the plurality of measures imposed on Germany actually weakened the will to persevere in their enforcement. The allies needed to decide what was the single most effective measure to strengthen France at Germany's expense and to persevere with that, rather than dispersing efforts and fostering the image of the vanquished as victims.

As so often after a great war, attitudes towards Germany were complicated by the difficulty of deciding exactly whom the allies had been fighting. If the war had been a struggle against the Kaiser and Prussian militarism then, once these had been removed and the democratic Weimar government installed, there was no intrinsic reason to insist on further punishment. On the contrary, the new government needed to be fostered as Louis XVIII's government had been in 1815. If, on the other hand, the war had been a struggle against the German people who remained expansionist, then it seemed not unreasonable that they should 'pay' for the war and it was only logical to weaken them in any way possible. But the allies were not agreed about their diagnosis; indeed, an individual statesman, like Lloyd George or Winston Churchill, might vacillate from one position to another. In 1815 the Prussians had refused to make the admittedly artificial distinction between Napoleon and the French; in 1919 the identification between the kaiser's policy

views see Jaffe, *The Decision*, p. 33. For Lloyd George's views see W. O. Shanahan, *Prussian Military Reforms 1786–1813* (Columbia University Press, New York, 1930), p. 15.

[10] See Chapter 2 above.

and the German people was made only too frequently by the victors.[11]

VERIFICATION PROBLEMS

The main body of allied disarmament inspectors was established in Germany at the beginning of 1920. During the previous year, individual allied officers had kept watch on events in the defeated nation, noting the slow decay of the once proud fleet, the red flags flying over the barracks, and the scrapping of many submarines and other weapons.[12] But the newly arrived Inter-Allied Commissions of Control were large, high-ranking, and intrusive. Divisions very quickly became obvious in their attitudes and approach.

Led by the tough staff officer, General Claude Nollet, most French inspectors took the view that the precise terms of the Treaty of Versailles should be enforced, however difficult this was and however much friction it caused with the German authorities. French officers were not to fraternize with Germans. Oddly, despite his initial scepticism about disarmament, Marshal Foch argued in 1921 that 'the allies were not safe until they had received from the Germans the last machine gun and the last rifle which had to be surrendered under the Treaty.' When allied inspectors passed through the French zone of occupation on their way to verify German disarmament, they were welcomed with speeches, a parade, and champagne. When they arrived in the British zone they were completely ignored.[13]

The British section of the Inter-Allied Military Control Commission (IAMCC) was commanded by Major-General Francis Bingham, who had been Director-General of Design in the Ministry of Munitions. He has frequently been criticized by historians for his naïvety about German behaviour.[14] But Bingham was representative of much of the British officer corps in taking a relaxed view of the German situation. Many British officers had never been in favour of imposing far-reaching disarmament on Germany. Sir William Robertson, the Chief of the Imperial General Staff for

[11] Jaffe, *The Decision*, pp. 120 ff.
[12] ADM/116/1939, 'Remarks on the General Situation and Food Conditions in the Following German Ports', 1–15 April 1919. See also Lt.-Col. S. Roddie, *Peace Patrol* (Christophers, London, 1932), chs 1–3.
[13] On Nollet see Williamson, *The Reluctant Occupiers*, p. 69. On the treatment by the British and French of the inspectors see Morgan, *Assize of Arms*, p. 37.
[14] Williamson, *The Reluctant Occupiers*, p. 70.

most of the war, and Sir Douglas Haig, the commander of the British forces in France, wanted Germany to survive as a major military power in order to balance French and Russian strength.[15] Enforced disarmament was either impractical or, beyond a certain point, it was undesirable.

Many serving officers had a natural empathy with the Germans. They had only to imagine German officers prying into Portsmouth Harbour, Vickers, or the Royal Arsenal to understand German resistance. When multilateral disarmament was discussed at League committees in the 1920s and 1930s, they were deeply opposed to intrusive inspection. They also disliked accusing an officer of deceit to his face. They felt that insistence on the minute details of the treaty was unnecessary and excessive. Bingham, Roddie, and others shared the fear of communist revolution, which was widespread among the Germany military. After all, such a revolution had been successful in Russia and there had also been abortive revolts in Hungary and Germany. The British General Staff itself supported German requests to maintain 200,000 men under arms in 1920 to deal with internal problems. One of the inspectors, Lieutenant-Colonel Stewart Roddie, made a personal appeal to the Prime Minister in support of the German position, and Lloyd George clearly sympathized with his point of view.[16]

Roddie epitomized the favourable view of Germany. His account of his work there, which was published in 1932, makes clear his concern for German poverty and demoralization in 1919 and his liking for the German liaison officers. Roddie denied that he ever received an 'insult or rudeness' from German officers. Just as the Duke of Wellington refused to allow attempts to assassinate him after 1815 to turn him against the French, so Roddie made light of threats to the inspectors' lives. He was well connected with the German aristocracy, whom he visited frequently, and he was horrified by the petty insults they suffered from the allies.[17] Bingham, his senior officer, noted in passing that inspectors were occasionally molested but said that, although he travelled all over Germany, he 'never had anything but the most polite and correct reception'.[18]

[15] Jaffe, *The Decision*, p. 32.   [16] Roddie, *Peace Patrol*, pp. 19 ff.
[17] Roddie, *Peace Patrol*, pp. 50 ff.
[18] Sir F. Bingham, 'Work with the allied Commission of Control in Germany, 1919–1924', *Journal of the Royal United Services Institution*, February 1924; *Quarterly Review*, October 1924; for attacks on Charlton's car see ADM/116/1941, Charlton letter of 24 October 1922.

Among the British inspectors, one group represented by J. H. Morgan disagreed strongly with the views expressed by Bingham and Roddie. Morgan was an acting brigadier but had been professor of constitutional law and legal history at University College London since 1908. He took a strictly legal view of what the Germans were supposed to do under the terms of the treaty.[19] Morgan loathed Germans, whom he regarded as boorish, arrogant, and deceitful. 'I knew by experience,' he wrote later, 'that Germans are only genial to Englishmen when they hope to make a fool of them. Geniality is not natural to a German.' Morgan believed that Germany was deeply imbued with militarism and that nothing but the strictest enforcement of German disarmament would keep the peace in Europe. His loathing was increased by German lies and evasions. According to Morgan's later account, 'almost every document put up to us by the Reichswehrministerium was found, after we had checked its statements by "control" inspections, to be false.'[20]

Morgan claimed that most of those who actually carried out the inspections supported his view of the Germans rather than Bingham's. Certainly they faced a good deal of obstruction. Sometimes the inspectors were simply hindered or told that their papers were not in order.[21] Sometimes opposition was more violent. On 6 March 1920 General Nollet complained to the German authorities that, when Colonel Irvine from Britain and Colonel Pollone from Italy tried to inspect the Prenzlau barracks, 'the soldiers standing along the railings shouted and threw at the various officers missiles, such as stones, bricks, glasses etc.'[22] A Belgian officer accompanying them was injured and the next morning, when the inspectors prepared to leave, they were insulted by groups of soldiers. That same month a team of naval inspectors was attacked in Bremen. In November 1920, when two British and two French officers visited the Grimmerhorn barracks in Cuxhaven, they were showered with dirty water and stones. Their car windows were smashed, water was put in its petrol, and the chauffeur was told he was to be

---

[19] Morgan, *Assize of Arms*, p. 36.

[20] Morgan, *Assize of Arms*, pp. 27, 123.

[21] ADM/116/1932, 'Violations and Infractions of the Naval Clauses of the Treaty of Versailles', 14 May 1920; ADM/116/1963, Report by James W. French, 25 May 1920.

[22] ADM/116/1941, Nollet to Mertens, 6 March 1920.

thrown in the river.[23] The officer in charge of the barracks knew what was happening but refused to take responsibility. At the Kustenwehr barracks a heavy bottle was thrown, knocking papers from the inspector's hands.[24] What was surprising was that none of the allied officers was badly injured.

Each side interpreted 'incidents' in its own way. The Germans complained that a naval team under Commander Fanshawe arrived late for an inspection and that Fanshawe then failed to apologize or to introduce his team. They also protested that Fanshawe had grumbled to the liaison officer about his clothes. Admiral Charlton replied that it was the German liaison officer's responsibility to introduce those present since he alone knew their names. Fanshaw had not criticized the liaison officer's clothes, merely suggested that it would be better if they all wore uniforms. More important, the managing director of the factory under inspection had concealed the presence of war materials. Furthermore, the German Admiralty had issued instructions to firms 'to the effect that they are to withhold from the visiting committee any information concerning the whereabouts of war material which is the property of the German government'.[25] The conflicting accounts suggest that Charlton and Fanshawe were right to complain that the Germans were being evasive, but that it would have been possible, with more tact and humanity, to reduce the friction involved in the inspection.

However, the most notorious incident could only be blamed on German trouble-makers. This occurred at the Hotel Adlon in Berlin, where the military inspectors were staying. On 6 March 1920 two French officers and their wives were dining. At another table Prince Joachim Albrecht von Hohenzollern was sitting with a group of German officers. They asked the violinist to play 'Deutschland über Alles' and, when the Frenchmen did not stand up, they threw bottles and the lighted candelabra at them. According to Roddie's eyewitness account, the incident deteriorated into a furious fight. Nollet asked for an apology from the German Foreign Minister. He also noted that Germany was expecting economic help from the allies but that German behaviour was hardly designed to make this more likely. The French complained that the

[23] ADM/116/1941, Report by Captain Forget, French Navy, and Charlton letter to German Ministry of Foreign Affairs, 25 November 1920.
[24] ADM/116/1941, Report by Gunner F. G. Worley RN.
[25] ADM/116/1963, letter from Commodore Gagern to Charlton, 4 May 1920, Charlton to Gagern, 6 May 1920.

Prince had only been fined 5 marks, though *The Times* reported that it was 500.[26]

Factory inspections would be arranged, only to be aborted by the absence of the German liaison officers or of those to be visited. On other occasions the liaison officers themselves hindered the inspectors. One told the directors of Lambrecht Pfalz and Brown Boveri that there was no need to answer allied questions. Liaison officers could also warn factory-owners to remove war material; 30 to 40 tons was taken from a Siemens factory to a private house in Berlin to keep it from the allies. The allied inspectors told the director of the Berliner Maschinebau company that he would have to destroy all machines for making torpedoes. He flatly refused to destroy more than three and the liaison officer supported him. When allied officers complained about the attitude of the liaison officers, the German authorities refused to accept the complaints and said that they were insulting.[27]

After his retirement to the governorship of Jersey, General Bingham gave a lecture on Germany to the Royal United Services Institute in London. Bingham lauded the success of the disarmament measures which the allies had imposed. There were a number of odd features about the occasion. The Prime Minister, Ramsay MacDonald, was supposed to take the chair but refused to do so at the last moment on the grounds that he was 'engaged elsewhere'. Against the Institute's custom, no questions were allowed. This was supposed to prevent any embarrassment to the government if the questions became too critical or touched on sensitive issues. In what can hardly have been a coincidence, Morgan's views appeared simultaneously in the October 1924 editions of the *Quarterly Review*.[28] Bingham stressed the 'melancholy' state of Berlin when the inspectors arrived, with 'food short, and people sullen, tired and yellow'. Conversely, what had struck Morgan most was that the shops were full of loot from France plundered by the General Staff, and that Berlin had become what he called 'a thieves' kitchen'. Bingham emphasized the unhappy state of the people;

[26] Roddie, *Peace Patrol*, p. 46; Morgan, *Assize of Arms*, p. 55.
[27] ADM/116/1969, Burhardt to Viel, 30 January 1923.
[28] Bingham was not completely uncritical of German behaviour. In January 1923 he advised the War Office against substituting Committees of Guarantee for the Commissions of Control because the Committees of Guarantee would lack the legal right to inspect; see AIR/5/343, Bingham to DMO and I, 11 January 1923.

Morgan thought the effect of the allied blockade much exaggerated.[29]

Bingham was responsible for the destruction of German military equipment, Morgan for insisting that the numbers in the German army were limited. Bingham argued that personnel were relatively unimportant and that limiting weaponry was the key to disarmament. He noted that, since the war, 4.5 million rifles had been destroyed by the IAMCC, 40,000 tons of powder, and 50,000 field guns. The inspectors had examined 7,000 factories to see whether they would have to be destroyed on the grounds that they could produce only war material. All but 80 had been cleared by 1924. Bingham acknowledged that rifles and machine-guns had been hidden, but he insisted that Germany was essentially disarmed and that it was the overall picture which was important. He found many of the attempted evasions of the treaty quite amusing. When the Germans wanted to keep their artillery range-finders, they said that they could use them for taking the heights of clouds; when they wanted to keep their flame-throwers, they said that they could use them to burn the insects off trees; the ramps round the powder factories were to be used for chicken-farming. Morgan found such incidents less amusing.[30]

Unlike Bingham, Morgan believed that the limitation of the personnel of an army was still of major importance. His greatest success was in working out how the Germans planned to avoid the limitation of their army to 100,000 men. Of course, some of the evasions were obvious. With the dissolution of the old imperial army, many soldiers had joined *Freicorps*, taking with them their rifles and even machine-guns. In theory, the *Freicorps* were independent bands of freebooters, but Morgan knew well enough that many of them had close links with the army. Others were backed by state governments in Bavaria and elsewhere. The so-called *Einwohnewehr* numbered as many as 300,000 in December 1920 and had 190,000 rifles and carbines. The German government also struggled to maintain the largest and most heavily armed police force that the allies would allow. To combat this, the allies became involved in laying down ever more detailed instructions on how the police could be armed and where they should be housed. It was all

---

[29] See note 18 above. Roddie sympathized with Bingham's view on this as on much else; see *Peace Patrol*, ch. 3; see also Morgan, *Assize of Arms*, p. 13.

[30] Bingham, *R.U.S.I. Journal*, February 1924, p. 754.

to little avail; by 1930 German officials did not deny that 'police' were involved with the army in military manoeuvres.[31]

Morgan regarded plans to expand the army through conscription as more serious than the existence of either the *Freicorps* or the para-military police. The army kept lists of all demobilized men so that they could be rapidly recalled to the colours. Thus the demobilization offices could effectively operate in reverse, should the opportunity arise. Furthermore, the Germans refused to hand over details of whom they were recruiting into the new army; its 4,000 officers and 40,000 NCOs were hardly necessary to look after 56,000 men. We now know that by 1925 the army planned, when the time came, to triple the seven existing infantry divisions. The three cavalry divisions were to be expanded to five and thirty-nine frontier defence divisions were to be recruited from classes of former conscripts. Clandestine depots contained 350,000 rifles, 600 light and 75 heavy cannon.[32]

Despite Morgan's efforts and the intrusiveness of allied inspection, the full extent of German evasion of the treaty's disarmament provisions was never discovered. Moreover, the verification system was undermined by the French invasion of the Ruhr in 1923. This gave the Germans an excuse to halt inspections for some 10 months. The German officer in charge at Wilhelmshaven wrote to the inspector there: 'the increasing number of breaches of the law on the part of the French government in extending its occupation of German territory, as well as the daily acts of violence on the part of the French soldiery . . . has caused among the population and among the officials and working men of the artillery depot such excitement as the occurrence of incidents in the course of inspection would still remain very probable.' The unfortunate allied inspector was also criticized by the Naval Commission of Control in Berlin for making a request for an inspection at such a time and thus giving the Germans the opportunity to refuse.[33]

Living conditions in Germany became increasingly difficult for

[31] For control of the police in the early postwar period see WO/155/2. For the subsequent situation see FO/371/14366, Tyrrell report of negotiations in Paris with the German government, 10 January 1930.

[32] Carsten, *The Reichswehr*, p. 221; Craig, *Germany 1866–1945*, pp. 402 ff.

[33] ADM/116/1932, Burghardt to Viel, 18 January 1923; Viel to Burghardt, 29 January 1923; Burghardt to Viel, 7 February 1923; Drax to Viel. See also AIR/9/20, Phipps letter of 15 April 1923, Foreign Office to Phipps, 19 April 1923. For Viscount d'Abernon's views see his autobiography, *An Ambassador of Peace* (Hodder and Stoughton, London, 1929).

the inspectors. In Wilhelmshaven the owner of the Loheyde Hotel, where the inspectors were staying, said he would refuse them accommodation. When German officials intervened on their behalf, the owner said he would provide no further meals. Restaurants in the town followed suit, and the inspectors believed the German police were circulating their photographs so that restaurant owners would recognize them. When one officer entered a café to drink a coffee he was manhandled into the street. The inspectors were reduced for more than a month to buying their own food and eating it cold.[34] They were the victims of the short-sightedness of the French government. The threat of invading the Ruhr was useful as a tool for achieving German compliance with the treaty. An actual invasion was a disaster because it showed that the French would suffer almost as much as the Germans. Berlin might have backed down in the end, but the French were unlikely to repeat the experiment.

INFORMANTS

The allied inspectors frequently received information about evasions of the treaty from Germans who needed money or who were anti-military. The German authorities responded by arresting and prosecuting such informers as spies. On 5 July 1922 a German workman approached the British inspector in Kiel and said that weapons were hidden in the marine arsenal there. The workman returned a second time and was given 1,000 marks but warned that he would be in danger if he approached the inspectors again directly. As a result of his information, 170 light machine-guns, 38 heavy machine-guns, 18 observation telescopes, and other equipment was discovered. On 14 July the *Volks Zeitung* reported that Heinrich Beck had been arrested and charged with high treason for giving information to the allies.[35]

Adolf Hitler later claimed that 'thanks to microphones installed in the seats of the enemy disarmament commissions, they sometimes succeeded in catching the traitors at work. When they did so, they at once had them hauled in by officials of the criminal police

---

[34] ADM/116/1941, letters from inspectors in Wilhelmshaven of 8 and 26 February 1923.
[35] ADM/116/1963, 'Concealed War Material at Marine Arsenal', report by Commander E. C. Brent RN.

[who passed themselves off as French] and at once arrested them.'
This may have been idle boasting, as it was probably easy to see the
informers approaching the inspectors. In any case, the main danger
did not come from the police, who sometimes co-operated with the
inspectors. According to Roddie,

a system of terrorism started and the informer seldom had an opportunity
of enjoying the fruits of his labour. Sometimes he would be found
afterwards—when flies drew one's attention to the body. Often it was
members of the secret police who in the course of their duty reported the
discovery of concealed stores of war material, and who were, therefore,
murdered. We never knew who was responsible for these removals, nor,
indeed, was it our business.[36]

Roddie's cavalier dismissal of the informers reflected his lack of
sympathy for those who sold their country's secrets, even if they
were helping the allies and backing up the treaty system.

In the case of the Kiel barracks, the German authorities claimed
that the weapons had been hidden there when radicals seized it in
March 1920. They had subsequently been forgotten. As for the
workman, the Germans said that the allies had no authority to
defend him under the Treaty of Versailles.[37] In 1930 a German
general justified his country' attitude towards informers on the
grounds that 'French allegations about secret preparations [for
war] are based upon the statements of informers and denouncers
who have poisoned the atmosphere of understanding year after
year. Germany will defend herself against the activities of these
people with the utmost rigour for the sake of understanding.'[38] He
was correct about the impact of informers' reports on Franco-
German relations, but it was a perverse logic which blamed the
informers rather than those in the armed forces who gave them
something to inform about.

FUNDAMENTAL PROBLEMS

Many allied problems were inherent in any attempt to compel an
industrial state to disarm on the scale they required. Just as British

[36] Roddie, *Peace Patrol*, p. 52. H. Trevor-Roper (ed.), *Hitler's Table-Talk*
(Oxford University Press, 1988), p. 406.
[37] ADM/116/1963, letter from von Lewinski at the German Foreign Ministry
to Charlton, 7 August 1922.
[38] FO/371/14366, Groener interview 29 November 1930.

pressure to keep Dunkirk demilitarized in the eighteenth century had threatened to ruin the port altogether, so a serious allied attempt to make it impossible for Germany to resume production of weapons would have seriously hampered civilian production and further reduced German standards of living. Article 168 of the Treaty of Versailles laid down that 'all establishments for the manufacture of arms, munitions, or any war material', other than the very small number needed for the new army, were to be closed.[39] But, during the war years, most factories had been used to help the war effort. Full enforcement would thus have been devastating.

Instead factories were divided into categories A and B. Category A factories could be destroyed because they had only military uses, but there were very few factories of this type. The German chemical industry had been extensively involved in the production of poison gases. Now it turned back to the manufacture of dyes and insecticides. However, at any stage the process could be reversed rapidly and this is precisely what happened in the 1930s when I. G. Farben advanced the art of chemical warfare by inventing nerve agents. Colonel Roddie was amused when an American lady approached him after her husband died in Germany. She told Roddie that the Germans had embalmed her husband's body so well for the return home that she felt bound to come and warn the inspector that their chemical industry was a threat to world peace. She was less naïve than he thought.[40]

These problems were raised in an acute form by aircraft and the aviation industry. Aircraft manufacture and design was advancing rapidly and becoming almost indispensable for a major industrial power. Germany was prohibited by the Treaty of Versailles from maintaining an air force, yet it could hardly be stopped from having civil airlines and civil airliners were virtually indistinguishable at this period from bombers. The compromise agreed was that single-seater aircraft of more than a certain power were prohibited; other types of aircraft would be allowed but limited in power to make them unsuitable for military purposes, and the number of aircraft

[39] Williamson, *The Reluctant Occupiers*, p. 22 argues that Lloyd George was primarily responsible for the limitations on German factories. In his own account of the negotiations Lloyd George claims he argued that such restrictions were a waste of time; Lloyd George, *The Truth*, p. 597. No doubt the Prime Minister's position varied over time.

[40] Roddie, *Peace Patrol*, p. 121.

and engines should not exceed the reasonable requirements of the civil airlines. Civilians could be trained as pilots but military officers should not receive flying training.[41]

Naturally, French representatives wanted to keep limits on the performance of aircraft as tight as possible, whereas the Germans were constantly pushing for them to be relaxed. In March 1925 officers from both sides met for the first time in Paris. The Germans wanted the 'ceiling' for civil airlines raised from 4,000 to 7,000 metres and the maximum permitted speed increased to 240 kilometres per hour.[42] The British view was that it was impossible to deny Germany the sort of airliners which could rapidly be put to military use and, in the event, by 1926 German airlines were bringing into service aircraft which could potentially carry 800 pounds of bombs over 180 miles. They could easily be equipped with bomb racks and sights.[43] The French may similarly have recognized the inexorable nature of the process, but they were determined to fight against it. The British view was that this was politically counter-productive and militarily ineffective.

If the Germans refused to disarm, the allies had to decide how they would compel them to do so. Invasion was possible, but maintaining forces in Germany was extremely expensive and would clearly arouse even greater resentment among the Germans. In any case, Britain's primary objective was to demobilize its armies as soon as possible. Given Germany's economic weakness after the war and the serious food shortage from which it was suffering, economic pressure could also be used. Indeed, the allies did continue to blockade the country even after the end of the fighting, but this would become difficult to defend in public as information spread about the state of the German people. An allied committee assembled at Foch's headquarters in Paris on 10 February 1919 to discuss whether pork and condensed milk should be sent to Germany. This was intended for sick children and nursing mothers but only if the Germans complied with the treaty and handed over merchant ships and submarines. Discussions were still continuing a month later, with the Germans saying they would not hand over

[41] AIR/5/391, letter from Wing Commander Sewell, Paris, 9 December 1924.

[42] AIR/5/391, Note on Revisions of Rules For Discriminating Between Civil and Military Aircraft.

[43] AIR/5/391, Folio 77a, Report from Wing-Commander Sewell in Paris, 18 March 1925;. AIR/9/20, 'German Air Menace against France', Note by the Air Staff, 16 July 1926.

the merchant ships until they were sure that the food would be delivered.[44] Such bargaining over the lives and health of civilians was clearly distasteful to many people. Once the blockade was lifted and normal trade began, the development of mutually beneficial economic links made it hard to reverse this process and again put economic pressure on Germany.

Already, when the allied leaders met at San Remo in April 1920, their powerlessness was causing them concern as German disarmament was not proceeding as fast as the allies had hoped. The French Premier, Millerand, pushed for an occupation of the industrial area of the Ruhr. Lloyd George countered with the ludicrous argument that 'Saxony and Bavaria and possibly Berlin would not much mind the occupation of the Ruhr which was not a sensitive part of Germany.'[45] Instead, the allies should meet German representatives and use diplomacy to achieve their ends. The Italian leader, Signor Nitti, also opposed an invasion and sympathized with the German government's efforts to maintain order and to stabilize the economy. This division between those who favoured the use of force and those who favoured persuasion lasted until Hitler overthrew the treaty system in the 1930s.

How long was the intrusive inspection of Germany to last? When the treaty was under negotiation, the French had wanted inspection to continue indefinitely; the British and Americans had insisted that this was an unacceptable infringement of German sovereignty. In the end the French negotiator, Tardieu, broke the deadlock by proposing that, after the end of the Control Commissions, the League of Nations Council would then ask for inspection, should it seem necessary, under Article 213 of the Treaty of Versailles.[46] The British believed that Germany had disarmed to the required extent by 1921 and that the Control Commissions should be withdrawn. However, the French wanted the AIMCC to continue and the Air Commission to be replaced by a small Committee of Guarantee which would be based in Germany and carry out the same functions. The Commissions of Control had been paid for by Germans; the new smaller committee would be paid by the allies. The service departments in Britain were doubtful whether it was necessary; the

[44] ADM/116/3223, Notes for Discussions with German Representatives, 6 February 1919 and Conference of 4 March with German Representatives.
[45] DFBP, First Series, vol. VIII, p. 6.
[46] Tardieu, *The Truth about the Treaty*, p. 138.

air staff argued that Britain had been aware of the size of the German armed forces in 1914 and would presumably be as well informed of German strength in the future without intrusive verification.[47] However, the British bowed to French requests and a small committee was set up with four British officers, three French, two Italians, two Japanese, and two Belgians. Its primary role over the next few years was to monitor German progress in civil aviation and to protest when it believed that this had direct military implications, thus clearly threatening to infringe the treaty.

The real change in attitudes towards the whole disarmament process occurred after the Locarno conference in October 1925. Until then the British had been prepared to put up with the friction with Germany caused by arguments over disarmament.[48] Subsequently, if the strategic advantages of disarmament had to be weighed against the political advantages of keeping on good terms with Berlin, the British government would choose the second alternative. The French government did not take the same view, but it had tried coercion when it invaded the Ruhr in 1923, and it did not want to repeat the process. Nevertheless, it insisted that the IAMCC remain until German disarmament was as complete as a strict reading of the treaty demanded. Conversely, the IAMCC was increasingly seen as nothing but a nuisance both in the British Foreign Office and in the service ministries.

In the atmosphere created by Locarno and the German decision to join the League of Nations in 1926, the French reluctantly agreed that the IAMCC should be withdrawn on 31 January 1927.[49] However, arguments were still continuing at that time about German failure to regulate the police force as the allies demanded and about other technical questions. So the allies left 'military experts' at their Berlin embassies to monitor the situation. The British continued to argue with the French and Belgians about the value of the experts: 'they were costing money and, as far as the British military authorities were concerned, they were doing no sort of good, all matters of any real importance to us having already been disposed of.' This was not because the British believed that the Germans were abiding by the treaty. On the contrary, in

[47] AIR/5/343, Air Minister and Foreign Office papers on inspection, February and March 1922.
[48] Williamson, *The Reluctant Occupiers*, p. 23.
[49] DBFP Series 1A, vol. V (HMSO, 1973, p. 3. Memorandum by Mr Perowne, 18 April 1928; p. 30, letter from Wigram in Paris, 18 May 1928.

August 1928 they had reliable information that the Germans were breaking it. But, as one diplomat put it, 'I doubt whether the mind of man could conceive a system under which, ten years after a war a country like Germany could remain absolutely tied both hand and foot . . . But for the moment, I should imagine that Germany is sufficiently hampered by the treaty to be incapable of sudden or dramatic aggression.'[50]

The French took a different view, particularly when the 'Locarno spirit' had begun to ebb. To a great extent, it was German potential which was the root of French fears. Even though the Germans had evaded many of the treaty's provisions, the French could easily have defeated the German armed forces in the early 1930s. Thus it was not the forces in being which were the problem, though German evasions seemed to Paris to confirm their malign intentions. If the Germans had reduced their army to 100,000 men, precisely as the treaty stipulated, the demographic balance between France and Germany would have meant that German military weakness depended purely on the maintenance of the Treaty of Versailles. Similarly, if German factories had to a great extent stopped producing weapons, the efficiency of that industry meant that the process could be reversed and German armaments could quickly threaten France once again.

All the efforts put into disarmament and inspection had reassured neither the French government nor their people, as became clear in 1930 when politicians in both France and Germany began to talk about their fears. The French government attempted to quieten anxieties, but the effect was somewhat reduced when the War Minister, Maginot, also announced the allocation of funds to begin the construction of his famous 'line' of fortifications. Privately, French generals told British officers that they believed German military revival had begun, and one said that the only way to increase security was to reoccupy the Rhineland from which allied forces had just withdrawn.[51] Fears were increased by debates in the Reichstag, where there were complaints about the imbalance between French and German military power, and by the tone of newspaper articles in the two countries.

When the British military attachés in Paris and Berlin looked at

[50] DBFP, Series 1A, vol. V, p. 253, letter from Nicolson in Berlin, 14 August 1928. See also FO/371/12895, fol. 182, 189.
[51] FO/371/14366, p. 63, and FO/371/14366, p. 77.

the issue, their contrasting views showed how differently the military situation was viewed in the two capitals. Colonel Needham in Paris sympathized with French fears about German evasion of the Treaty of Versailles and the clandestine improvement in German military capability.[52] Colonel Marshall-Cornwall in Berlin argued that French fears were the irrational product of an inferiority complex. He denied that the Germans were secretly storing arms or that their military co-operation with the Soviet Union was significant.[53] The acting ambassador in Berlin agreed with Marshall-Cornwall and so did most of the officials who read the despatch in the Foreign Office, though some warned of the dangers of dismissing French fears. In terms of reassurance, enforced disarmament and intrusive verification had been a failure. Soon after Hitler's accession to power in 1933 it became clear that it had done nothing to reduce Germany's military potential.

WEIMAR, THE NAZIS, AND DISARMAMENT

The Weimar republic was weakened from its inception by the shame of accepting the Treaty of Versailles. Any other government would have had to do the same because the high command had advised that the military situation was hopeless. But the Socialist government could be presented by nationalists as having betrayed Germany. Even more unfortunately, the unrest within Germany during the early years of the new republic meant that the Socialist government had to rely on the army to keep order. The opportunity to reform or even to control the army was lost because of threats to the government from nationalists and from the communists or Spartacists. The army came to be dominated by the Chief of Army Command, General von Seeckt, who devoted all his efforts to evading the Treaty of Versailles and rebuilding German strength.[54]

Thus, even if the government wanted to carry out the peace treaty, it could not easily do so because the armed forces had a parallel policy of resistance, a policy which led Seeckt to forge links with Japan and produce weapons in Sweden and Austria. But it was co-operation with the Soviet Union which was, for a time, most important. By January 1921 the French were aware of

---

[52] FO/371/14366, p. 80,
[53] FO 371/14366, p. 102.
[54] Carsten, *The Reichswehr*, pp. 246 ff.

German plans to set up air routes to the Soviet Union so that contacts could be maintained and the treaty evaded. Allied officers were asked to take note of all aircraft they saw flying east of Berlin to try to track down what was happening.[55] Despite their efforts, German pilots received extensive training in the Soviet Union, where armaments factories were established by Junkers and other German companies and where experiments were also conducted with tanks, poison gas, and combat aircraft.

Nobody epitomized German ambiguity more than Gustav Stresemann, who was Chancellor briefly in 1923 and Foreign Minister from then until 1929. Britain and France came to see Stresemann as the mainstay of *détente* and reconciliation, yet Stresemann was a staunch nationalist who had supported the annexations outlined in the Treaty of Brest-Litovsk. He knew about the army's secret relationship with the Soviet Union, about the links with the *Freicorps*, and about plans to expand the size of the army. Stresemann pushed the allies to withdraw the control commissions and evacuate the Rhineland as soon as possible. Of course, his efforts were not enough to satisfy von Seeckt and the army, but his aim was not essentially different from theirs.[56] When he was Chancellor, Stresemann did apparently try to halt some of the short-term courses which the army conducted for civilians in contravention of the treaty. He also wanted to bring in laws against links between student organizations and the Reichswehr. But the Weimar republic was dependent on the army and Stresemann's efforts came to nothing.[57]

Parallel efforts by the Prussian government were also frustrated. The Prussian Interior Ministry was particularly concerned because of the secret links between landowners, the army, and extreme right-wing political organizations.[58] Protests about clandestine rearmament from the Inter-Allied Control Commissions went some way to strengthen the Prussians and the central German government in relations with the army. But the balance of power still lay

[55] For links with Japan see S. Asada, in D. Borg and S. Okamato, *Pearl Harbor as History* (Columbia University Press, New York and London, 1973). For links with the USSR see H. L. Dyck, *Weimar Germany and Soviet Russia: A Study in Diplomatic Instability* (Chatto and Windus, London, 1966). See also ADM/116/1932, Aeronautical Inter-Allied Commission of Control, Report by Smyth Piggot, 27 November 1920.

[56] H. W. Gatzke, *Stresemann and the Rearmament of Germany* (Johns Hopkins Press, Baltimore, Md., 1954).

[57] Carsten, *The Reichswehr*, p. 233.   [58] Carsten, *The Reichswehr*, p. 229.

with the military authorities who were able to ride out the various protests and ensuing scandals until Hitler became Chancellor in January 1933.

When the Nazi government showed its determination to rearm quite openly, the British government was confronted with the same dilemma which had faced Gladstone in 1870: should the allies go to war to maintain disarmament or, if not, how could they avoid humiliation and a breach of international law? In retrospect, it would have been better to fight, indeed this was probably the only opportunity of fighting a limited rather than a world war. However, the British people would not have gone to war to maintain the treaty and the French were afraid to act alone. In February 1935 the British and French governments issued a communiqué which asserted that 'neither Germany nor any other Power whose armaments have been defined by the Peace Treaties is entitled by unilateral action to modify these obligations.'[59] Yet four months later the British negotiated a naval treaty with the Germans which allowed them to build 6 capital ships, 44,000 tons of aircraft carriers, 18 cruisers, as well as smaller vessels and submarines. The French, not unreasonably, protested and rightly warned 'that Germany would violate the agreement as soon as it suited her'.[60] The British government persisted until the spring of 1939 in treating Hitler and the Nazis as if they were just like any other government and could be trusted to abide by the agreements they made. The longer the war was postponed, the further the military balance moved from that established by the Versailles Treaty and the more the allied military position deteriorated.

During the First World War the Germany army had proved superior to any one of the allied armies. Thus the imbalance of power created by Germany's defeat depended on the maintenance of the allied coalition and the reduction of German power by forced disarmament. The same might have been said about France's strategic position after the Napoleonic Wars, but we can now see that Napoleon's wars brought to an end the period of continental dominance begun by Louis XIV. Allied statesmen ascribed French superiority in 1815 partly to Louis's frontier fortifications, which

[59] Viscount Simon, *Retrospect* (Hutchinson, London, 1952), p. 200.
[60] S. R. Roskill, *Naval Policy between the Wars*, vol. 2 (Collins, London, 1976), pp. 302 ff.

they tried to counteract by strengthening those in Belgium and Germany. In fact, it was not their efforts but the changing economic and demographic balance, together with France's continuing isolation, which preserved the Peace of Paris for four decades.

Unfortunately for the reputations of the allied statesmen gathered in Paris in 1919, the First World War was by no means the last gasp of the German thrust for world power. German economic and demographic predominance remained, while the coalition the allies had welded together was even more fissiparous than the anti-French alliance had been in 1815. Russia had collapsed and the United States withdrew into isolation. British power was vastly over-stretched by its imperial commitments, and Italy and Japan were dissatisfied with the peace treaties. Thus the disarmament measures, which Germany was forced to accept, occupied a pivotal position. In one sense this justifies the emphasis placed on such measures and their far-reaching nature. But every previous forced disarmament measure in modern history had eventually come to an end. How was this to be avoided or dealt with in the German case?

The British government's answer was apparently either that once militarism had been overcome Germany would cease to be threatening, or that all armaments should be reduced and consequently Germany would cease to resent the limitations imposed upon it. It is difficult to know which of the two arguments was more absurd. Militarism could hardly be defined let alone eliminated by international agreement.[61] Conscription could hardly be the root of the problem, despite Lloyd George's claims, because most European states maintained conscript armies and many were not particularly aggressive. The suggestion was a gratuitous insult to Britain's continental allies.

As far as general disarmament was concerned, in the unlikely event of far-reaching measures being negotiated, strategic stability would be reduced not enhanced. Military strength is relative, as the French government kept trying to explain to their purblind British colleagues. There was no strategic difference between France disarming down to the German level or Germany rearming. Either way the German government would be in a position to recover its

[61] For an early attempt at definition see A. Vagts, *A History of Militarism*, rev. edn. (Hollis and Carter, London, 1959).

'lost' territories as it did in the 1930s.[62] The implicit French answer
to the conundrum was that the allies should continue to use force—
go to war—whenever it became necessary and before a great war
was involved. French leaders knew that the British never accepted
this. Thus they would have to act alone and they lacked the
ruthlessness and determination necessary.

In 1815 the allies had a coherent strategy for dealing with
France. Their political objective was to install the Bourbons and
prevent Napoleon regaining control. Their military objective was
to weaken France by reducing its fortifications or building up those
belonging to neighbouring powers so that any French government
would feel a reduced temptation to expand. In 1919 there was far
less coherence in allied strategy. The new Socialist government in
Germany should have been welcomed enthusiastically as a repudi-
ation of the expansionism of the past. Had a strong and radical
government been in power in Germany in 1919, it might have been
able to establish an army which was willing to obey the legal
authorities rather than carry out a parallel policy of resistance. It
would also have been able to demobilize the *Freicorps* and to
discipline Bavaria and the other states which refused to obey its
orders. To bolster such a government, only those territories which
voted to join Poland or other states should have been separated
from the new republic. Reparations should have been limited to
paying for the damage to northern France and Belgium, for which
even the Germans accepted responsibility, and which would not
have left Germany permanently indebted.[63]

It was not unreasonable to destroy German weapons in 1919
and so postpone the moment when Berlin was in a position to seek
revenge. It was only reasonable to insist that Germany remained
disarmed, if the allies were ultimately prepared to force it to do so.
Moreover, they had to be ready to use force quickly because of
Germany's intrinsic power; the French were afraid of Germany in
1930, not because of German evasions of the Treaty of Versailles
but because of German industrial and demographic strength. Yet
any extensive attempt to weaken Germany's ability to revive
its weapons industry would have had cataclysmic effects on the

[62] P. Towle, 'British security and disarmament policy in Europe in the 1920s',
in R. Ahmann, A. M. Birke, and M. Howard, *The Quest for Stability* (Oxford
University Press, 1993), p. 127.
[63] Temperley, *The Peace Conference*, pp. 308 ff.

German economy as a whole. Such despoliation was perfectly possible in the ancient world, as the Carthaginians learnt to their cost, but was inconceivable for the modern democracies even after four years of total war. Self-imposed limitations of this sort made forced disarmament both more important to the victors and much more difficult to maintain.

5

The Disarmament of
Central Europe

At the end of the First World War the Austro-Hungarian Empire disintegrated, leaving a power vacuum in the centre of Europe. Czechoslovakia, Austria, Yugoslavia, and Hungary for the first time became independent states. All were politically weak but most were fiercely nationalistic. Hungary and Austria were bitter at their impoverishment and the loss of their predominant position.[1] Bulgaria too was angry at its loss of territory to Yugoslavia and Greece. On the other hand, the Czechs and Yugoslavs were euphoric at their new-found freedom. Despite their optimism, like all the states in the region, they harboured large and dissatisfied minorities; this caused tension and instability throughout the inter-war years.

The period began with the forced disarmament of Austria, Hungary, and Bulgaria, and the attempt to disarm Turkey; it finished with Anglo-French insistence that the Czechoslovak government appease Germany by abandoning its line of fortifications in the Sudetenland. Both of these processes were far-reaching. Czechoslovakia in 1938 was as vulnerable without its defensive line as Athens had been without its walls. Germany's former allies were only allowed to maintain armed forces which were a fraction of the size of those mobilized by their neighbours in the 1920s. This made it impossible for them to use force to regain their lost territories but it also increased their bitterness.

The earlier examples of forced disarmament studied in this

[1] Yugoslavia was originally known as the Kingdom of the Croats, Serbs, and Slovenes. For Hungarian problems see B. K. Kiraly, P. Pastor, and I. Sanders (eds), *War and Society in East Central Europe: A Case Study of Trianon* (Brooklyn College Press, New York, 1982) and Sir R. Donald, *The Tragedy of Trianon: Hungary's Appeal to Humanity* (Thornton Butterworth, London, 1928). For Austria see M. Bullock, *Austria 1918–1938: A Study in Failure* (Macmillan, London, 1939).

book were related to major powers. The disarmament imposed on Austria, Bulgaria, and Hungary was unusual because they were such minor actors and could not threaten the allies directly. The measures taken against them were part of the new international system, based on the League of Nations, where the Great Powers not only protected their own interests but were responsible for security worldwide. They were intended to demonstrate allied fairness, particularly minor enemies being treated in the same way as the major one, Germany. The allies hoped that they would build confidence in Central Europe and the Balkans. Unfortunately, the former enemies did not regard such measures as 'fair' and, for example, they were completely baffled by allied insistence that they abandon conscription. The allies' hope that the limitation of the armaments of the former enemy powers would set a regional trend was also disappointed. Such limitations prevented Hungary and Bulgaria from trying to recapture territory lost to their neighbours but did not reassure those neighbours sufficiently to persuade them to reduce their forces. They knew that Budapest and Sofia harboured revisionist aspirations even if they could not realize them.

If the disarmament imposed on minor powers was unusual, so was the disarmament of Czechoslovakia in 1938. States can sometimes be brow-beaten into surrendering their armaments or positions without fighting if they can be persuaded that opposition would be futile. The Carthaginians handed over their weapons to the Romans before the Third Punic War because they knew that the Romans would defeat them if it came to battle. In the end, the French withdrew their garrison from Eyemouth without fighting in the sixteenth century because the Scots turned against them and they believed that, in the circumstances, it was not worth going to war to maintain their position in Scotland. What made the Czech case so exceptional was not only that they were persuaded to disarm without defending themselves, but that it was their allies who talked them into abandoning the Sudetenland in the vain hope that this would appease Nazi Germany. Only Prussia's betrayal of Poland in the eighteenth century offers a partial parallel.

AUSTRIA

Hungary and Austria protested to the allied governments in 1919 against being treated as defeated enemies, rather than as successor states like Czechoslovakia or Yugoslavia. This raised the question of blame for the earlier conflict in an acute form. Weimar Germany was in an obvious sense the successor of the kaiser's *Reich*, but were the truncated territories of Hungary and Austria the successors of the Habsburg regime and how did they differ from Czechoslovakia? The Austrian government wrote to the French Premier, Georges Clemenceau, on 2 July 1919, denying that their new state had any connection with the Austro-Hungarian Empire and any responsibility for the First World War. There was no difference, Chancellor Renner argued, between Austria and any of the other states which had emerged from the wreck of the empire. The Habsburg monarchy had been the 'prison of the peoples', all of whom had suffered from its domination, except the Hungarians who had occupied a predominant position. Austria was being made liable for the foreign debts of the previous regime, a burden its 7 million impoverished citizens were quite unable to sustain.[2] Unfortunately, Austrian pleas were ignored. Although the new state had no more connection with the Austro-Hungarian Empire than Czechoslovakia or Yugoslavia, Austria was treated as a defeated enemy while the others were treated as allies.

The Habsburg army collapsed after the revolution of 12 November 1918. In the confusion that followed, militias were organized by various soldiers' councils. However, these added to the disorder and the new Austrian government planned to establish an army of its own. The allied leaders meeting in Paris decided what shape this would take. By the end of April 1919 the negotiators had completed the disarmament terms for Germany, and the British military representatives began working on the Austrian treaty. They wanted to continue the process of reducing military power begun by the provisions for Germany and to leave Austria with only enough force to maintain internal order. If Germany was to end conscription, then so must the other enemy states too. The representatives were fully aware of Austria's poverty and so they envisaged allowing it an army of only 40,000 men.

The military representatives of the major powers discussed the British draft on 11 May. The French and Italians strongly opposed

[2] For Chancellor Renner's plea see ADM/116/3230, letter of 2 July 1919 to Clemenceau. For the general situation in Austria see C. Pribram and K. Brockhausen, 'Austria-Hungary' in *These Eventful Years* (Encyclopaedia Britannica, London, 1924), vol. 2, pp. 123 ff. and on conditions in the early 1920s FO/381/8537.

banning conscription, on the grounds that a professional army would be too expensive and too difficult to raise. The issue was passed to the politicians on 15 May. Clemenceau then precipitously conceded to the British and Americans, isolating the Italian Premier, Orlando, who maintained his objection to the Anglo-American view of conscription. This apart, the Council of Four wanted to reduce the size of the army permitted to the Austrians, as it seemed excessive when compared to the 100,000 allowed the Germans. Lloyd George claimed that 10,000 to 12,000 troops would be sufficient to maintain internal order, Clemenceau proposed 15,000, and Orlando agreed that 40,000 was excessive. The issue was then referred back to the military representatives, who met the political leaders on 23 May.[3]

General Bliss from the United States defended the limits proposed by the military representatives. He pointed out that they had always believed that the restrictions imposed on Germany should have been set at 200,000, not 100,000. As far as Central Europe was concerned, it was currently in chaos and was likely to continue to be exceedingly turbulent. If Austria were limited to 15,000 and the surrounding countries were restricted in parallel, then 'they would be converted into mere vassals of the two Continental Powers of the Entente.' Order would have to be maintained by France and Italy. European peace and civilization might also be threatened by a combination of Germany and the Slav and Asiatic races. The four political leaders conceded the strength of Bliss's arguments and re-examined the question on 4 June. President Wilson proposed that they should agree to limit the Austrian army to 40,000, as suggested by the military representatives. Clemenceau warned that this would further anger the Germans, and Lloyd George came up with the compromise figure of 30,000. The Austrians claimed later that the treaty permitted them to have 30,000 men with the colours and 30,000 in reserve. The allies never allowed this and, to make sure that Vienna did not evade the agreement by increasing its reliance on police and gendarmes, these were also limited to the number of policemen the former Austro-Hungarian Empire had raised within the geographical area of the new republic.[4] All further military

---

[3] *Papers Relating to the Foreign Relations of the United States: The Paris Peace Conference 1919* (United States Printing Office, Washington, 1946, hereafter FRUS 1919), vol. 5, pp. 627 ff., 873 ff.

[4] H. W. V. Temperley (ed.), *A History of the Peace Conference of Paris* (Henry Frowde and Hodder and Stoughton, London, 1921), vol. 4, pp. 144 ff.

organizations were prohibited. As in the case of the other defeated powers, the most modern and feared types of military equipment, such as tanks, poison gases, flame-throwers, military aircraft, and submarines, were banned.

Although the disarmament provisions imposed on Austria were far-reaching, this was not because of concern among the allies that the new republic would be belligerent. Their anxiety was rather that it might be so weak that it would collapse altogether. For the first few years after the war, there were constant pleas from Austria and from the diplomats and bankers familiar with its problems that the allies should bolster the new government with financial assistance.[5] In 1922 the allies provided a loan of 650 million gold crowns. A new national bank was established and the runaway inflation was eventually brought under control.

In the early years the disarmament of Austria caused a good deal of friction between the allies. The Austrians were allowed by the treaty to keep only enough rifles, machine-guns, and mortars for the 30,000-man army. The British would have liked all the other weapons destroyed, as they were in the German case. The Italians wanted them handed over for their own use. They had been able to seize many of the Austrian weapons after the November 1918 armistice of Villa Giusti and they delayed the entry into force of the Treaty of St Germain with Austria so that they could continue to take Austrian equipment. The Austrians signed the treaty on 10 September 1919, despite their vehement opposition to the prohibition of conscription. The British members of the Inter-Allied Commission of Control were ready to leave for Vienna the following month, but it was not until July 1920, nine months later, that the allies ratified the agreement. Advance parties of the Control Commission had gone to Austria in the spring of 1920, but they could do little until the treaty came into force.

Finally 130 allied officers and 582 men were detailed to see that Austria had actually disarmed. They were to be paid by the impecunious Austrians. They included 24 naval officers and 76 naval ratings, even though Austria had lost its coastline and its naval 'power' was confined to three patrol boats on the River Danube. The inspectors were an unhappy group. The Japanese were represented simply to assert a presence as a Great Power and

[5] Sir G. Franckenstein, *Facts and Features of My Life* (Cassell, London, 1939), pp. 221 ff.

took little part in the proceedings. The British were dissatisfied with the way the Control Commission carried out its work. Its main role appeared to be to burden the Austrians because the British officers believed that their Italian and French colleagues were not interested in enforcing the formal terms of the agreement. The Italians continued to separate the material they believed they were entitled to take for their own use from the equipment left to the Austrians.[6]

One of the treaty's stipulations was that Austria, like Bulgaria and Hungary, should be allowed only one state-owned munitions factory which would then be easy for the allies to inspect and monitor. The Austrian government agreed that the factory should be at Wollersdorf but could not afford to move production there. There were many other outstanding issues. The British inspector, Colonel Sherbrooke, produced a whole list of complaints about Austrian behaviour. An Austrian official was supposed to be look-ing after six guns belonging to the allies in Linz.[7] Inspection showed that the guns had disappeared and had presumably been sold. The Austrians were also trying 'German' prevarication tactics. When the allied officers wanted to visit one particular factory, the Austrians sent a policeman to accompany them. He then explained that he needed permission from the President of Police. When that difficulty was overcome, he said he wanted authority from the Austrian Foreign Office, and so it went on. Eventually the allied inspectors insisted on the inspection going ahead regardless. They found the reason for this procrastination when large quantities of empty shells were uncovered. Sherbrooke believed that the Austrians were not only hiding military activities but deliberately emulating the Germans in the not unreasonable expectation that the allies would quickly lose patience with the whole enterprise.[8]

The allied governments were inclined to take a relaxed attitude to such allegations and the British Foreign Office was not very supportive of Sherbrooke, whom it suspected of harbouring 'diplo-matic' ambitions. But the allies did take a stand against Vienna over both its determination to build up a 30,000-man reserve and the number of its naval vessels on the Danube.[9] The Austrian

---

[6] For arguments with the Italians over Austrian equipment see Temperley, *The Peace Conference*, p. 149. Figures for the contingents to the Inter-Allied Commissions come from ADM/116/2051 and 2059.

[7] FO/371/8554, c 17612.   [8] FO/371/c 21181.

[9] Temperley, *The Peace Conference*, p. 155.

government believed it should have the same number of boats as Hungary and began building armed motor launches. The allies told the Austrian Chancellor in July 1923 that they did not accept Austria's right to numerical equality, as the number of boats should be proportional to the length of river controlled. The Austrians continued to protest, especially when the Ambassadors' Conference in Paris rejected their appeals in November 1923.[10]

Ironically, given its inability even to mobilize the forces allowed by the allies, Austria was inspected for much of the 1920s. The Inter-Allied Military Commission of Control with its bloated staff came to an end in February 1921, but it was replaced by a smaller 'Organ of Liquidation'. This was still at work in 1927, largely because the Austrians were unable or unwilling to destroy weapon-manufacturing equipment banned by the allies.[11] The inspectors were aware that rifles had been spread across the country. They believed that socialist workers had some 7,000 in Vienna and that right-wing organizations kept similar armouries. However, they felt that the government was not strong enough to seize these and that an attempt to do so would only produce a crisis. In December 1927 the British, French, Japanese, and Italian ambassadors sent a final protest to the Viennese authorities about their weapon-manufacturing capability. The Organ of Liquidation was withdrawn in February 1928, even though the British believed the Austrians had not complied with allied demands.

HUNGARY

Immediately after the First World War, Hungary's internal affairs were as chaotic as Austria's but far more violent. The government was furiously denounced in Parliament for signing the Treaty of Trianon in June 1920. This treaty took away two-thirds of the historic state of Hungary and left 3.4 million Magyars in Romania, Czechoslovakia, and Yugoslavia. The more the peace was denounced, the more afraid those states became and the more Budapest acquired a reputation for revisionism. There were strong royalist forces in Parliament and outside supporting a Habsburg

[10] FO/371/8554, C 19393.
[11] DBFP, Series 1A, vol. 4, p. 33, no. 15, Viscount Chilston to Sir Austen Chamberlain, 29 September 1927; no. 94, p. 187, Chilston to Sir Austen Chamberlain, 14 December 1927 and no. 133, p. 246, Marquess of Crewe to Sir Austen Chamberlain, 8 February 1928.

restoration, but the allies refused to agree to this, partly because it would be taken as a symbol of Hungary's determination to regain its former territories.[12]

Hungary was surrounded by the Little Entente of Czechoslovakia, Romania, and Yugoslavia, who were united by their belief that Budapest had designs on their newly acquired territory. The British Minister in Budapest believed that the Little Entente was secretly pleased by royalist diatribes against the peace treaty because they confirmed their anti-Hungarian prejudices. From time to time there were border clashes, as in April 1923 when a Czech frontier guard was killed.[13] Given the extent of the bitterness on both sides, allied diplomats were surprised that these clashes were not more frequent or more bloody.

Hungary had been taken over in March 1919 by a radical left-wing government under Béla Kun. The experiment lasted only until August, when Budapest was 'liberated' by Romanian troops. With some difficulty, the allies persuaded the Romanians to withdraw with their loot, and a Hungarian delegation was invited to Paris to discuss peace terms. Eventually a strongly conservative government was established under Admiral Horthy, while for a period there was a 'white terror' against any suspected of left-wing leanings. Middle-class Hungarians continued to recall the Béla Kun experience with horror and were determined that it should not be repeated. They also believed that the communists had mainly been Jewish and their historic anti-Semitism grew accordingly. Gangs from the 'Awakening Hungarians' and other organizations smashed the offices of newspapers which voiced liberal opinions or belonged to Jews.[14] Bombs were planted where liberal politicians were expected to speak.

Amid all this chaos, political strife, and instability, the Treaty of Trianon laid down that Hungary must be disarmed very much as Austria had been. The Hungarians were made to abandon conscription and restrict their army to 35,000 men, serving for a minimum of twelve years, of which six would be with the colours. The armed forces protested vociferously that they would not be able to protect their frontiers with so few or to attract enough volunteers into the

---

[12] For arguments over frontiers see J. K. Hoensch, *A History of Modern Hungary* (Longmans, London, 1988) and FO/371/8856, C 13049 and C 15148.

[13] FO/371/8846, C 7497. The Czech guard had nineteen bayonet wounds.

[14] FO/371/8856, C 16088 and C20917.

army. Instead, they wanted a conscript army numbering 85,000. They also wanted to increase the permitted number of police and frontier guards. On the other hand, the Hungarians were worried by the size and cost of the Commission which was coming to inspect them and for which they would have to pay.[15] The allies rejected Hungarian appeals to alter the treaty terms, but they tried to reduce the cost of control by using the staff of the Inter-Allied Military Commission of Control in Austria and the Military Mission of Generals, which had been established for some time in Budapest. They also had to damp down Hungarian fears that the Little Entente countries would be represented among the inspectors.

The French generally backed the Little Entente, while the British were sympathetic towards some of Budapest's fears. The Royal Navy protested strongly against allied plans to send five flag officers to inspect the handful of boats on the Danube; a single French frigate captain would, it believed, be more than sufficient, but the French insisted that the full commission should go ahead. The Hungarians did not help their own case by grumpily demanding compensation for units of the former Austro-Hungarian fleet seized in the Adriatic. Many of the ships were decrepit and even useless, but it was still galling for the Hungarians to watch as the destroyer *Ulan* and six torpedo boats were handed over to Greece and three monitors were given to Romania.[16]

The allies were particularly angered by Hungarian threats to hang four 'spies' who told allied officers where hidden weapons caches were to be found.[17] Hungarian newspapers reported on 26 August 1923 that the court at Pecs had condemned Leopold Izelstoger and Kalman Melzer to be hanged.[18] The French persuaded the Papal Nuncio to protest to the Hungarian government and, to lower the temperature, the Hungarians allowed an allied officer to visit another man, who was condemned for the same offence, in his cell. The allied officer said that the man, Schuller,

[15] For British views on the number of inspectors see ADM/116/2051, Rear-Admiral Watson, letter to Secretary of the Admiralty and the message from the Conference on Ambassadors in Paris, 17 February 1921.

[16] ADM/116/2051.

[17] FO/371/8554, C 9119, Hohler to Miles Lampson, 16 May 1923; FO/371/8872, C 9119, p. 156.

[18] FO/371/8852, C 16950, translation from Hungarian papers of 26 August 1923.

was in a 'passable' condition but, as the Hungarian government intended, these cases showed how dangerous it was for any Hungarian to aid the allied inspectors.[19]

There were also isolated attacks on allied officers, and the allies protested strongly against what they regarded as Budapest's initial failure to punish those responsible. One of the most serious incidents occurred at Kecskemet, where a riot broke out against the allied officers who were searching houses for arms. The officers themselves were threatened and their car windows were smashed. After allied complaints, one of the workers who threw stones was sentenced to fifty days in prison. The police officer responsible for the village was given four days' imprisonment for not doing his duty and his second in command lost 10 per cent of his pay for a year. Another policeman, who was not at his post during the incident, was dismissed. The British Minister in Budapest thought that the punishment was light but probably enough to deter most attackers.[20]

Bitter against France because of its backing for the Little Entente, the Hungarians looked to Britain for support. Their ambassador in London told the Foreign Office that orders for coal-extracting machinery were placed in Britain to strengthen links between the two countries. All the same, the British made clear that they backed allied complaints about Hungarian obstruction of the inspectors and demanded action to stop anti-Semitic riots.[21] They grumbled that the Hungarian government often refused to say where its troops would be stationed and this made it difficult for allied officers to check on their numbers. Information provided by the Hungarian government on the size of its army proved inaccurate and allied inspectors received numerous reports of hidden arms and ammunition.

Some of these reports were clearly false and were produced by *agents provocateurs* or by frauds hoping for money. On one occasion, the allies were told that sixty aircraft engines were hidden in a factory. Inspection showed that there were no engines and the factory was far too small to contain sixty of them. On another occasion, a photograph allegedly showing material concealed in a factory was so obviously forged that investigation was useless. The British suspected that the covering letter had been written in one of

---

[19] FO/371/8852, C 17272 and 17405.
[20] FO/371/8850, C 1140.   [21] Ibid.

the Little Entente states. Nevertheless, hidden stocks of arms were discovered from time to time. On one occasion 100 tons of ammunition were found buried in the Hajmasker woods alongside 300 rifles. The Hungarian government claimed that they were buried by Béla Kun, but the allies doubted this. Before the Manfred Weiss factory was inspected in September 1923, the Hungarians said it was making cars. On inspection, hundreds of shell cases were discovered. The director of the factory then said this was an old order being fulfilled. The Hungarians were fined 24,000 francs.[22]

There were also complaints that Czechs living in Hungary were being forced to join the army, even though conscription was prohibited.[23] The technique was to order all men of military age to assemble at a certain place and then to put maximum pressure on them to 'volunteer'. More legitimately, volunteers were offered farms in return for their service to the state.[24] But in October 1923 the Hungarian Prime Minister openly admitted to the British inspector, Colonel Selby, that they would not be able to field an army of 35,000 if it were truly voluntary.[25] The Hungarians also increased their power, as the Germans did, by fostering paramilitary organizations. They claimed that the 'Society for the Protection of Work' was a voluntary and unarmed organization, yet its members had the right to bear arms, although Article 112 of the treaty prohibited sporting clubs from occupying themselves with military affairs. The allies were also suspicious that the police reserve was being used for military purposes. Even though an inspection in September 1923 failed to reveal any hidden arms, the allies asked for the organization's dissolution.[26]

Colonel Selby, who was sympathetic to the Hungarians amid all their difficulties, strongly advised them to be more open and honest. He believed that the inspectors would not have insisted that the police reserve should be abolished if the Hungarians had not tried to hide its existence. He knew that prevarication and obstruction only increased the determination of the French inspectors to help their allies in the Little Entente by following up every rumour. But Selby's advice was not taken and the British Foreign

[22] FO/371/8850, C 11484 and 12271; FO 371/8852, C 16950.
[23] FO/371/8850, C 11873.
[24] FO/371/8852, C 17402.
[25] FO/371/8852, C 18117.
[26] FO/371/8852, C 17405 and 17866.

Secretary, Austen Chamberlain, again tried to persuade the Hungarian Prime Minister, Count Bethlen, to co-operate, when they met in Geneva in December 1925. Bethlen promised to do what he could, although he insisted that no Hungarian government could accept the existing frontiers.[27]

Hungary's clandestine rearmament measures received most publicity in January 1928, when the Austrians intercepted arms being sent from Italy to Hungary in breach of the treaty's ban on arms imports. They found 591 cases of machine-gun parts, leading the Little Entente nations to protest vigorously to the League of Nations.[28] Such revelations were magnified by Hungary's enemies, but Budapest remained far too weak to attack Czechoslovakia or Yugoslavia during this period. According to the British statistics, given in answer to parliamentary question in April 1921, the military balance was as set out in Table 1.

Table 1   Men under arms in Central Europe.

Czechoslovakia	147,300
Romania	160,000
Yugoslavia	200,000
Austria, Hungary, and Bulgaria combined	less than 100,000

The figures show clearly that any war between victors and vanquished would have led to a crushing defeat for the former enemy powers, and the British were afraid that, if Hungary did not faithfully carry out the Treaty of Trianon, the Little Entente 'would proceed to take matters into their own hands, and if necessary, to employ direct measures to secure the execution of the Treaty'.[29]

BULGARIA

Like the Hungarians, the Bulgarians bitterly resented their loss of territory at the end of the First World War, in this case amounting

---

[27] FO/371/8852, C 17866 and C 18117.

[28] DBFP, Series 1A, vol. 4 (HMSO, London, 1971), no. 130, p. 241, Marquess of Crewe to Sir Austen Chamberlain, 6 February 1928, and no. 150, p. 274, Sir Austen Chamberlain to Sir R. Graham, 22 February 1928.

[29] DBFP, Series 1A, vol. 1, no. 137, p. 223, record of a discussion between Sir Austen Chamberlain, Mr Lampson, and Count Bethlen, 8 December 1925.

to 5,000 square miles. They defended themselves against claims that their troops had massacred Serbs during the fighting and wrote to the allied governments in September 1919, expounding their case and arguing that Bulgaria had no history of aggression or expansionism. They admitted that they had made a grave mistake in joining the Central Powers, but said that they had already been punished by losing 400,000 men in the war and now only wanted plebiscites in disputed territories to ensure that 'Wilsonian' principles of national self-determination were followed.[30]

Terms for Bulgaria were laid down in the Treaty of Neuilly, though arguments over frontiers rumbled on until the Lausanne conference in 1923 and even beyond. Because thousands of Bulgars now lived in Yugoslavia and Greece, a Macedonian Revolutionary Organization was established to fight for their 'freedom'. The first postwar Bulgarian Prime Minister, Stambouliiski, who co-operated with the Yugoslavs, was murdered by nationalists in June 1923.[31] Faced with such threats, it was not surprising that governments hesitated to improve relations with other Balkan states, even if they needed to do so for strategic reasons. Bulgaria's weakness was compounded by allied reparations policy. The Bulgarians were initially asked to pay 90 million pounds in reparations, though this was later reduced to 22.5 million pounds.[32]

At the end of the war, the allies sent the French General Franchet d'Esperey to Sofia with orders to collect the breech-blocks for all Bulgarian artillery. Subsequently, the Bulgarian armed forces were forced to end conscription, limit their manpower to 20,000 serving for a minimum of twelve years, and close all but one military school. As with the other defeated states, precise numbers of rifles, machine-guns, mortars, and artillery were laid down for each 1,000 men. The Bulgarians were allowed to build one new arms factory but had to give up all their warships except four torpedo boats and six motorboats. As in the other former enemy countries, Sofia had to pay the costs of the allied inspectors.[33] The Bulgarian army believed that the forces allowed were far too small and that

[30] ADM/116/3234, Bulgarian delegation to Clemenceau, 29 August 1919, and to Paul Dutasta, 2 September 1919.
[31] C. Woods, 'The country that guessed wrong', in *These Eventful Years*, pp. 232 ff., 237.   [32] Temperley, *The Peace Conference*, pp. 166 ff.
[33] ADM/116/3234, record of a meeting of military, air, and naval representatives, Versailles, 5 June 1919, and Bulgarian letter to Clemenceau, 45 September 1919.

'encouraged by our military weakness . . . our neighbours may take advantage thereof to occupy certain portions of our territory.' They maintained that the prohibition on conscription was particularly hard on them because they had no large towns to provide recruits, and conservative peasants were most unwilling to leave the land for twelve years. However, the Bulgarians were allowed to increase their strength by keeping 10,000 gendarmes and 3,000 frontier guards under the control of the Ministry of War. These were armed only with rifles and the number of gendarmes remained well below the limit allowed. As with Hungary, the Bulgarian armed forces were greatly outnumbered by each of their neighbours throughout the period. Greece alone had 64,000 men under arms in 1931 and the Turks 140,000.

The Turkish threat to Bulgaria would have been reduced had the allies' original plans been realized. In the Treaty of Sèvres, which was presented to Turkish delegates in June 1920, the sultan's territories were reduced from 613,500 square miles to 175,000 and Turkey's population from 20 to 8 million. Like other enemy powers, Turkey was banned from maintaining an air force, and it was restricted to a coastal navy and an army of 50,000 men. The sultan's government signed the treaty in August 1920, but real power had long since moved from the sultan to Kemal Ataturk's nationalists in Ankara, and they totally rejected the Sèvres Treaty. For a time it looked as though the nationalists might be defeated by Greek armies which invaded their territories. However, the nationalists drove out the Greek forces and compelled the allies to negotiate with them. As a US diplomat wrote later, 'it was evident that the Turks were in a position of great strategic advantage. They were the only ones prepared to fight if necessary in defence of fundamental principles . . . All the old methods of an out-worn diplomacy—threats, bluster, cajolery and earnest pleadings—were unavailing.'[34]

The Treaty of Lausanne between the new Turkish government and the allies was signed in July 1923. There was no question now of enforced disarmament but, to reduce tension between Greece, Turkey, and Bulgaria, the treaty partly demilitarized their common frontier for 30 kilometres on either side and laid down that all fortifications within this zone were to be destroyed. The Turks

[34] P. M. Brown, in *These Eventual Years*, p. 145. For force levels in the Balkans and the Treaty of Lausanne see *League of Nations Yearbook 1932*.

were to keep 5,000 frontier guards in the area, the Greeks and Bulgarians 2,500. The demilitarized zone may have marginally reduced the chances of armed clashes on the frontier but, in any case, the military balance would have made Bulgarian aggression against Turkey, Greece, or Yugoslavia suicidal.

THE DISARMAMENT OF THE FORMER
ENEMY POWERS

Gradually the various control commissions were removed from the former enemy states as their armed forces settled down to abide more or less by the terms of the treaties imposed on them. According to the figures they supplied to the League of Nations, their armed forces were now as listed in Table 2.

Table 2 Men under arms in the defeated powers.

Officers, NCOs, and men	1926	1927	1930
Austria	22,914	20,411	21,238
Bulgaria	20,302	19,922	19,956
plus gendarmes etc.	9,800	9,495	9,800
Hungary	34,705	35,103	35,035

Thus the disarmament provisions imposed on the Central European powers had a number of advantages. First, they saved Hungary and Bulgaria considerable military expenditure. Second, in the heated atmosphere of the time, rumours of vast military preparations circulated only too easily in Central Europe and the Balkans. The presence of allied inspectors and military attachés in Hungary and Bulgaria made such rumours less plausible. Third and most important, the two states did have extensive claims on their neighbours' territories, claims which they could not pursue by conventional military power while the treaties of Neuilly and Trianon remained in force.

The disadvantage of the various commissions was that they were expensive and intrusive. The proud Hungarians, Bulgarians, and Austrians naturally resented allied interference in their national life. The Hungarians correctly regarded the French as the allies of their enemies and deeply distrusted the presence of their officers on

Hungarian territory. They also genuinely feared attacks by the smaller allies because their disarmament did not give these countries sufficient confidence in their security to follow suit.[35] In fact, allied statesmen had foreseen this problem during the Paris peace conference and had tried to limit the postwar establishment of allied armies in the Balkans and Central Europe.

As soon as the disarmament of Austria had been discussed in May 1919, Lloyd George had suggested that the armed forces of the smaller allied states should be restricted. These restrictions should fall on Czechoslovakia, Yugoslavia, Romania, and Greece. Poland should also be included, but it was at war with the Soviets and thus it was in no position to think of disarmament until the war was over. Clemenceau, Orlando, and Wilson agreed. The military representatives were asked to come up with figures for the various armies, but they wanted to impose higher limits than the political leaders thought advisable. Table 3 shows both the difference between the proposals made by the military and political leaders and the much greater contrast with the actual numbers mobilized by the smaller allies in the 1930s.[36]

Table 3   Limits proposed by allied military and political leaders compared with League figures for actual numbers in the early 1930s

	Military Proposal	Political	Actual
Austria	40,000	15,000	21,238
Hungary	45,000	18,000	35,035
Bulgaria	20,000	10,000	29,756*
Czechoslovakia	50,000	22,000	138,788
Yugoslavia	40,000	20,000	184,448
Romania	60,000	28,000	240,501
Poland	80,000	44,000	265,980
Greece	20,000	12,000	64,622

*includes gendarmes

On 5 June 1919 the four allied leaders met with their equivalents from Poland, Romania, Serbia, Greece, and Czechoslovakia to

---

[35] *League of Nations Yearbook 1932*, pp. 25, 48, 146.
[36] *FRUS 1919*, vol. 5, p. 388.

discuss the question of general East European military restrictions. The outcome was hardly surprising and the discussions had some comic overtones.[37] The smaller states had had hints of what was coming in private discussions with individual allied leaders. They were therefore able to prepare their 'defence'. The Serbian or Yugoslav representative immediately protested about being treated like an enemy and worse than states which had remained neutral in the war. He claimed that his country had gone to war to defend the freedom and sovereignty of nations. Such freedoms would be restricted by what was proposed, and it would be very difficult for him to persuade his people to accept allied ideas. Venizelos, the Greek representative, agreed and suggested that disarmament should be considered later by the League of Nations.

The Romanian representative said that his country was in a state of war with the Bolsheviks in Russia and Hungary. His government was even unsure whether its eastern neighbour would be the Ukraine or Russia but, in any case, Romanian armaments could only be considered in relation to Russian ones. For the Czechs, Benes said that he was in favour of arms limitation, 'but in deciding on the limitation of armaments, it was impossible to overlook Russia and the Neutral States or, for that matter, the Western Powers.' Limitations of armaments could only be considered as a world question by the League of Nations. Finally Paderewski, the Polish Premier, pointed out that his country was menaced by Bolshevism on one side and by more than 300,000 German soldiers on the other. If Poland were to disarm it would have to be protected by the allies.

Lloyd George denied that allied proposals threatened the sovereignty of the small states or that allied leaders were advancing ideas that they did not themselves accept. Britain would be reducing its forces as soon as possible and its army would probably be smaller than the Romanian or Polish ones. Clemenceau supported him, stressing that the allied leaders were not out to repress the sovereignty of small nations but to produce a general settlement. However, given the current tensions and even wars in Eastern Europe, the issue should be postponed until it could be dealt with by the League of Nations. So it was agreed and the consequence was the imbalance of forces outlined above.

[37] *FRUS 1919*, vol. 6, pp. 202 ff.

One striking difference between enforced and negotiated disarmament measures is that the first can be decided in a moment. Thus Austrian force levels for the postwar period were eventually decided in a very brief discussion between Lloyd George, Wilson, and Clemenceau. Negotiated limits take months or even years to decide, because each country stresses its vulnerabilities and needs. Compromises between the various positions only emerge gradually, if at all. No doubt each country's representatives will exaggerate their need for armaments, but their arguments cannot be dismissed. It was notable in 1919 how the military representatives of the allied powers believed that Central European states genuinely needed large numbers of men under arms to keep order and to control their frontiers. They also saw how the region could not be isolated from Russia, Turkey, and other neighbouring powers.

The failure of the disarmament measures imposed by the allies to increase confidence showed that it was ethnic disputes which lay at the bottom of Central European tensions. Unless these could be solved there was little hope of a permanent improvement in relations. Western statesmen periodically urged their Central European counterparts to negotiate a regional 'Locarno', but it was doubtful if the Hungarian and Bulgarian governments could have survived if they had accepted the 'loss' of the minorities.[38] When Hitler came to power in 1933, regional rivalries and economic weakness left Central and Eastern Europe wide open to increasing German influence. In the end, these frictions led to the destruction of Poland and Czechoslovakia, and the other states in the region became 'protectorates' first of the Reich and then of the Soviet Union.

POSTSCRIPT: THE DISARMAMENT AND DESTRUCTION OF CZECHOSLOVAKIA

Despite the size of its armed forces, between the wars Czechoslovakia was generally regarded by Britain and France as a model democracy in an area dominated by dictators. However, from its foundation it had not only large numbers of Hungarians but also more than 3 million Germans within its frontiers, many in the so-called Sudetenland. With Hungary and Germany so weak their doubtful loyalty could be ignored but, once Germany had

---

[38] See note 29 above.

recovered its power under Hitler, then the situation became extremely threatening.

According to a strict reading of Wilsonian principles, much of the Sudetenland would not have joined Czechoslovakia. But the area was important for the country's economy, and it was there that the Czechs built a defensive line similar to the more complex Maginot Line which covered part of France's eastern border with Germany. Brigadier Stronge, the British Military Attaché in Prague at the end of the 1930s, said that he 'had been greatly impressed with the defensive strength of the whole system, the skill with which it had been designed, permitting economy of force in garrison formations . . . By the autumn [of 1938] it was to become truly formidable.' The Czech defences contained minefields, pill boxes, and heavy artillery. The Czechs had a renowned arms industry and they had built up a well-equipped army, which was backed by over a million reserves who had passed through the system and received periodic refresher training.[39]

Czechoslovakia's weaknesses were internal. The German minority was encouraged by the Nazis to protest and demonstrate against the Czech government. On 12 September 1938 German mobs smashed Czech and Jewish shops, knowing that any repression by the Prague government would give Hitler the excuse to invade.[40] France was committed by a treaty dating back to 1925 to help the Czechs should this occur, but the French army was deeply pessimistic about its prospects in a war with Germany. It was also defensive-minded. The British feared air attacks against London, which they could not protect because neither their new generation of fighter aircraft nor their radar chain were yet fully operative. The British army was tiny, as Lloyd George had forecast it would be in June 1919, and its ability to contribute to a continental campaign was derisory. The willingness of the democracies to fight for the status quo had been undermined over the years by criticism of the peace treaties on both ethical and practical grounds.

[39] Brigadier H. C. T. Stronge, 'The Czechoslovak Army and the Munich Crisis: a personal memorandum', in B. Bond and I. Roy (eds), War and Society (Croom Helm, London, 1975), p. 162. See also K. Ben-Arie, 'Czechoslovakia at the time of Munich: the military situation', Journal of Contemporary History, 25 October 1990. For the attitude of the German army see G. Weinberg, 'The German Generals and the outbreak of the Second World War', in Adrian Preston (ed.), General Staffs and Diplomacy before the Second World War (Croom Helm, London, 1978), p. 24.

[40] A. Palmer, The Lands Between (Weidenfeld and Nicolson, London, 1970), pp. 228 ff.

Thus, in September 1938, the British and French governments pressured the Czechs into abandoning the Sudetenland and with it their defensive lines. The independent status of the rump of the republic was then guaranteed by France, Britain, Italy, and Germany, a guarantee which Hitler upheld only until he destroyed Czech independence in March 1939. The disarmament of Czechoslovakia is unique. Most of the other examples of forced disarmament in this book concern defeated enemy powers. With the partial exception of Poland in the eighteenth century, no other nation has been persuaded to disarm by its own allies in order that they could avoid their treaty obligations. Just as the 'crime' of the Polish partition hung over Europe during the nineteenth century, so the humiliation of Munich hung over the democracies for the rest of the twentieth century.

The Czech case shows that, in exceptional circumstances, states can be compelled to disarm even without going to war against them. The Czech government was weak and cautious. It looked to the Western democracies for aid and it accepted the view of their governments that resistance to German demands was doomed. It was frightened and overawed by Hitler and the Nazis. It was weakened by the activities of its own German minority and by the knowledge that, in Wilsonian terms, they should not have been included in the Czech state. Thus it erroneously believed that the disadvantages of resistance outweighed the disadvantages of surrender. The result was that it was absorbed piecemeal into the German Empire.

Czechoslovakia's fate was a reminder that no part of Central Europe could be sealed off from contiguous areas. This was a point made by the smaller allies in 1919 when Lloyd George and the other leaders had tried to push them into disarmament. Greece had to maintain defences against Turkey to the east as well as its Balkan neighbours to the north, Poland had to guard against the Soviet Union to the east and Germany to the west, the Czechs had to arm themselves against Hungary to the south and Germany to the west. Thus the Czech army dwarfed the Hungarians and Bulgarians, while being completely unable, in the eyes of the British and French, to stand up to the army mobilized in 1938 by its German neighbours.

6

The Disarmament of
Vichy France

Forced disarmament has frequently been a preliminary to the
destruction or subjugation of a defeated nation. Had Napoleon not
been defeated, it is probable that the disarmament of Prussia and
Austria would have led to the loss of their independence and their
incorporation within the French Empire. In the case of Vichy
France, we can see the whole process of national destruction and
imperial expansion gradually unfolding.

After the stunning defeat of the French armies in 1940, most of
France was occupied by Germany. The rump of the French state,
with its capital at Vichy, maintained a vulnerable and uneasy
independence. The new government under Marshal Pétain was
permitted to keep only 100,000 men under arms. French officers
were relieved that they were allowed to maintain an army at all,
but it suited Hitler to show leniency because this made it less likely
that the French colonies would align themselves with Britain. It
also made it easier for the French military to lay down the greater
part of their arms, and it meant that the responsibility for keeping
order in the unoccupied part of France was in the hands of the
French. In November 1942 these advantages waned when the allies
overran French North Africa and consequently Hitler decided to
strike. The remains of the army were disarmed by the Germans and
the fleet was scuttled by the French themselves. The Vichy experiment was over.[1]

---

[1] The classic analysis of the armistice army is R. O. Paxton, *Parades and
Politics at Vichy: The French Officer Corps under Marshal Pétain* (Princeton
University Press), 1966. The best source for material on Vichy attitudes towards
enforced disarmament is the records of the armistice discussions, A. Costes (ed.),
La Délégation française auprès de la Commission Allemande d'Armistice
(Imprimerie Nationale, Paris, 1947–1957).

THE GERMAN EMPIRE

In the two years that the Vichy experiment lasted, France was reduced to the level of Germany's third-rate 'allies', Hungary, Slovakia, and Romania. Countries such as Poland and the Czech heartland, where Hitler intended to destroy or enslave the people entirely, were not allowed to maintain forces. Hungary and Slovakia were treated with slightly more respect and permitted to align themselves with Hitler's forces. In 1939 the Slovak army joined in the attack on Poland.[2] Two years later the Hungarian army helped the Germans invade Yugoslavia. When the Germans attacked the Soviet Union in June 1941, they were joined by Hungarian, Romanian, and Slovak armies which suffered terribly as the Russians fought the invaders to a standstill. The Second Hungarian Army of 200,000 men, for example, was destroyed by the Soviets in January 1943.[3] Despite such setbacks and quarrels among themselves, Romania, Slovakia, and Hungary were the ideal models from Hitler's point of view. They provided forces which could be expended in his campaigns and obeyed the orders of the Reich, albeit somewhat reluctantly. They also sent the food and other goods demanded by the German military machine.

Unlike Hungary and Slovakia, France had been a major military power. Many of Hitler's generals had been reluctant to attack France in 1940 because they feared the strength of the French army. Hitler himself said that he never slept at all during the night of 9 May when the Nazi onslought on France began.[4] But the French were surprised by the German attack through the Ardennes. They were also stunned by German *Blitzkrieg* tactics. Just as the theorists of armoured warfare had hoped, the French armies fell back in confusion as German armoured columns raced behind their lines and Stuka dive-bombers attacked from the air. Military defeat accentuated divisions within the French army and state. Many older officers, including heroes of the First World War like Marshal Pétain, quickly became convinced that further struggle was hope-

---

[2] On Poland see R. Umiastowski, *Poland, Russia and Great Britain 1941–1945* (Hollis and Carter, London, 1946).

[3] On Hungary see J. K. Hoensch, *A History of Modern Hungary* (Longman, London, 1988), pp. 146 ff. On Slovakia see J. Lettrich, *A History of Modern Slovakia* (Atlantic Press, London, 1956); see also A. Palmer, *The Lands Between* (Weidenfeld and Nicolson, London, 1970), pp. 228 ff.

[4] H. Trevor-Roper, *Hitler's Table-Talk* (Oxford University Press, 1988), p. 70.

less. Instead of resisting, as the Russians were to do from 1941 onwards or the Germans from 1944, Paris and other French towns were declared 'open' or undefended.[5] On 16 June Paul Reynaud, the Prime Minister, was replaced by Pétain. Days before an armistice had been negotiated, Pétain broadcast a call for the French armies to cease to fight. On 22 June General Huntziger signed an armistice agreement in the railway carriage where the Germans had accepted allied terms in 1918.

Most of France was occupied by German troops. Pétain's government ruled the remains of the state bordering on the Mediterranean in the south. Under Article 1 of the armistice the French government had to order resistance to Germany to cease in its colonies in Africa and Asia. Those who tried to go to North Africa to resist were regarded as criminals. French troops fighting for Britain were to be treated as insurgents rather than prisoners of war. Under Article 4,

French armed forces on land, on the sea and in the air are to be demobilized and disarmed in a period still to be set. Excepted are only those units which are necessary for maintenance of domestic order. Germany and Italy will fix their strength. The French armed forces in the territory to be occupied by Germany are to be hastily withdrawn into territory not to be occupied and discharged. These troops, before marching out, shall lay down their weapons and equipment at the places where they are stationed at the time the treaty becomes effective. They are responsible for orderly delivery to German troops.[6]

Soldiers in the unoccupied territories, who were still resisting, were to give up their weapons. Some were to be allocated for the use of the remaining Vichy army, but the rest were to be handed over to the Germans or Italians, who were to use them extensively in their next campaigns. All weapons manufacture in Vichy territories was halted for the time being. All fortifications in the occupied territories were to be handed over in good order, as well as barracks, industrial facilities, docks, and communication centres. The French were to provide the manpower to keep railways rolling. They were also to give the exact locations of minefields in the

[5] H. F. Armstrong, *Chronology of Failure: The Last Days of the French Republic* (Macmillan, New York, 1940), p. 114. On Weygand see *The Private Papers of Paul Baudouin* (Eyre and Spottiswood, London, 1948), pp. 47, 57, and J. Charmley, *Lord Lloyd* (Weidenfeld and Nicolson, London, 1987), pp. 245–6.

[6] Armstrong, *Chronology of Failure*, p. 142. Costes, *La Délégation française*, vol. 1, 1947, contains the French version of the Armistice.

occupied territories or to clear them away. No flights were to take place in Vichy territory without German permission and all air-fields were to be handed over to the Germans and Italians to stop Frenchmen escaping to Britain and North Africa. France had to bear the cost of the occupation forces, while 1.5 million French troops were kept as prisoners of war in Germany until the end of hostilities.[7]

The final Article of the armistice laid down, 'The German government may terminate this agreement at any time with immediate effect if the French government fails to fulfil the obligations it assumes under the agreement.' In effect, this meant that the Germans could simply annul the armistice whenever they wanted. If the war continued, it was inevitable that some troops would join the British. Indeed, General de Gaulle was already encouraging them to do so in radio broadcasts from London. But this was a breach of Article 10 of the agreement. Since Hitler's power was total, he had no real need of an excuse to destroy the Vichy regime, but Article 24 was a threat which he could hold over Pétain's government.

When he was sent to negotiate an armistice with the Nazi leaders, General Huntziger was told that there were certain terms which he could not accept, particularly the handing over of the empire or the fleet.[8] The size of the remaining French army was not laid down in the armistice, but the Germans told Huntziger that it would be restricted to 100,000 men. Hitler intended this as a humiliating reminder of France's mistakes at Versailles. Leaving France with an army also suited Hitler's convenience because it would encourage Pétain to accept the terms and to call on the French colonies to do the same. Thus he could prepare the invasion of Britain in the knowledge that his rear was secure, just as Napoleon had set out to secure his rear in 1808 while he took his armies into Spain. Once Britain had capitulated, then the French could if necessary be crushed, as the Poles and Czechs had been in Eastern Europe.

Hitler meditated on the German evasion of the Treaty of Versailles and the possibility that the French would also try to avoid the armistice terms. In his view, the Weimar government had shown its weakness by not evading allied terms far more success-

[7] Armstrong, *Chronology of Failure*, pp. 142 ff.
[8] Paxton, *Parades and Politics*, pp. 3 ff.

fully. German industrialists should have hidden thousands of guns from the allies and the government should have been much fiercer with those Germans caught betraying evasions of the treaty to the allied authorities. 'Nowadays it's the duty of our High Command to make sure that the French aren't playing this game with us,' Hitler told his closest associates in April 1942. He then went on to say that one of the most powerful figures in the Vichy government, Admiral Darlan, had talked about French 'precautions for the future' and that he had not yet had time to question the admiral about this. 'In any case I could have drawn his attention to the fact that he seems to be hatching certain ideas that were not unfamiliar to me at the time of my struggle. And I'd have added that the tricks of a small conjuror cannot deceive a master-conjuror. It will be France's fate to atone for the error of Versailles for the next fifty years.'[9]

FRANCE AND BRITAIN

While Hitler revenged himself on them, many Frenchmen blamed Britain for abandoning their country in 1940. The French had frequently asked Britain to send more squadrons of fighters across the Channel; the British had kept 25 squadrons at home and there were few Frenchmen who knew that Britain lost over 900 aircraft in the Battle for France.[10] Instead of attacking southwards in May, as the French requested, the British expeditionary force had withdrawn north to Dunkirk. What the British viewed as a glorious escape across the Channel could hardly be seen in the same light by the French, although they still complained that not enough French soldiers had been rescued from the beaches. Hostility to Britain vastly increased on 3 July 1940, when the Royal Navy attacked the French fleet in Mers el Kebir in North Africa. Article 8 of the armistice laid down,

The French war fleet is to collect in ports to be designated more particularly, and under German and [or] Italian control there to be demobilized and laid up—with the exception of those units released to the French government for the protection of French interests in the colonial empire.

[9] Trevor-Roper, *Hitler's Table-Talk*, p. 407.
[10] John Terraine, *A Time for Courage: The Royal Air Force in the European War* (Macmillan, New York, 1985), p. 118. For French ignorance of British losses see *Baudouin Diaries*, p. 55.

The peacetime stations of ships should control the designation of ports
. . . All warships outside France are to be recalled to France, with the
exception of that portion of the French war fleet which shall be designated
to represent French interests in the colonial empire.[11]

The same article solemnly declared that Germany would not use
the French war fleet for its own purposes, except for guarding the
coast and sweeping for mines.

But the British Prime Minister, Winston Churchill, could not
trust such assurances. General de Gaulle naturally bewailed what
had happened but admitted, 'there is not the least doubt that from
principle and necessity, the enemy could have used [the ships]
against England or against our own empire.' The French fleet was
the second largest in Europe and its acquisition by the Axis would
have been a devastating blow to a Britain already fighting for its
life. There were two modern battleships at Mers el Kebir, *Dunkerque* and *Strasbourg*, two older battleships, several light cruisers,
as well as destroyers, submarines, and other smaller vessels. Admiral Gensoul in charge of the French fleet in Mers el Kebir was
given the alternatives of scuttling his ships, joining the allies, or
sailing to some distant French port such as Martinique. He not
only refused but subsequently suppressed the offer of sailing to a
French port. The British opened fire, causing 1,269 casualties. This
attack halted the trickle of French officers who were joining de
Gaulle's resistance movement in London.[12] French Equatorial
Africa did join the Free French in the autumn of 1940, but North
Africa and Syria remained loyal to Vichy. On 23 and 24 September
a joint British and Free French force tried and failed to capture
Dakar, the capital of Senegal, after causing more French casualties.
In the summer of 1941 Syria and Lebanon were captured by the
allies, again after bitter fighting, though the Vichy authorities were
at least grateful for the honourable terms subsequently granted by
the British.[13]

From the British point of view, the French fleet still represented a
major threat to their position after the attack on Mers el Kebir.
Before the US entry into the war, Churchill persuaded Roosevelt to

---

[11] Armstrong, *Chronology of Failure*, p. 144.
[12] Paxton, *Parades and Politics*, p. 32; *Baudouin Diaries*, pp. 134, 157 ff.
[13] Paxton, *Parades and Politics*, p. 122; on Dakar see *Baudouin Diaries*,
pp. 246 ff.; on the fighting in Syria see M. Dayan, *The Story of My Life*
(Weidenfeld and Nicolson, London, 1976), pp. 46 ff. For Vichy responses to the
surrender terms see Costes, *La Délégation française*, vol. 4, pp. 627 ff.

put pressure on Marshal Pétain over the use of the fleet. Roosevelt warned Pétain, 'the fact that a government is a prisoner of war of another power does not justify such a prisoner in serving its conqueror in operations against its former ally.' When rumours grew that the French government was considering moving two of the most powerful ships, *Jean Bart* and *Richelieu*, to home ports for completion, Roosevelt pressed the Vichy government to sell them to the USA. Pétain replied, 'even if I wanted to, I cannot sell these ships. It is impossible under the terms of the Armistice, and even if it were possible, it would never be permitted by the Germans. France is under Germany's heel and impotent.'[14]

LIBERALIZING THE ARMISTICE TERMS

Pétain's bitter complaint precisely expressed the Vichy government's point of view. France could not resist; it had to win concessions through diplomacy. The Vichy government had few friends in the Second World War or afterwards. In part, this was because it had to offend French patriotism by co-operating with the Nazi conquerors, but Vichy ideology created suspicions that the government actually wanted to co-operate. Pétain and some of those around him blamed the democratic governments of the 1930s and the 'decadence' of the French for their defeat. They wanted France to become a more authoritarian, more religious society. They were also imbued with vicious anti-Semitism. In the early months of the new regime they complained to the Germans when Jews fled to France from occupied territories.[15] They maintained that the refugees were 'undesirables' and that Vichy was over-populated. Later they co-operated with the Nazis in the persecution of French Jews.

Yet, however odious their racism, the Vichy authorities struggled manfully to defend the remains of French power, the vestiges of independence, and the rights of the majority of French people against German encroachments. They refused to hand over German citizens living in France or the French gold reserve, which was hidden in the African colonies.[16] Above all, unlike the Prussians in 1812, they refused to join the war against their former allies, even

[14] W. Churchill, *The Second World War: Their Finest Hour* (Reprint Society, London, 1951), pp. 410 ff.
[15] Costes, *La Délégation française*, vol. 4, p. 97.
[16] On French gold see A. L. Smith, *Hitler's Gold: The Story of the Nazi War Loot* (Berg, Oxford, 1989).

though the attack on Mers el Kebir gave them a far better excuse than the Prussians had ever possessed. The arguments over these issues took place in the Armistice Commission established at Wiesbaden. This was subdivided into military and economic sections. The French negotiators were led by Huntziger and then by General Doyen, the Germans by General Stulpnagel and later by General Vogl. Documents left by Vichy about their negotiations with the German Commission were published by the French government from 1947 onwards. They reveal the tenacity of the French representatives, who were no more willing collaborators than the German officers who had been dealing with the allies in the 1920s.[17]

To win concessions, Huntziger and Doyen repeatedly emphasized that French weakness made their colonies vulnerable to seizure by the allies. They asked to be able to send reinforcements to Indochina and Africa, to recruit in the occupied parts of France, and to arm their forces with heavier weapons. The Italians and Germans promised to look sympathetically on these proposals, provided that the French allowed them the bases in French North Africa which had been refused. Nevertheless, Hitler postponed some of the measures of naval disarmament and suspended air force demobilization as far as this was 'necessary to repel English attacks in the Mediterranean'. The Germans also allowed six French warships to leave the Mediterranean for West Africa. It was these three cruisers and three destroyers which stiffened resistance in Senegal and prevented its defection to the Free French.

General Huntziger continually pressed the Germans for concessions. At the end of October 1940 he asked for permission for the armistice army to recruit in the rest of France, an increase in the North African army from 30,000 to 120,000 men, the creation of a motorized division in Senegal, and an increase of 16,000 men in the navy. The French air force would also be expanded and modernized. Hitler allowed only the reinstitution of two groups of transport aircraft, the formation of a motorized unit in West Africa, and the replenishment from France of ammunition expended at Dakar. The French could not obtain more at that time without committing themselves to handing over bases, though they were later to be allowed 115,000 troops in North Africa and 60,000 in the West

---

[17] The introduction to Costes, *La Délégation française*, vol. 1, explains the limitations of the documents.

African territories. Despite the plea, carefully designed to appeal to
the Nazi mind, that the position of the white race was at stake,
they were not allowed to send reinforcements to the Far East and
few to their African colonies.[18] The Germans also wanted the
French to produce weapons to assist their war effort against the
allies. The French temporized, pointing out that, if they manufactured weapons for the occupiers, they would become targets of
allied bombing raids. Thus they needed more weapons to defend
their factories. The Germans offered to compromise; French aircraft factories could restart production if four out of five aircraft
went to Germany. The rest could be used to re-equip the French air
force.[19]

Vichy's negotiators had to balance the advantages they gained
from such deals against the growing enmity of the allies. They may
have bowed too much to German pressure, but they could not be
accused of ignoring French interests or of supporting the German
cause for its own sake. When the Germans were particularly press-
ing in April 1941, Doyen made a list for Vogl of some of the issues
which prevented harmony between the two nations; so little food
was allowed to the people of northern France that they were near
starvation; in other areas the meat ration was derisory while the
German occupation troops were well fed; French civil guards, who
had captured German airmen, had been treated as guerrillas
and condemned to death, and French soldiers were being kept
as prisoners even though they were needed in France to work
the land. From the French record General Vogl appears to have
accepted the justice of some of the complaints, but the situation
was deteriorating as food became scarcer and the number of
Frenchmen executed by the Germans continued to mount.[20]

French negotiators also stressed the internal threats to the
regime. When France was defeated in 1870, the revolutionary
Commune was established in Paris, leading to civil war in the
nation's capital. Many of the highly conservative French officers
feared that a new uprising would break out in 1940. Thus they
were delighted that a French army was to survive and to be able to
maintain order.[21] Hitler accepted the validity of these fears, though

[18] Costes, *La Délégation française*, vol. 4, pp. 155, 198.
[19] Costes, *La Délégation française*, vol. 4, pp. 18, 55.
[20] On executions see Costes, *La Délégation française*, vol. 4, pp. 200, 501, and
524;. on Doyen's general complaints see pp. 340 ff.
[21] Paxton, *Parades and Politics*, p. 10.

he had no faith in Vichy's ability to put down a real revolt. In May 1942 he told his close associates, 'if France is at the moment safe from disintegration, protected against the threat of a *coup de main* or a civil war, she owes it all to the presence of our occupation troops, who constitute the only real power in the country.'[22]

Within the French army, as within the Prussian army after 1806 or the German army in the 1920s, there were those who planned and hoped for the chance to redeem themselves, but their problems were greater than those faced by General von Seeckt and his colleagues. Germany was united in the 1920s in its hostility to the Treaty of Versailles and to the allies. Vichy's position was far more complex. First of all, there were ambiguous feelings about Britain and its behaviour. Secondly, however much they hated Germany, many officers preferred Pétain's government to the democracy of the Third Republic. It would have been hard to find German officers in the 1920s who preferred the Weimar republic to the kaiser's Germany.[23]

Yet the Germans did little to conciliate the Vichy government. French negotiators at Wiesbaden repeatedly argued that the Germans were treating their countrymen far more harshly than the Germans had been treated after 1918. French people in the occupied zone were executed for harbouring escaped prisoners of war; Germans in the Rhineland had never been treated in this way.[24] Stulpnagel and Vogl replied that the war had ended when France occupied the Rhineland, but they were still at war with Britain and consequently had to take stronger measures. The French said it was against honour and law to demand that German exiles should be handed over to the German authorities. The Germans responded that the émigrés in France stirred up hatred against their own country and reminded the French that they had been asked to hand over their own officers to the allies to be tried after the First World War. The French said it was against their tradition to hand over foreigners to another government. The Germans claimed that the tradition had only developed since the French Foreign Legion had begun to recruit criminals and deserters in the mid-nineteenth century.[25]

---

[22] Trevor-Roper, *Hitler's Table-Talk*, p. 478.
[23] Paxton, *Parades and Politics*, pp. 21 ff.
[24] Costes, *La Délégation française*, vol. 2, p. 73 and vol. 4, p. 139.
[25] Costes, *La Délégation française*, vol. 4, pp. 25, 89, 187.

Doyen complained to Stulpnagel and his successor about German and Italian hostility to Vichy. He pointed out that the French forces in North Africa had created no trouble for the Italians when Italian armies were falling back before the British. For France the war was over; they had signed the armistice agreement and they were not given to kicking a neighbour who was in trouble, yet the Axis powers continued to treat them as enemies. There were too few Europeans in their North African forces, but Axis (and particularly Italian) suspicions prevented them from sending more than fifty soldiers at a time as reinforcements.[26]

The Germans had continually hampered the allied inspectors in the 1920s, but the Nazis could now take far more severe reprisals against Vichy than the allies had previously been able to take against Germany. Indeed, they could take more ferocious measures than any of the other victors described in this book have been able to take in modern times against a defeated enemy. In January 1941 the forage cap of a German soldier was stolen by a French civilian in Montpellier. The next month, the car belonging to two German officers was vandalized while they were dining at the Hôtel de Bellevue in Mâcon. Two wheels were removed and the car suffered other 'degredations'. The Armistice Commission demanded the condign punishment of the offenders and threatened to increase the number of inspectors in Vichy France. German officers visiting Montpellier found the area particularly hostile and put this down to the influence of the officer commanding the local 16th Division, General Altmayer. Civilians made derogatory remarks about them in the shops and French soldiers pointedly ignored them. The Germans quickly made clear that such behaviour would not be tolerated and Altmayer was ordered to apologize for sending an insufficiently obsequious letter to the German authorities.[27] There was nothing except convenience stopping the Germans moving to the Mediterranean and crushing the remnants of French independence. The French High Command knew this only too well and never systematically evaded the armistice terms as Seeckt and his fellow officers had done.[28]

General Doyen's position typified the views of many senior officers. He began as a supporter of Pétain and Vichy's policy

[26] Costes, *La Délégation française*, vol. 4, pp. 106 ff.
[27] Costes, *La Délégation française*, pp. 125, 177 ff.
[28] Paxton, *Parades and Politics*, ch. 10.

of appeasement. He resigned from the armistice delegation in July 1941 and explained to his superiors the reasons for his growing disillusionment. He argued that Germany would never accept another power on the European continent and that its ideologists believed that France was becoming ever more decadent because of the mingling of Mediterranean blood with its racial stock. The Germans had insisted on a brutal and rapid disarmament of French forces. They had deliberately fermented trouble between France and Britain. In particular, they had used French airfields in Syria in 1941 when they knew that this would provoke a British attack on the French colony. At the same time they had deliberately weakened French colonial forces. In Doyen's view, no German promise could be believed, because they felt justified in taking any action to improve their military position. Thus France should limit its co-operation with Germany to the minimum possible and bear in mind that the German campaigns, culminating in the attack on the Soviet Union, were becoming ever more adventurous and (though this was merely implicit) likely to end in defeat. Quite surprisingly, considering the moment when he was writing and the audience for his memorandum, Doyen argued that France should put its trust in the United States, because it was only the US which could restore France's integrity, as indeed it had in 1918.[29]

EVADING THE ARMISTICE TERMS

If appeasement offered limited scope for improving France's position, outright evasion of the armistice was made more difficult by the efficiency of German inspection.[30] The Germans behaved very much as the French inspectors had done under the Versailles treaty. The Armistice Commission at Wiesbaden had nine subcommissions working from a headquarters in the occupied zone at Bourges. These carried out inspections wherever they wished inside Vichy France. They were diligent in noting disparities between the various lists of weapons and searching for hidden dumps. The French would never have dared mob the German inspectors as German civilians and soldiers had mobbed their allied equivalents in the 1920s. Nor could the French liaison officers practise non-

---

[29] Costes, *La Délégation française*, vol. 4, pp. 645 ff.
[30] Costes, *La Délégation française*, vol. 2, p. 69.

co-operation in the way their German predecessors had done.[31] They tried to retain their self-respect by emphasis on pomp and ceremony, but the very process of inspection and the general political background made co-operation difficult.

By February 1941 the Germans were convinced that most weapons had been handed over and that those which remained were of limited use. They discovered how wrong they had been when they took over Vichy France in November 1942 and found some 536 secret arms dumps.[32] After the initial defeat, individual French officers and troops had hidden their weapons. The first Vichy War Minister, General Colson, may even have given the order to do this as early as July 1940. Colson was succeeded by Huntziger in September. Huntziger wanted to convince the Germans of French loyalty, while planning a cadre army capable of expansion. However, the German Control Commissions had started to operate the previous month and they tightened control over depots of arms to prevent 'seepage' to the Vichy army. Nevertheless, an organization known as the Conservation du Matériel or Camouflage du Matérial did operate under Major Emile Mollard, who was head of the Material Section of the First Bureau. This had its headquarters in the Hôtel Mart at Royat and was supposed to be concerned with transport. In fact, it collected and hid weapons and other equipment.[33]

The Germans were insistent that Vichy's army should move only on foot, by bicycle, or by horse. Its immobility would mean that its powers of resistance were limited in the extreme. Thus one of Mollard's first tasks was to ensure that trucks requisitioned by the French army before its defeat were restored to civilian use so that they could be recalled at short notice by the army. New companies were set up to run trucking businesses, often with officers and non-commissioned officers on leave overseeing the vehicles. The German Control Commissions noted that the French were starting to smuggle the better vehicles out of depots and change registration numbers. Eighteen truck companies, known as the Sociétés XV, with a total of 3,720 vehicles were eventually established. But there

---

[31] Paxton, *Parades and Politics*, p. 97.
[32] Paxton, *Parades and Politics*, p. 283.
[33] Paxton, *Parades and Politics*, p. 285; on Huntziger's plans see *Baudouin Diaries*, p. 229.

was constant pressure from the Germans for more vehicles to be handed over to assist them with their war effort.[34]

Mollard and his associates also managed to hide weapons and maintain them in good order. These included between 60 and 100 anti-tank weapons and enough rifles, machine-guns, and mortars to increase the size of the Vichy army by perhaps 80 per cent.[35] The German Armistice Commission records show that some 46,000 individual weapons were hidden, 28 million rounds of ammunition, 5,828 machine-guns, and 3,193 mortars. French figures were much higher and, of course, the French army in North Africa also hid substantial quantities of weaponry.[36] The French even hid parts for a number of armoured cars. These were based on General Motors chassis which the French army had bought before the surrender but never used. Armour was taken from an armoured train and the design was produced by J.-J. Ramon, director of tank production at Renault. In April 1943 the German Control Commission found a walled-up cave near Sarlat containing 38 of these dismantled vehicles.[37]

In the summer of 1941 the French Chief of Staff, Colonel Picquandar, ordered the head of his operations bureau to begin secretly planning operations against the Germans. Lieutenant-Colonel Alain Touzet du Vigier and his colleagues hoped to be able to raise sixteen more divisions to add to the eight divisions of the army. Remembering their own behaviour under the Weimar republic, the Germans had closed all French recruiting offices which might have been used to raise further troops or keep in touch with those who had been demobilized. Thus the French plotters had to use the new National Statistics Service of the civilian Finance Ministry. This had the first data-processing system in France and comprehensive information about Frenchmen of military age. The head of this service, René Carmille, collected the names of 220,000 former French soldiers living in Vichy France. He and Major Pierre Jacquey divided the troops by locality so that they could be mobilized and their orders printed within a matter of hours. The system was never tried before the armistice army was destroyed. Carmille died in Germany after being deported for other activities.[38]

[34] Paxton, *Parades and Politics*, p. 287.
[35] Paxton, *Parades and Politics*, p. 289.
[36] Paxton, *Parades and Politics*, p. 290.
[37] Paxton, *Parades and Politics*, p. 291.
[38] Paxton, *Parades and Politics*, p. 284.

Picquandar, Mollard, and others were not the only ones to meditate attacks on the Germans but such plans were never co-ordinated. Some planned to seize Paris if the Germans had to weaken their occupying forces because of the demands of the Eastern front. Others saw the armistice army helping an Anglo-French landing on the Mediterranean coast. Yet others conceived a plan to seize La Rochelle and allow an allied landing.[39] General Giraud, who escaped from a German prison and was eventually taken from France in a British submarine, saw the army moving northwards into Alsace to throw confusion into the German ranks and facilitate an allied landing. All such hopes faded when the army was demobilized after the German take-over in November 1942. Instead, more and more Frenchmen began to join the resistance. Thus French national morale was restored not by the hidden stocks of weapons, most of which fell into German hands at the end of 1942, nor by the professional army's plan to use Vichy's forces against the occupiers, but by the sanguinary guerrilla struggle which continued to intensify right up to the allied landings in Normandy in 1944.

Once the French armies had been destroyed in 1940, there was little chance of effective resistance against the Germans. The armistice army was unpopular among many civilians and was never able to recruit enough men to reach its 100,000 limit. Evasions of the armistice were more important for the army's morale than for their practical value. However, they showed that, even faced with a regime as brutal and determined as the German, and with a leadership as divided and demoralized as the French, it was still possible to organize some opposition to the occupation forces. Vichy's main strategy was to persuade the Nazis gradually to liberalize the armistice terms, to defend French rights, colonies, and gold for as long as possible, and to await developments. Covert rearmament and preparations for war against Germany were in conflict with this strategy. Guerrilla resistance in the occupied areas also threatened efforts to reduce German oppression.

Hitler saw parallels between Weimar Germany and Vichy France, but the analogy between Prussia in 1808 and France in 1940 is more suggestive. Some would argue that all forced

---

[39] Paxton, *Parades and Politics*, p. 295.

disarmament is imperialistic; however, the allies in 1815 and 1919 had no intention of crushing the independence of their vanquished enemies completely. They wanted to remove the threat to their security, but the idea of trying to incorporate their former enemies into their territories never occurred to them. Napoleon and Hitler, by contrast, were naturally predatory and imperialistic.

As far as the defeated leaders were concerned, Pétain and Frederick William shared a fear of social revolution and reform. Scharnhorst, Clausewitz, and other Prussian reformers saw their defeat as a reflection on the inadequacy of both the Prussian state and the army. Their response was to try to persuade the king to accept conscription as well as political and social reforms. Even though the reformers were never entirely successful and most of them lost office after 1815, they were regarded as national heroes and left behind traditions which never entirely died out. Pétain and his army left nothing but humiliation and disgrace. Pétain turned against the modern world and saw defeat in 1940 as a justified punishment for the Third Republic's anti-clericalism and materialism. The tenacity with which Doyen and others struggled to minimize German control over France, protect German refugees, and expand the armed forces went almost unremarked and unremembered. They lacked the social and political vision of their Prussian predecessors, but their military achievements were comparable. Most of the secret attempts to evade the armistice were forgotten, while Prussian successes were exaggerated. It was Vichy's persecution of the Jews which was remembered with appropriate shame. Yet, to be fair to Pétain and his colleagues, although individual Fascists joined the Axis forces, they never allowed the Vichy army to fight alongside the Germans as Frederick William allowed himself to be coerced into joining Napoleon's invasion of Russia in 1812. Pétain's government took greater risks and saw the last vestiges of French independence crushed by the Nazis.

7

Allied War Aims and Disarmament
in the Second World War and
Afterwards

The heterogeneous alliance, which defeated the Axis states in the
Second World War, was united by its determination to demand the
unconditional surrender of the enemy powers and to prevent their
resurgence. For the Russian people the war was a struggle for
survival in which many of their great cities were destroyed and
some 20 million died. The Western democracies saw it as a crusade
against the forces of evil. The allied leaders, Stalin, Roosevelt, and
Churchill, agreed that enemy governments should be removed and
Nazism and Fascism should be eradicated. While the fighting was
continuing, they could also agree that the defeated nations should
be totally disarmed and kept demilitarized. Disarmament was not
an afterthought, as in 1918, but a central aim throughout the
struggle. For Churchill, in particular, it was the key to maintaining
peace in the postwar world. Roosevelt added to it a determination
to partition Germany in order to prevent its resurgence and Stalin
insisted on the destruction of the elites in the defeated nations
and extracting reparations, both to weaken them and to pay for
repairing some of the damage which their aggression had caused.[1]

[1] Virtually all the major Western leaders and senior officials who were influen-
tial during the Second World War subsequently wrote their memoirs. Among
those autobiographical accounts which discussed forced disarmament and the
Morgenthau plan are *The Memoirs of Cordell Hull* (Hodder and Stoughton,
London, 1948), vol. 2; J. F. Byrnes, *Speaking Frankly* (Heinemann, London,
n.d.). Byrnes produced a second volume, *All in One Lifetime* (Museum Press,
London, 1960) but it adds little to this topic. See also *The Memoirs of Harry S.
Truman: Year of Decision, 1945* (Hodder and Stoughton, London, 1955); W. D.
Leahy, *I Was There* (Gollancz, London, 1950); W. S. Churchill, *The Second
World War: The Hinge of Fate* (Reprint Society, London, 1953); H. L. Stimson,
On Active Service in Peace and War (Harper, New York, 1948); J. M. Blum,
From the Morgenthau Diaries: Years of War 1941–1945 (Houghton,
Boston, 1967).

Churchill, Roosevelt, and Stalin were thus united in their determination to make a permanent alteration in the balance of power,
though they disagreed on the way to do this most effectively.

Given the immense political experience of the three allied leaders,
one would have expected them to produce a realistic peace treaty.
Stalin had emerged from the wreckage left by the Russian Revolution and civil war to dominate and industrialize his country. Roosevelt had served as Assistant Secretary of the US Navy from 1913 to
1920. As President from 1932, he had steered the United States
through the worst depression in its history and brought it united
into the Second World War. Churchill had held high office before
and during the First World War. He had served as a soldier in India
and on the Western Front. He had been a war correspondent in the
Boer War and had studied war throughout his life. None of the
three could be accused of being ignorant of the problems inherent
in peace-making.

Yet, apart from the Nuremberg and Tokyo trials of enemy
leaders and the immediate demobilization of enemy forces, none of
their war aims was achieved without rancour between them. As the
Axis lurched towards defeat, arguments about frontiers, reparations, and, above all, about the type of governments established in
the countries freed from the Axis, eroded allied links and led to the
Cold War. The physical disarmament of the enemy was laborious
but relatively simple, because the allies were in total control of
their territories. The Western allies also proposed legal barriers
against their rearmament. The United States gave Japan a constitution which prohibited the maintenance of armed forces. The US
and Britain wanted to impose treaties on the enemy states which
would keep them disarmed for the next decades. All such plans fell
victim to the Cold War. The Japanese constitution was to be
'reinterpreted', while the two halves of Germany were rearmed.
The 'Byrnes' treaties, which would have forced the former enemies
to disarm for up to forty years, were almost forgotten.

CHURCHILL'S WAR AIMS

Churchill put forced disarmament at the centre of his war aims. In
February 1943 he sent Roosevelt his proposals for the future in a
document called 'Notes on Post-War Security'. He suggested that
'so far as possible total disarmament of guilty nations will be

enforced. On the other hand no attempt will be made to destroy the peoples or to prevent them gaining their living and leading a decent life in spite of all the crimes they have committed.' This was a position the Prime Minister held consistently, except for a temporary aberration during and after the second Quebec conference. The Axis countries were to be totally disarmed, not partially disarmed as they had been in the 1920s or deliberately weakened by economic measures. They would somehow be 'deprived of all power to rearm' and prohibited from having a General Staff, any type of aircraft, or practising the art of flying.[2]

Roosevelt gave Churchill consistent support over this issue, while Soviet policy seemed to wobble slightly in 1943. In May Stalin announced that he would not destroy the German army after the war, and the Soviets established a Free German Movement and a Union of German Officers from among their captives. Such moves worried Western leaders but, at the Moscow Foreign Ministers' Conference, Molotov and Stalin accepted allied disarmament proposals with enthusiasm. It seems likely that Soviet actions in 1943 were simply designed as propaganda to weaken the German will to continue the war and reassure them that they would not be totally destroyed by the allies. Nevertheless, the democracies were uncertain about the Soviet position and US planners wrote in 1944, 'there is apparently no [Soviet] intention of destroying Germany as a nation, or of disarming it completely, although the Soviet government intend to limit the German military machine to the point where it could not be a menace to Soviet security.'[3]

Churchill's enthusiasm for the total forced disarmament of the enemy was particularly interesting, both because of his wide knowledge of history and strategy, and because he had been no friend of the general disarmament negotiations under the League of Nations. These, he felt, increased tensions because they concentrated so much attention on force levels. He also believed they were based on the illusion that equality of armaments was conducive to peace.[4]

---

[2] W. F. Kimball, *Churchill and Roosevelt; The Complete Correspondence* (Princeton University Press, 1984), vol. 2, p. 129. See also Churchill, *The Hinge of Fate*, p. 552.

[3] National Archives, Washington, T 1221, CAC 71, 'Soviet War Aims'. See also H. Feis, *Churchill, Roosevelt, Stalin* (Princeton University Press, 1957), p. 219.

[4] P. Towle, 'Winston Churchill and British Disarmament Policy', *Journal of Strategic Studies*, 2 (December 1979).

Churchill was one of the few British politicians who had the insight to see that the status quo powers needed superiority in order to keep the Axis revisionists in check. This inequality was to be perpetuated after the surrender of the enemy. The Prime Minister was also only too familiar with the failure of attempts to disarm Germany in the 1920s and fully aware of the need to maintain disarmament by force if it was to be effective. He never appears to have explained how previous mistakes were to be avoided, but clearly the Soviets, Americans, and British had far more power to impose disarmament upon their enemies than the British and French had had in the 1920s.

ROOSEVELT'S WAR AIMS

Roosevelt announced at the Casablanca conference in January 1943 that the allies would demand the unconditional surrender of the enemy forces because 'peace can come to the world only by the total elimination of German and Japanese war power.'[5] He agreed with Churchill that it was essential to disarm the Axis, but he evidently felt that this was not enough to ensure future security or to punish the aggressors. Roosevelt's Secretary of State, Cordell Hull, made plans for a new international organization to replace the discredited League of Nations. But again, while the President backed what became the United Nations, he was too much of a realist to believe that it would be sufficient to keep the peace. At the Teheran conference with Churchill and Stalin in November 1943 and on many previous occasions, he proposed breaking Germany down into separate states. Over this Stalin and Roosevelt saw eye to eye, while Churchill vacillated, putting forward his own plan for partition and then emphasizing the disadvantages of 'Balkanizing' Europe. When the British Foreign Secretary, Anthony Eden, visited Moscow in December 1941, Stalin suggested splitting off the Rhineland, setting up an independent Bavaria, and giving Eastern Prussia to Poland.[6] Both evidently felt that partition would weaken Germany more than disarmament alone.

[5] Churchill, *The Hinge of Fate*, p. 550; Leahy, *I Was There*, p. 174; Feis, *Churchill, Roosevelt, Stalin*, p. 109; for Hull's criticism of the policy see Hull, *Memoirs*, pp. 1570 ff.
[6] On the Teheran conference see D. Dilks (ed.), *The Diaries of Sir Alexander Cadogan, 1938–1945* (Cassell, London, 1971), p. 620. On Eden's visit to Moscow in December 1941 see Feis, *Churchill, Roosevelt, Stalin*, p. 26.

Cordell Hull and many other members of the administration were dubious about partition and the US postwar policy committee argued in a paper dated 23 September 1943 that it would be destabilizing because it would have to be maintained by force. The British government was as undecided as its leader. In March 1943, Eden told Hull that Britain was coming round to supporting dismemberment but, at the first Quebec Conference five months later, he said that, while some members of the British government were in favour, the majority believed it was impractical.[7] The Foreign Ministers were very cautious in their pronouncements on this issue at their conference in Moscow in October 1943. Eden said that British Ministers would prefer Germany to break apart and wanted to encourage any separatist tendencies. Molotov said that his government had not studied the issue carefully but was in favour of doing anything which would weaken Germany. Reflecting the divisions between the President and himself, Hull said that the administration was undecided and would prefer to keep an open mind.[8]

Despite the President's consistent support for partition, arguments within the US administration intensified after the Treasury Secretary, Henry Morgenthau, became involved in the issue in 1944. The 'Morgenthau plan' envisaged the total break-up of Germany, with parts handed over to Poland, Denmark, and France. Hull and the State Department objected. They reiterated their view that, 'because of the high degree of economic, political, and cultural integration of Germany, it must be anticipated that partition would not only have to be enforced but maintained by force.' The Secretary of War, Henry Stimson, agreed. Roosevelt was eventually persuaded that the economic aspects of the Morgenthau plan were impractical, but he held generally to his view that some dismemberment was essential.[9]

The President was more convinced than Churchill that the German people had to be punished to make them change their behaviour. 'We have got to be tough with Germany and I mean the German people, not just the Nazis. You either have to castrate the German people or you have got to treat them in such a manner so

[7] Hull, *Memoirs*, p. 1165; Feis, *Churchill, Roosevelt, Stalin*, p. 124. For the views of the US postwar planning committee see National Archives T 1221, CAC 13, paper of 23 September 1943.

[8] Hull, *Memoirs*, p. 1233.   [9] Hull, *Memoirs*, pp. 1606–7.

that they just can't go on reproducing people who want to continue the way they have in the past.'[10] Roosevelt's comment was unusual for a Western statesman because it touched on policies going far beyond what was acceptable in a civilized but victorious power. Apart from the trials of the enemy leaders, it was not punishment but the re-education of the German and Japanese people which eventually became a Western war aim. US planners called in April 1944 for 'the psychological disarmament of the German people' by removing Nazi teachers, reforming the school curriculum, and placing all media under surveillance.[11]

As with forced disarmament, the democracies turned to re-education at the end of the war because the alternatives were ruled out. In both Britain and the US, re-education was extensively debated in the media. In Britain, the former Deputy Under-Secretary in the Foreign Office, Sir Victor Wellesley, argued that the revival of militarism could best be prevented in the defeated nations by educational reform and the breaking down of economic barriers between the nations. Even someone who hated the Germans as much as Wellesley's former superior, Lord Vansittart, could only call vaguely for the indictment of the German nation and its forced reform for an extensive period.[12]

On the other side were many who doubted the practicality of re-education. How could peoples be persuaded to oppose militarism and support democracy simply by education and allied propaganda? Even if democratic values were instilled in enemy peoples, by no means everyone accepted the liberal assumption that democracies were intrinsically less belligerent than autocracies. However, there was little opposition in the West to imposing democratic constitutions on the enemy. The impact of allied re-education in support of these constitutions is still debated among historians, but the autocratic ideologies were probably discredited by the Second World War itself and by the revelations about the mass murder of Jews and the mistreatment of prisoners of war rather than by allied

---

[10] Kimball, *Churchill and Roosevelt*, vol. 3, p. 317.

[11] National Archives T 1221-3, CAC 167, paper of 17 April 1944. See also N. Pronay, *The Political Reeducation of Germany and Her Allies after World War Two* (Croom Helm, London, 1985).

[12] Sir V. Wellesley, *Diplomacy in Fetters* (Hutchinson, London, n.d.), pp. 143 ff.; R. G. Vansittart, *Lessons of my Life* (Hutchinson, London, n.d.), pp. 235–6. For a sceptical view of re-education see C. Morgan, *Reflections in a Mirror* (Macmillan, London, 1946).

propaganda. Whatever the reason, democracy has been successful in Germany and Japan since 1945 beyond the sober expectations of many of the allied officials involved in peace-making.

STALIN'S WAR AIMS

The original Soviet plans for the postwar world emphasized the need for changes in the frontiers of Eastern Europe. When the British Foreign Secretary visited Moscow in December 1941, Stalin asked for the restoration of those provinces which his country had lost since the German attack the previous June. The Soviet Union would re-incorporate the Baltic republics, parts of Finland and Romania, as well as Poland east of the Curzon line.[13] Eden said that he would report Stalin's requests to his government, though Stalin immediately made clear that he would regard any hesitation as a major slight on the Soviet Union. Alterations in frontiers remained an issue between the allies up to and beyond the end of the war, but in 1945 Stalin had the power to impose his solutions on Eastern Europe. The Soviet Union wanted buffer zones to protect it against further invasion, and it was determined that nothing would prevent it from gaining them.[14]

The members of the US and British governments were by no means agreed upon war aims, but they could discuss these openly with their colleagues in allied governments. The Soviets could hardly be open about all their plans and methods without shocking the democratic leaders and causing tensions within the alliance. Stalin had ordered the execution of Polish officers after his troops invaded eastern Poland in 1939. Undoubtedly he envisaged the 'removal' of the elites in all the countries separating the Soviet Union from Central Europe. He told the allied leaders at Teheran that he would expect to execute 50,000 to 100,000 Germans for war crimes. In the event, once Soviet armies had taken over the rest of Eastern Europe, the old elites were either crushed or forced to flee.[15]

If disarmament was the British contribution to the solution of the German problem and partition was Roosevelt's, Stalin's main

[13] Hull, *Memoirs*, p. 1166; Feis, *Churchill, Roosevelt, Stalin*, p. 24.
[14] H. Seton-Watson, *The East European Revolution* (Methuen, London, 1961); A. Palmer, *The Lands Between* (Weidenfeld and Nicolson, London, 1970), pp. 290 ff.
[15] Dilks, *Alexander Cadogan*, p. 620; Feis, *Churchill, Roosevelt, Stalin*, p. 273.

interest, apart from frontier alterations and the removal of elites, was in reparations. Western leaders were sceptical. Churchill told Stalin at Yalta that reparations had been tried after the First World War and had produced nothing. Moreover, the German people had to be kept alive. If you wanted a horse to pull your cart, you had to feed it, a point reinforced when the allied armies discovered that a fifth of all machines and a seventh of all German houses had been destroyed during the fighting. Roosevelt said that the United States was not interested in reparations for itself and would not subsidize Germany so that it could pay reparations to others, as it had done in the 1920s. However, he seemed willing to go some way to meet the Soviets, a concession which caused tension between the allies subsequently.[16]

The Soviets started from the premise that the Germans should pay for some of the immense damage for which they alone were responsible. More than forty years later the long-serving Soviet Foreign Minister, Andrei Gromyko, wrote in his memoirs, 'Stalin and the rest of the Soviet delegation wondered what Roosevelt and Churchill were thinking of when they discussed the question. Did they realize that, if the Germans were made to pay even twenty or thirty billion dollars, it would represent no more than a drop in the ocean?' Stalin claimed later that his country had been 'cheated' by the allies out of the reparations it was owed.[17] The allies started from the premise that the Germans must not be allowed to starve; this meant that, although some factories were moved from the Western zones of Germany to the Soviet Union, reparations on the scale Moscow wanted were effectively ruled out.

THE MORGENTHAU PLAN

Economic war aims had been extensively discussed in the US administration following the visit of Henry Morgenthau, the Treasury Secretary, to Europe in August 1944. Unlike Stalin, Morgenthau was not primarily concerned about recompense for losses; his

[16] Byrnes, *Speaking Frankly*, p. 27. On the devastation of Germany by the fighting see E. N. Peterson, *The American Occupation of Germany* (Wayne University Press, Detroit, 1977), p. 114. See also N. Annan, *Changing Enemies: The Defeat and Regeneration of Germany* (Harper Collins, London, 1995).

[17] *The Memoirs of Andrei Gromyko* (Hutchinson, London, 1989), pp. 80 ff.; Byrnes, *Speaking Frankly*, p. 28; Leahy, *I Was There*, p. 355. See also A. Cairncross, *The Price of War: British Policy on German Reparations 1941–1949* (Basil Blackwell, Oxford, 1986).

chief objective was to produce a change in the European balance of power by weakening Germany and strengthening Britain. In a broadcast he made just before leaving Britain, he said, 'it is not enough for us to disarm Germany and Japan and hope that they will come to behave as decent people; hoping is not enough.' He also wanted to punish the German people for their crimes. His aims could be achieved, so he believed, by destroying the industrial region of the Ruhr and reducing Germany to a subsistence economy. Morgenthau maintained that this would benefit Britain: 'If the Ruhr were put out of business, the coal mines and steel mills of England would flourish for many years.' His opponents, led by Stimson, the Secretary of War, argued that German recovery was essential if the European economy as a whole was to revive. They also said that millions would starve if the Ruhr were destroyed. To this Morgenthau replied, 'Just strip it. I don't care what happens to the population . . . I would take every mine, every mill and factory and wreck it.'[18]

Morgenthau had the opportunity to press his ideas on war aims at the second Quebec conference in September 1944. The discussion lasted for three hours. Stimson and Hull were absent and thus unable to put their case. Roosevelt was ill and silent. Churchill initially countered with his own plans for German disarmament. 'I'm all for disarming Germany but we ought not to prevent her living decently. There are bonds between the working classes of all countries, and the English people will not stand for the policy you are advocating.'[19] Unfortunately Lord Cherwell, Churchill's scientific adviser, had accompanied him to Quebec, and within forty-eight hours he had persuaded Churchill to change his mind. At Quebec the Prime Minister even helped to draft the 'Morgenthau Plan' for turning Germany into an agricultural nation.

Hull and Stimson were furious. They believed that Churchill had agreed to the deal simply because Britain was offered financial assistance worth some 6.5 billion dollars. When Roosevelt returned to Washington, Hull told him that this went against all previous US planning and that US promises of assistance should be used in subsequent bargaining with the British government. He was able to make the President see the unreality of the Morgenthau Plan. The

[18] Blum, *Morgenthau Diaries*, pp. 339, 351–4.
[19] C. M. W. Moran, *Winston Churchill: The Struggle for Survival* (Constable, London, 1966), p. 177.

allies could neither let millions of Germans die after they had
surrendered nor keep them alive if they were not allowed to produce enough to survive. Roosevelt agreed. The aim, he stressed,
must be to stop Germany using its industry again for military
purposes. 'No one wants "complete eradication" of German industrial productive capacity in the Ruhr and Saar. It is possible,
however, in those two particular areas to enforce rather complete
controls.'[20]

The Morgenthau Plan was a radical attempt to address the
problems caused since 1871 by the predominance of German
power in Europe. It also fully recognized the impossibility
of distinguishing between those factories capable of producing
weapons and those devoted to the civilian sector. Churchill's
counter-arguments about disarmament lost weight precisely because they failed to do this. Lord Moran, Churchill's doctor, who
watched the whole debate at Quebec, concluded that Churchill had
spent too much time thinking about minor details of military
strategy and not enough about peace-making. 'He was frankly
bored by the kind of problem which might take up the time of the
Peace Conference.' The result was that Churchill briefly made the
Morgenthau Plan his own. In Moscow the following month, he
agreed with Stalin that the industry of the Ruhr and Saar should be
put out of action for a generation and Germany deprived of its
metallurgical and chemical industries.[21]

Thus it was left to a later US Secretary of State, James Byrnes, to
put flesh on the bones of the forced disarmament measures for
which Churchill had long been the primary advocate among the
allied war leaders.

THE BYRNES TREATIES

The allies' general strategy towards Germany was co-ordinated at
the great wartime conferences. The Foreign Ministers meeting in
Moscow in October 1943 agreed to establish a European Advisory
Commission staffed by officials to deal with the detailed problems
which the end of the war in Europe would bring. The zones of
occupation for the allied powers in Germany, the terms of sur-

---

[20] Hull, *Memoirs*, p. 1620.
[21] Moran, *Winston Churchill*, p. 180. On Churchill's visit to Moscow see
M. Gilbert, *Churchill: A Life* (Heinemann, London, 1991), p. 800.

render, the arrangements for Berlin and Vienna were all worked out by this Commission. Representatives of the three Powers were divided for many weeks over a number of issues, including the status of German soldiers who surrendered and the role of the minor allies in the occupation of Germany. What they could agree on was 'complete disarmament and demilitarization, as they deemed requisite for future peace and security'.[22] How this was to be maintained in practice proved far more difficult to decide.

With the allied armies advancing across the world towards their Axis enemies, so the divisions within the coalition became steadily more obvious. As we have seen, Stalin's first priorities were for changing frontiers, replacing the East and Central European elites, and exacting reparations. But for the democracies these were either morally repellent or impractical if carried too far. Partition of Germany never became agreed allied policy, not least because there was no consensus on how the German state might be divided and how the various pieces were to be kept apart. As all these questions loomed larger, so even those aims which the allies could agree upon, such as the disarmament of the enemy, began to be obscured by disagreements. In any case, disarmament seemed relatively less important as allied armies achieved it de facto.

1945 saw changes in the US and British governments. Attlee and Bevin replaced Churchill and Eden. Truman and Byrnes became President and Secretary of State. Byrnes had been Director of War Mobilization and Reconversion under Roosevelt. As Secretary of State he took the initiative in trying to perpetuate the disarmament of the enemy. In his memoirs Byrnes explains the origins of his proposals. He attended the Yalta conference in February 1945 some months before he became Secretary of State. At the conference, the alternative ways of weakening Germany were losing their appeal. The idea of breaking Germany up into smaller units received much less attention than it had done at Teheran. Churchill and Roosevelt wanted to defer action until after the surrender. Byrnes believed Stalin concluded that ultimately the democracies would reject partition. In the end the allies were to achieve a de facto division of Germany for forty years, thus making this by far

[22] W. Strang, *Home and Abroad* (André Deutsch, London, 1956), p. 211; on the Commission see also G. Kennan, *Memoirs 1925–1950* (Hutchinson, London, 1968), p. 164. On British planning see *The Memoirs of Lord Gladwyn* (Weidenfeld and Nicolson, London, 1972), pp. 109 ff.

the most enduring of the means used to limit its power. However, this came about not by deliberate agreement but because the temporary occupation zones eventually coalesced into two separate states.[23]

In the meantime there had been a good deal of public discussion in the US about the need for a treaty to keep the enemies disarmed, following a speech made by the influential Senator Vandenberg on 10 January 1945. Vandenberg had been a Republican senator for Michigan since 1928. His speech reflected the concerns of many Poles living in Michigan, who were becoming increasingly anxious about the likelihood that the Soviets would dominate Eastern Europe. Thus Vandenberg saw the forced disarmament of Germany as a possible substitute for such control, though he believed that 'America has this same self-interest in permanently, conclusively and effectively disarming Germany and Japan.' A treaty to this effect should be signed immediately and the President should have the right to use US armed troops to make sure that it was permanently enforced.[24]

Vandenberg's speech was given headline treatment across the US, partly because it was a total rejection of his earlier isolationism and partly because it was the sort of idealistic proposal the US public was looking for. Walter Lippmann argued that Vandenberg had offered the US a coherent policy because he had 'seen what so many of our anguished idealists have not seen, that what our allies are seeking first of all is security against the revival of German militarism.' On the other hand, the speech was attacked by isolationist newspapers like the *Chicago Tribune*, which saw it 'pledging us to maintain a well-nigh permanent police force in Germany, in exchange for vague concessions'. Some papers felt so strongly that it was a betrayal of US national interest that they believed it heralded the break-up of the Republican party and the emergence of a 'third force'.[25]

Roosevelt made little public response to Vandenberg's initiative, except to invite him to join the US delegation to the San Francisco conference which was to establish the United Nations. It was not until the autumn of 1945 that the Truman administration officially

[23] Byrnes, *Speaking Frankly*, pp. 21 ff. See note 16 above.
[24] A. H. Vandenberg Junior (ed.), *The Private Papers of Senator Vandenberg* (Gollancz, London, 1953), p. 136.
[25] Vandenberg, *Private Papers*, pp. 138–44 for a summary of this debate.

endorsed Vandenberg's specific proposal, though with a more immediate objective in view. The Senator's aim had been to reduce Soviet control over Eastern Europe; Byrnes used the idea to break the deadlock which had emerged at the Foreign Ministers' conference in London. Byrnes asked for a private discussion with Molotov, and reminded him that Stalin had talked at Yalta about the successive attacks which had been made on Russia through Poland. He went on to say, 'As you know, the US, historically, is reluctant to enter into political treaties, but I want to ask you if the Soviet government would consider desirable a twenty-five-year treaty between the four principal powers for the demilitarization of Germany.'[26] If the Soviets were interested, Byrnes promised to recommend the idea to the President and to Congress. Molotov replied that it was 'a very interesting idea' which he would refer to his government. But, at the Moscow conference three months later, the Soviet Foreign Minister dismissed the Byrnes treaty as 'wholly inadequate'.

Not easily thwarted, Byrnes brought up the idea with Stalin himself when they were drinking coffee after a Christmas Eve dinner. Stalin said that Molotov had mentioned the idea to him but there had been little discussion. 'Such a treaty will give all European states assurance that the United States would not return to a policy of isolation,' Byrnes informed the Soviet dictator. He admitted that the US people had always been opposed to long-term commitments 'but our experience in trying to stay out of Europe's wars has been so disastrous I am confident our people would support a treaty under which the major powers would join forces to keep Germany disarmed.' Stalin promised that, if Byrnes fought for such a treaty in Congress, it would have Soviet support.[27] Stalin may have assumed that Byrnes's proposal was doomed by US isolationism or he may have been procrastinating. He had to weigh the proposed US involvement against the promised benefits, The Cold War was only just taking shape and US–Soviet relations were not yet resolutely antagonistic. Accepting an exiguous US presence in

---

[26] Byrnes, *Speaking Frankly*, p. 100. Vandenberg's comments do not suggest that he had been closely involved with Byrnes's plans for approaching Molotov and he did not attend the London Conference; Vandenberg, *Private Papers*, p. 264. For the text of the treaty see *FRUS 1946*, vol. 11 (US Government Printing Office, Washington, 1970), pp. 190 ff.

[27] Byrnes, *Speaking Frankly*, p. 172. See also *FRUS 1946*, vol. 11, p. 62.

Europe might be worthwhile if it left the Soviets in a strong position to enforce German demilitarization.

According to Byrnes's account, he started preparing the draft German treaty as soon as he returned to Washington. He followed as closely as possible the allied declaration of 5 June 1945 on the demilitarization that was carried out immediately after the allied armies occupied Germany. Byrnes argued in his memoirs that 'such a compact would eliminate the need to maintain large armed forces in Germany. A disarmed Germany would never fail to comply with an order from the Allied headquarters if the government knew a violation would bring the air forces of one or more of the four powers over their land within a few hours.'[28] In other words, Byrnes did not originally envisage the US keeping substantial ground forces in Europe to enforce the treaty but being committed to the use of airpower, should this become necessary to maintain the disarmament of the enemy powers. Conversely, British officials believed that the experience of the 1920s showed that troops had to be stationed within the disarmed state. Otherwise, nations would not be prepared to initiate the use of force to keep it disarmed.

Separate though similar draft treaties were prepared for Germany and Japan. Initially they proposed that the defeated enemy should be disarmed for 'as long as the peace and security of the world may require'. This meant that no 'military or para-military organizations in any form or guise shall be permitted' and that 'the manufacture, production or importation of military equipment' would be prevented.[29] Once the actual occupation of the defeated powers had been ended, the role of the occupying forces in overseeing disarmament would be taken over by a commission of control staffed by the four Great Powers. Byrnes envisaged that this would contain engineers with the knowledge 'to prevent the establishment or conversion of industries capable of producing weapons of war'.[30] They would have the right to conduct 'such inspections, inquiries and investigations as [the commission] may deem necessary to determine whether the disarmament and demilitarization provisions . . . are being observed'. If the commission believed rearmament was taking place, it would inform the Great

[28] *FRUS 1946*, vol. 11, p. 62.
[29] FO/371/64160 C 11372. See also note 26 above.
[30] Byrnes, *Speaking Frankly*, p. 172.

Powers which would 'take such prompt action—including actions by land, sea or air forces—as may be necessary to assure the immediate cessation or prevention of such violation.'[31]

The British redrafting of the treaty suggested that inspection should begin while the allies were still in occupation of the defeated powers. This was intended to end the arguments which had broken out between the allies about whether or not all enemy forces had been disarmed in the separate occupation zones. Then, when the occupation ended, the commission of control would inherit the inspectors. The commission would have greater power than the Americans allowed so that it could take action in the event of a breach of the treaty and before the Great Powers had responded.[32] These were minor revisions and the Foreign Office was determined that they should be. Britain's primary aim was to keep US troops in Europe, protecting Europe against both a resurgent Germany and the Soviet Union.[33] Nothing else was important in comparison with the achievement of such an aim.

The original draft of the treaty allowed for action against breaches only when all four powers were agreed. Later this was changed to a majority vote, although Byrnes subsequently admitted that this might have increased Soviet opposition to his proposal. Later drafts also gave the defeated more latitude by allowing them to have civil airlines and to manufacture aircraft. Already the 'purity' of the vision of disarmament was sullied by practicality. With civilian aircraft the defeated enemies could reconstitute some of their war potential; without them their civilian manufacturing capacity would be sorely handicapped.

The French expressed their warm support for Byrnes's proposal, though they made clear that the treaty would not be enough to reassure them. They wanted allied garrisons permanently stationed on the Rhine. French anxieties were difficult to satisfy, but the real problems came from Molotov, who warned Byrnes of his continued hostility and flatly opposed the agreement at the Paris conference in 1946. Molotov claimed that the treaty would actually delay German disarmament, though he also argued that, if a satisfactory treaty could be negotiated, it would have to last for forty years. Byrnes immediately accepted this extension. Molotov argued that the formula was insufficiently comprehensive; Byrnes said it was

[31] See note 29 above.   [32] Ibid.
[33] FO/371/64160 telegram from William Strang, 22 October 1947.

taken from the declaration issued by Generals Zhukov, Montgomery, Eisenhower, and de Lattre de Tassigny on 5 June 1945 and that they were the best qualified to draft a disarmament programme.[34] That was only a debating point; the Soviets may well have been concerned about the revival of German industry and thus of its potential military power. After all, the democracies were refusing the massive reparations Moscow was demanding, which might have kept Germany at subsistence level for many years. But the Byrnes plan did allow for intrusive inspection of Germany industry, and this was the best scheme the Western Powers could devise for reducing the threat which its revival would present.

Despite the difficulty of distinguishing between civilian and military factories, it seems strange that the Soviets should reject a plan which promised to reduce the strength of Germany and Japan, two of the greatest threats to Soviet security. Forced disarmament had originally been Churchill's idea not Stalin's, although Stalin had never expressed hostility to the proposal. But there were two major aspects of the treaties which were clearly against Soviet interests: international inspection and a permanent US presence in Europe and Japan. Long before the Byrnes treaties were rejected, the issue of openness constantly divided the victors. At the Potsdam conference the British and Americans complained about Soviet behaviour in Romania and Bulgaria and the gradual erosion of democratic freedoms there. The Soviets countered with complaints about the British war against the communists in Greece. The British replied that anyone could go and see what was happening in Greece, and outside observers had been invited to Greek elections. Even British diplomats could not move around Romania and had to remain 'penned' in their mission.[35]

When the Council of Foreign Ministers met in London in September 1945, Western representatives proposed that international inspectors should make sure that Romania had been effectively disarmed. Bevin argued that small states could cause as much trouble as large ones and that therefore inspection was essential. Byrnes recollected, 'Mr Molotov said it had never occurred to him that "if one disarmed a state it would have a quiet life".' He went

---

[34] Byrnes, *Speaking Frankly*, p. 174. FO/371/64145 C 4796 and C 5071. For French views see *FRUS 1946*, vol. 2, pp. 56 ff.
[35] Byrnes, *Speaking Frankly*, pp. 74, 99. See also H. Feis, *From Trust to Terror* (Anthony Blond, London, 1970), pp. 129–35, 218–20.

on to inquire sardonically whether the West had enough people to spare to carry out such inspection. It was at the same conference that Byrnes proposed to Molotov the negotiation of the disarmament treaties for Germany and Japan.[36] It was inevitable that the Soviets would make the connection. The Soviet Union had helped Germany evade disarmament in the 1920s, so Soviet leaders knew a good deal about techniques of evasion. Intrusive inspection would be needed to ensure that this was not repeated, but intrusive inspection would lead to the revelation of what the Soviets were doing throughout Eastern Europe. Stalin had to balance the dangers of such revelations and of US involvement in Europe's destiny against the possibility that the 'German problem' would be solved for the next decades.

The British welcomed the Byrnes treaties above all because they believed that they meant the US would have to keep some forces in Europe. Indeed, Byrnes had suggested to Stalin that this was one of their positive advantages. But, given the steady deterioration in US–Soviet relations through 1946, this must have seemed ever more unattractive in Moscow. In his memoirs Byrnes noted, 'the Soviet High Command or Politbureau concluded that they did not want the United States involved in the maintenance of European security for the next twenty-five or forty years.'[37]

Byrnes continued to back the treaty in speeches in Germany and France. On 3 October 1946 he told the American Club in Paris, 'so long as such a treaty is in force, the Ruhr could never become the arsenal of Germany or the arsenal of Europe. That is a primary objective of the proposed treaty. The United States is firmly opposed to the revival of German military power.'[38] Nevertheless, officials in London and Washington recognized that agreement was becoming steadily less likely. In January 1947 General Marshall replaced Byrnes as Secretary of State, though US policy did not change immediately. In April the Soviets tabled their own version of the Byrnes treaty. Given the history of the previous eighteen months, the Western allies were immediately inclined to regard this as a covert form of rejection.

[36] Byrnes, *Speaking Frankly*, p. 99. The published British official documents on these talks ignore the Byrnes Treaties, showing how much they were a US initiative. See R. Bullen and M. E. Pelly (eds), *Documents on British Policy Overseas* (HMSO, London, 1985), series 1, vol. 11.

[37] Byrnes, *Speaking Frankly*, p. 176.

[38] Byrnes, *Speaking Frankly*, pp. 189, 193.

Their greatest problem was with the proposal that the Ruhr should be placed under four-power control. The democracies had toyed with this idea but had increasingly turned against it as the Cold War intensified and the Soviet zone became ever more separate. By 1947 it was clear that four-power control of the Ruhr would give the Soviets influence in the West with no corresponding Western influence in the East. The Soviets also proposed the transference of all German industries to state ownership, the break-up of the large landed estates, and the distribution of land to the peasants.[39] The Soviets were already carrying out these policies in the East but, even if they had been acceptable to Western governments, they would have threatened further disruption at a time when the allies were desperately trying to encourage industrial growth. In the Soviet draft, Germany's 'industrial war potential' was to be liquidated, although how this was to be achieved without going back to the Morgenthau plan was unclear.

The gap between the two sides was growing and there was some desultory discussion between the Western governments in 1947 on the advantages of negotiating a Byrnes treaty which applied only to the Western zones. But that idea too was overtaken by the Cold War. Rearmament, not disarmament, was becoming the order of the day.[40] It was Washington which had originally proposed the Byrnes treaty and it was Washington which was the first to turn openly against it. In February 1948 General Marshall told President Truman that the idea had been overtaken by events. The State Department paper pointed out that Bevin had invited the Benelux countries to discuss security with Britain and France. The long-term US policy was to bring Italy and the Western zones of Germany into such a security relationship.[41]

In the Western camp it was the French and Belgians who were made most anxious by this change in US policy. They argued that some way would have to be found of guaranteeing them against a revival of German military power before they would agree to the unification of the three Western zones or the restoration of German

[39] For the Soviet Treaty see 'Treaty on the Demilitarization of Germany and Prevention of German Aggression', 14 April 1947, National Archives, RG 43 Box. For earlier British and French views on the Ruhr and Rhineland see Bullen and Pelly, *British Policy*, pp. 191–2.
[40] FO/371/64160, telegram from William Strang, 1 November 1947.
[41] *FRUS 1948*, vol. 2, 1973, p. 60, memorandum of 11 February 1948 and State Department paper, 'Security against Germany'.

industry. The British government favoured allied military occupation of the Ruhr and Rhineland for forty years as the best way of dealing with a revival of the German threat. British, French, and Benelux representatives met US officials to discuss the problem in London in February 1948. The US representative stressed the overriding importance of the Soviet threat, though he also told Washington that the French would need some sort of guarantee against Germany.[42] Marshall replied that the administration might be prepared to give the sort of guarantee of US assistance which had been implicit in the Byrnes treaty. In the event this gradually evolved into the North Atlantic Treaty, which was signed the following year, committing the allies to consider an attack on one of them as an attack on all. It was to be another five years before the NATO allies began the rearmament of the Federal Republic of Germany, but the premises on which the Byrnes treaty had been based were already discarded.

THE LESSER ENEMY POWERS

The division between East and West also determined the treatment of the lesser enemy powers. By 1946 Soviet armies were occupying Hungary, Bulgaria, and Romania, just as the Western armies dominated Italy. Draft peace treaties with the defeated enemies were prepared by the Council of Foreign Ministers in July 1946 and amended at the Paris Peace Conference, where all the victorious nations were represented. The draft treaties proposed the detailed arms limitations on the lesser enemy powers outlined in Table 4. These were much less ferocious than the restrictions placed on Hungary, Bulgaria, and Austria in 1919. Hungary and Bulgaria were allowed more than twice as many men under arms as they had been after the First World War. They were also allowed to maintain air forces and larger naval forces. In 1919 the allies had tried to restrict the forces of the former enemy powers so that they were capable only of maintaining internal order; now this was clearly no longer the case.

In any case, as the Cold War intensified, only the neutral states were to be restricted for any length of time.[43] Italy was almost immediately co-opted into the Western security system and NATO.

[42] *FRUS 1946*, vol. 2, pp. 93, 111, 12
[43] The original draft peace treaties are in *FRUS 1946*, vol. 4, 1970.

Table 4   Postwar treaty limits for the forces of the lesser enemy powers.

	Army personnel	AA	Navy	Ships	Air Force	Aircraft
Romania	120,000	5,000	5,000	15,000 tons	8,000	150 (100 combat)
Bulgaria	55,000	1,800	3,500	7,250 tons	5,200	90 (70 combat)
Hungary	65,000 (includes AA and river flotilla)				5,000	90 (70 combat)
Finland	34,400		4,500	10,000 tons	3,000	60
Italy	185,000 (plus 65,000 carabinieri)		22,500	specified 25,000 2 battleships/16 torpedo-boats 4 cruisers/4 fleet destroyers 20 corvettes		350

Pressure to abolish the limitations on Italian forces intensified and in 1951 the US, Britain, and France agreed to nullify the restrictions imposed four years before.[44] In Eastern Europe the treaties were simply put to one side. The Western Powers were never allowed to verify that Romania, Hungary, and Bulgaria were abiding by the terms laid down. Hungary surpassed the treaty limits in 1948, when it bought 102 aircraft from Czechoslovakia and the Soviet Union, and manpower restrictions were exceeded by the army two years later.[45] By 1968, Western governments estimated that all the former enemy powers, except Finland, had far more military power than the treaties had originally allowed, as Table 5 makes clear.[46]

Table 5   Force levels of the former enemy powers in 1968.

	Army	Navy	Ships	Air Force	Aircraft
Romania	150,000	8,000	63 small coastal vessels	15,000	240 combat
Bulgaria	125.000	6,000	2 destroyers 29 small coastal vessels	22,000	250 combat
Hungary	95,000			7,000	140 combat
Finland	31,400	2,000	3 frigates 46 small coastal vessels	3,000	50 combat
Italy	265,000	40,000		60,000	400 combat

Faced with an enemy as vile as the Nazis and a war which produced tens of millions of dead and left many of the world's most productive regions in ruins, it was hardly surprising that allied leaders should expend so much effort on ways of preventing the revival of

[44] I. Poggiolini and L. Nuti, 'The Italian Peace Treaty of 1947' in F. Tanner (ed.), *From Versailles to Baghdad: Post-War Armaments Control of Defeated States* (UNIDIR, 1992), pp. 36 ff.

[45] M. Fulop, 'The military clauses of the Paris Peace Treaties with Roumania, Bulgaria and Hungary', in Tanner, *From Versailles to Baghdad*, pp. 51 ff.

[46] ISS, *The Military Balance 1968–1969* (London, 1968).

the enemy powers. Their discussions were not as dispassionate, analytical, and authoritative as those carried on by their predecessors in 1815, but the very nature of the alliance militated against agreement on first principles. They were divided over the demarcation of Europe's frontiers, reparations, and the complexion of the governments of the smaller powers.

Stalin was in a position to reduce conquered nations to colonial status; the democracies could occupy them temporarily but they could plan neither for permanent occupation nor for the destruction of the enemy peoples or their economies. When the Morgenthau plan was leaked to the US press in 1944, it caused an outcry. British and US policy-making was thus circumscribed by the leaders' own ethical standards and by what they believed was acceptable to the informed public. In 1815 and 1919 British leaders said that the public demanded more stringent peace terms than they would themselves have chosen. In 1945 public opinion polls might show a widespread desire for vengeance, but the political elite and the media regarded this as totally unacceptable. Even Nazi leaders had to be tried by the courts. Reparations could not be imposed upon starving peoples and, if Germans were to be moved from Poland, it should be with the minimum of violence. Stalin faced no such limitations, but he did not want to appear too bloodthirsty to Churchill and Roosevelt. In a roundabout way Western public opinion thus had some impact on at least the public face of Soviet policy.

Partition was acceptable in principle to the Western elite and it was conceivable that Germany might have been deliberately divided in that way, though most Western planners were deeply sceptical. In any case, such a policy was never seriously advanced for Japan and Italy. Because the war represented a clash of civilizations, democratic capitalism against Nazism, Fascism, and Oriental imperialism, re-education in the virtues of democracy became an important part of Western policy; however, this modern version of forced religious conversion had never been tried before on any scale and it was rightly regarded with some caution.

It was partly because of the lack of alternative ways of strengthening allied postwar security that Churchill emphasized forced disarmament as the main policy for weakening the enemy and preventing another war. The plan had electoral appeal, as the response to Senator Vandenberg's 10 January speech made clear. It was supported by the idealists, who saw it as a step towards general disarmament, and by the realists, who simply wanted to reduce the power of former enemies. Thus, despite all the difficulties encountered in Germany in the 1920s, forced disarmament became the core of British and, to some extent, of Anglo-American policies.

All Western leaders can be faulted for their lack of realism and prescience. Throughout the war years Churchill and Roosevelt had overlooked the ways in which current enemies become allies in the next struggle. Each generation believes that its circumstances are unique, and the nature of the Nazi regime and the total character of the war made it easy for even the most astute and realistic of leaders to ignore the way wartime coalitions fall apart once victory has been achieved. Yet, within a decade, Japan, Italy, and the Federal Republic of Germany had become major links in the Western alliance system, while Bulgaria, Hungary, and Romania were founder members of the Warsaw Pact.

But the Soviets also miscalculated. In retrospect, we can see that it was in their interest to accept the Byrnes treaties. The West gained far more from the rearmament of the Federal Republic of Germany, Italy, and Japan than the Soviets gained from the re-armament of the East European states and the German Democratic Republic. US troops remained in Europe even though the Byrnes treaties were rejected. Had they signed the treaties, the Soviets could have found ways of circumventing or restricting allied inspection in Eastern Europe. Stalin was no better than Western leaders at seeing more than two moves ahead in the international chess game.

8

The Disarmament of Germany
after the Second World War

In striking contrast to the situation after the First World War, Germany offered virtually no resistance to its disarmament by the allies in 1945. Effective opposition would have been much more difficult than in the 1920s because the allies occupied every part of the country, the German armed forces were utterly crushed, and the power available to the allies was far greater than it had been twenty-five years earlier. There was no central German government or clandestine general staff to plan resistance. However, the Germans could have waged guerrilla warfare against the allies had they had the will to do so. It was the will to resist which had largely died with the defeat and the revelation of Nazi atrocities.[1]

The main difference between Germany and Japan was that Germany was allowed no government of its own in 1945 and was divided into four occupation zones. The form of Japan's demilitarization was largely determined by the United States, but it worked through a Japanese government and the Emperor retained his title. The Soviets protested against their lack of influence in Japan, but they would have protested much more strongly if they had had no say in German disarmament. Germany was regarded as much the most fearsome enemy in 1945, and the importance of destroying German power was correspondingly greater. The allied occupation

[1] For allied policy towards Germany in 1945 see *The Memoirs of Harry S. Truman: Year of Decision* (Hodder and Stoughton, London, 1956), pp. 220 ff.; R. Murphy, *Diplomat among Warriors* (Greenwood Press, Conn., 1964), pp. 226, 180 ff.; H. Zink, *The United States in Germany 1944–1955* (Van Nostrand, Princeton, 1957); E. N. Peterson, *The American Occupation of Germany: Retreat to Victory* (Wayne State University Press, Detroit, 1977); D. Botting, *In the Ruins of the Reich* (Allen and Unwin, London, 1985); N. Annan, *Changing Enemies: The Defeat and Regeneration of Germany* (Harper Collins, London, 1995); J. Cloake, *Tiger of Malaya: The Life of Field Marshal Sir Gerald Templer* (Harrap, London, 1985), pp. 149 ff.

zones were intended to be temporary, but the intensification of the Cold War made reunification less and less likely. As a British official put it in February 1946, 'a German puppet regime for the Soviet Zone will now soon be an accomplished fact . . . We can kiss goodbye to democracy on the Western pattern for what is practically half of pre-war Germany.'[2]

As arguments over partition and reparations intensified, the drive put into disarming Germany steadily diminished. There were really only two years when a major effort was made. They were also the years when it was most difficult to keep the German people from starving and so the tension between rebuilding Germany for humanitarian and economic reasons and curbing its military potential was most acute. From 1945 to 1947 the allies tried to reduce German power in three ways: by destroying German military equipment, demobilizing military personnel, and undermining its industrial capacity to make war.

The destruction of German weapons and equipment was physically the most difficult and politically the easiest of these tasks. Finding weapons scattered around the battlefields of Europe took time. The actual destruction of the weapons was sometimes dangerous. Much was done which would be inconceivable in a more environmentally conscious age. The British threw hundreds of thousands of tons of highly toxic chemicals into the North Sea. The allies protested only that they were not proceeding quickly enough.

The demobilization of German personnel was administratively the most difficult of the three types of demilitarization. The task of screening not only 11 million German troops but hundreds of thousands of former soldiers from other parts of Europe to assess whether they had committed war crimes proved beyond allied resources. But, at the time, far more tension was caused by the Western policy of using German soldiers as labourers to clear minefields and repair damage than by failures in the screening process. Although the Soviets kept millions of German prisoners for the same purposes, they constantly complained about the Western decision to do so because they alleged that troops had not been effectively demobilized.

The destruction of German industrial capacity to prevent a resurgence of militarism proved conceptually the most difficult

---

[2] FO/371/55586, C 1480, minute by Franklin, 9 February 1946.

issue of all. This problem had surfaced during the war with the Morgenthau plan. It caused increasing tension between the Soviet Union on one side and the British and Americans on the other. The British zone included the German industrial heartland of the Ruhr. Much of it was ruined by bombing and the people were near to starvation, partly because they were cut off from the farmlands in the Soviet zone. Within months, if not weeks, it became obvious that, unless millions were to die of famine, the priority must be reconstruction, not reparations or demilitarization. The Americans came to the same decision slightly later, the French at a still later date, and the Soviets never openly accepted the point at all. They complained constantly that no destruction of Germany's industrial capacity had taken place in the Western zones. The bitterness with which this issue and the linked problem of reparations were pursued was both a symptom of the Cold War and a cause of its intensification.

GERMAN RESISTANCE TO DISARMAMENT

It is inaccurate to say that there was absolutely no German resistance to the occupation, but it was far less than expected and caused very little concern to the occupation forces. In November 1945 the British reported that some sabotage had taken place and a few stores of hidden arms had been discovered. In particular, some Hitler Jugend had apparently hidden ammunition and explosives.[3] In January 1946 there were attempts to block roads in the Hanover area. The following month there was a case of sabotage, a small cache of arms was discovered at Eckernforde, and some explosives on the island of Borkum.[4] In May 1946 there were nine separate discoveries of arms and a sabotage attempt against an ammunition dump near Brunswick. Fortunately, the British managed to control the fire; otherwise a poison gas store containing phosgene would have been destroyed, with dire effects on the Germans living nearby. Machinery in a steelworks near Brunswick had also been damaged several times.[5] In November 1946 the British noted, 'no

[3] FO/371/55380, C 10, BAOR Disarmament Progress Report no. 6, month ending 15 November 1945.
[4] FO/371/55380, C 3545, BAOR Disarmament Progress Report no. 9, month ending 15 February, 1946.
[5] FO/371/55384, C 7614, BAOR Disarmament Progress Report no. 12, month ending 15 May 1946.

major acts of sabotage have been reported during the last month though the type and seriousness of incidents has increased slightly.' These included four attacks on allied personnel and two explosions and attempted explosions. In February 1947 the British reported three explosions and two fires, but none was serious.[6] Some secret arms caches had been discovered and a few German suspects arrested. In March 1947 the British did find some exiguous sort of German 'underground movement' in Bremen and Stade. There was little public reaction in Germany when arrests were made.[7]

Such isolated cases of resistance were barely noted in the occupation reports. Compared with the difficulty of dealing with millions of refugees, feeding a vast population, and restarting the economy, they were regarded as insignificant. Occupation forces were hardly needed in the primary military role, although their administrative and organizational skills could play a very important part. The American army had tried to train specialists for this purpose during the war, but their plans had been hindered by Roosevelt's refusal to allow advance planning. The Morgenthau plan was rejected, but its legacy was seen in US orders against fraternizing with Germans or allowing any former Nazis to occupy positions of importance. Both policies proved completely impractical.[8] The other Western allies had made even less provision, though this at least made it easier for them to take the common-sense decision to allow some former Nazi party members to carry out routine tasks. Mistreatment of the German population was frequent. There were numerous rapes and thefts, but still there was remarkably little active German resistance.[9] If disarmament eventually failed, it was certainly not because the Germans undermined allied efforts.

DESTRUCTION OF GERMAN MILITARY EQUIPMENT

There was no disagreement with the idea that German military equipment had to be destroyed unless one of the four powers wanted to assess its utility for their own forces. Most military

[6] FO/371/64154, C 43/2/18, Disarmament Progress Report no. 18, month ending 15 November 1946; FO/371/64157, C 6025, BAOR Disarmament Progress Report no. 21, month ending 7 February 1947.
[7] FO/371/64155 C 4520.
[8] Murphy, *Diplomat among Warriors*, pp. 283–4; Zink, *The United States in Germany*, p. 135.
[9] Murphy, *Diplomat among Warriors*, p. 293; Botting, *In the Ruins*, p. 16.

equipment came under Schedule A which had to be destroyed; conversely, Schedule B equipment could be retained if it had some civilian applications. Equipment such as detonators, which could be used in quarries, came under Schedule B and could be kept for that purpose. But should the Germans be allowed to manufacture dynamite for mining? The Czechs believed that they had enough capacity to supply all Germany's civilian requirements. On the other hand, if the Germans could not manufacture equipment of this sort, another German factory was left without a role and there were more civilians in need of allied assistance.[10]

Conventional ammunition was destroyed, while chemical weapons were thrown into the sea. By December 1945 nearly 80,000 tons had been disposed of in this way.[11] In May 1946, 4,000 tons a week were being taken out in ships from Wilhelmshaven and 3,000 tons from Lübeck. In November 1946, 5,007 tons of chemical weapons were taken out to sea from Emden. The rate of such dumping depended upon the weather and the availability of ships. In February 1947 only 318 tons were dumped because the ports were ice-bound.[12] The other allies tended to regard such explanations as excuses and put pressure on the British authorities to speed up the process.

Sometimes it was actually difficult to find all the weapons abandoned, hidden, or wrecked in areas devastated by battles. The British reported that this was especially the case in the heavily wooded areas round Aachen. Nevertheless, by 1947 the British had destroyed 1866 tanks, 1,362 single-engined aircraft, 277 warships, and 264 submarines. The French had destroyed 250 tanks and 400 single-seat aircraft; the Soviets had demolished 5,730 tanks, 3,820 aircraft, 34 warships, and 94 submarines. Meanwhile, the US occupation forces had destroyed 2,016 tanks, 4,780 single-seat aircraft, 20 warships, and 21 submarines.[13]

Occupying powers could keep items of enemy equipment they wanted for testing and research. The British authorities compiled a list of 122 items of technical interest which they hoped to find in

---

[10] FO/371/55384, C 6947.

[11] FO/371/55380, C 1122, BAOR Disarmament Progress Report no. 7, month ending 15 December 1945.

[12] FO/371/64157, C 6025, BAOR Disarmament Progress Report no. 21, month ending 7 February 1947.

[13] FO/371/64154, 'Progress report on disposal of German war material in British Zone', to January 1947.

their zone and send back to Britain for assessment. However, only six of these could be found in November 1945, and there were increasing doubts about whether there really were examples of the wanted equipment within the zone.[14] Nevertheless, 125 different types of ammunition were sent to Britain for examination during that month alone and 180 tons of radar equipment were ready to be sent to Woolwich Arsenal when transport became available.

The sheer volume of destruction to be carried out caused problems. In January 1947 the British representative on the Co-ordinating Committee of the Allied Control Committee reported that they had still to destroy 160 airfields; another 92 were in use by the British services and 156 by the Control Commission.[15] Sometimes the authorities put on demonstrations to illustrate the scale of the tasks demanded of them. The British used 6,700 tons of explosives to destroy the various military facilities on Heligoland. The eighty journalists invited to the scene watched the smoke rise to 7,000 feet. The problems involved were practical. There were shortages of engineers to overcome them, but there was never any doubt that they would be overcome and that Germany would be comprehensively disarmed by the end of 1947.

ARMED FORCES PERSONNEL

The allies faced daunting administrative difficulties before they could disperse the German armed forces. For every soldier the Prussians had when Napoleon set out to reduce their power in 1808, the Germans had about 100 in 1945. The allies also faced highly sensitive political problems in 1945 of a type which were not met with elsewhere or in previous cases of forced disarmament. While all the soldiers returned to Japan were of Japanese nationality, in Germany millions of soldiers of various nationalities were mixed together. Some wanted to return to their homes; others knew that to return meant certain death. There were regiments of General Anders's Polish army whose country was now under Soviet control. There was also the Royal Yugoslav Army, whose country was dominated by Tito and his bloodthirsty partisans. Some of these minorities had committed war crimes; others were accused of

---

[14] See note 3 above.
[15] FO/371/64154, Allied Control Committee Authority Coordinating Committee, January 1947.

doing so, even if they were innocent. Verification of such accusations would have taken years, even if it had been possible at all. In the British zone alone at the end of 1945 there were 3,200 Estonians and 21,000 Lithuanians and Latvians whose countries had been seized and absorbed by the Soviet Union. At the end of the war the Soviets enjoyed accusing the allies of harbouring such 'war criminals' and demanding their return. But the British felt that this was to gain a propaganda advantage, rather than because they really wanted the Baltic citizens repatriated.[16]

Conditions in Germany were inevitably very harsh. Long before their victory the British and Americans had been convinced that they would not be able to treat all surrendered personnel as prisoners of war. They could not find the food to give them the same rations as allied soldiers, and this was what international law would have demanded. Instead, in a remarkable sleight of hand, they were categorized as disarmed enemy personnel. In June 1945 demobilized soldiers, who worked for the allies, were allowed 2,900 calories a day, non-working ex-soldiers were given 2,000 calories, and civilians 1,550. Until provisions could be moved around more easily, fertilizer could be produced, and the first postwar harvest had been gathered, little more could be done.[17]

The numbers of enemy personnel over-taxed the administrative capacity of the allied armies. Demobilized soldiers poured into Germany from all parts of the former German Empire—340,000 came from Scandinavia alone. By the middle of November 1946, 2.8 million soldiers had come to the British zone, nearly 44,000 had left for the Soviet zone, and nearly 375,000 had gone to the US zone. According to a US report in June 1946, 8 million personnel had passed through their zone and been disarmed. Of those still being held, 143,437 were in labour units, while 75,594 were detained because they had been in the SS and over 20,000 were in hospitals. Among those interned there were 22 admirals, 661 army generals, 182 air-force generals, 37 generals of para-military organizations, and 398 general staff officers of field rank.[18]

Numbers caused administrative problems; what gave rise to

[16] FO/371/55480, C 1788, Foreign Office minute to Wilberforce in Control Office, 1 March 1946. See also Annan, *Changing Enemies*, p. 155.
[17] WO/219/192, SHAEF message 2 June 1945; Cloake, *Templer*, p. 155.
[18] FO/371/55385, C 8005, 'Status report on demilitarization and industrial disarmament—US zone'. On numbers of ex-soldiers from Scandinavia see WO/219/192, SHAEF X15/23.

more tension than anything else was the British (and, to a lesser extent, the American) decision to use German prisoners of war for mine clearance and other labouring tasks. In May 1945, when the surrender took place, the British immediately began to allow German staff officers to command these groups because there was such a shortage of allied officers.[19] Not only were the British short of troops, but they thought it was appropriate that German soldiers should carry out such difficult and dangerous jobs as mine clearance.[20] In May 1946 the British were employing 120,000 officers and men in these ways. The numbers gradually decreased, and in the three Western zones there were only some 93,500 by the beginning of 1947.

Although the Soviets used former German soldiers in exactly the same way and in far greater numbers, they began in December 1945 to claim that the British had not demobilized the German army within their zone. The British admitted that ex-soldiers sometimes wore uniform, but said that it was difficult to stop this as they often had nothing else to wear.[21] However, this provided marvellous propaganda for the Soviets. In February 1946 the *Red Star* maintained that the Soviets had disarmed their part of Germany, but that 'a very different picture is presented in the Western occupation zones.' The British had kept German minesweepers in action from Kiel and German soldiers were still in formations elsewhere. The Royal Yugoslav Army and General Anders's Poles had formations in Germany.[22] The allies in turn complained that they had no information about the 3 million ex-soldiers they believed the Soviets were still holding and forcing to work for them.

Despite their angry reaction to Soviet accusations, the British had set up 'operation Clobber' to speed the demobilization of personnel well before the *Red Star* attack quoted above. Within a month from the middle of December 1945 to the middle of January the following year they dispersed no less than 250,000 ex-soldiers.[23] Unfortunately, these efforts were undercut when the well-known American columnist, Walter Lippmann, added his voice to the

[19] WO/219/192, minute 31 May 1945.
[20] FO/371/64154, BAOR Disarmament Progress Report, no. 18, month ending 15 November 1946, paragraph 6; see also FO/371/64155 C 4513.
[21] FO/371/55480, C 1788, Allied Control Authority, 11 February 1946.
[22] FO/371/64154, *Red Star*, article, 2 February 1947, translated.
[23] FO/371/55380, C 2104, BAOR Disarmament Progress Report, no. 8, month ending 15 January 1946.

Soviets' criticisms. In May 1946 he repeated allegations in his *Herald Tribune* column that armed Wehrmacht officers were operating in the British sector.[24] The Soviet press then began to quote Lippmann's article, while the British encouraged other journalists to refute his claims. The *New York Times* editorial said that the British and Americans had already disproved Soviet charges of this sort. Edgar Mowrer in the *New York Post* denied Lippmann's assertion that the British had fenced off their zone with a 'silken curtain' to keep out foreign journalists. The British commander in Germany, General Sir Brian Robertson, wanted to invite Lippmann to come to the British zone. But the Ambassador in Washington, Lord Inverchapel, said that Lippmann would interpret this either as flattery or an attempt to rub his nose in his humiliation.[25]

The Americans mentioned the various accusations at the Paris Foreign Ministers' Conference and proposed that the four powers should carry out inspection to end such rumours. The British said they had no objection if all zones were equally open to inspection.[26] Bevin came to feel that even Byrnes had some suspicions about what his country was doing. Similarly, General Robertson's political adviser said that he suspected the American commander, General Clay, of inspiring Lippmann's reference to the 'silken curtain'.[27]

Articles flowed into the Foreign Office from capitals as far away as Lima in Peru, reproducing Lippmann's criticisms. The British Embassy in Paris also reported that the French press were very critical of British policy. Many believed Lippmann was right and that the British were building up their zone against the Soviet Union, arming Germans and opposing French policy in the Rhineland and Ruhr.[28] General Robertson did his best to refute such criticisms by telling the press that 'there was only one way of ensuring that the German people would not seek to reorganize themselves for war—to change the heart of the German people and to direct their energies to the pursuits of peace, and, while it was not easy to undo the work of centuries, the British authorities had set themselves to this task.' Robertson welcomed any journalists who wanted to visit the British zone.[29]

[24] FO/371/55381, C 5176.
[25] FO/371/55383, C 6133 and C 6348. Inverchapel telegram 5 June 1946.
[26] FO/371/55381, C 5276.
[27] FO/371/55382, C 5451, telegram to Strang, 13 May 1946.
[28] FO/371/55384, C 6651, Duff Cooper letter, 7 June 1946.
[29] 'British Zone of Germany', *The Times*, 15 June 1946.

Upset by Soviet accusations at the Paris Foreign Ministers' conference, Bevin told the Foreign Office, 'I must have a clean bill of
health on this and be sure that I have lived up to Potsdam. I would
be grateful if you would have the most searching inquiries made in
the War Office, Control Office and Control Commission' about
the disarmament of the British zone.[30] Consequently, the British
appointed a commission under Major-General R. G. Stone to visit
Germany to look into the various allegations. However, the Allied
Control Commission accepted the US proposal that there should be
a joint investigation. The British decided that General Stone's
commission should be integrated with this.

British commanders in Germany were not opposed to a four-
power investigation, although they pointed out that the Soviets
might be suspicious of the former German military scientists living
close to research establishments and working for the British. They
offered to send 300 of them to Britain. There was particular
concern about the naval research establishment at Minden. Here
nine German scientists and their assistants were working under
British direction. The centre had been set up by the Admiralty in
October 1945 to study advances in German gun aiming and in
guided missiles. Given the 'threat' of an international investigation,
the government decided to close the establishment immediately
and prepare to move the scientists to Britain.[31] Minden was one of
ten military research establishments in the British zone which the
allies had agreed to close or convert. One had been so devastated
by bombing that it could be ignored. Three were cleared for other
work, and three more were made unserviceable in June 1946. The
Trauen rocket-motor establishment was to be moved to Britain;
sixteen of the forty staff were offered posts there, though the British
knew the French were offering better terms.[32] Twenty of the eighty-
six scientists at an aeronautical laboratory were also offered posts
in Britain.

In the meantime, plans for the four-power investigation ran into
increasing trouble. The British wanted the investigators to fan out
and look at all zones simultaneously, rather than give the Soviets
opportunity to make propaganda about conditions in the British
zone. The Soviets wanted to investigate each in turn. The British

[30] FO/371/55384, C 6934G, Bevin to Prime Minister, 13 May 1946.
[31] FO/371/55384, C7336 and C 6931.
[32] Ibid.

wanted the group to make sure that economic disarmament was taking place; the Soviets said there was no economic disarmament in the Western zones and thus nothing to investigate.[33] The Soviets were determined to make sure that allied inspectors could not see what they were doing with industries within their own zone. Consequently, General Stone's investigation eventually went ahead on its own, though it was hardly likely than an investigation in the British zone by a serving British officer would convince any hostile foreigner of Britain's good intentions, let alone the Russians.[34]

THE CONTROL OF GERMAN INDUSTRY

The allies agreed at Potsdam that the ability of German industry to produce weapons and military equipment should be reduced as far as possible, without so impoverishing the country as to make it a permanent drain on allied resources. Reparations should be extracted, though Germany should be provided with a standard of living comparable with but not above the rest of Europe.[35] The British, who were occupying much of the German industrial heartland, initially interpreted this to mean that German industry should be reduced by one-third over the 1938 level. Aircraft manufacture would be ended, metal and engineering industries would be reduced by 60 per cent, private consumption and food consumption would be between 25 and 30 per cent less than in 1938. All this lent a spurious notion of precision, which was remote from the situation on the ground. In practice, the British authorities found themselves caught between German efforts to feed their hungry population by infringements of the letter of allied agreements, for example, by building deep-sea trawlers, and allied criticism that they were being too generous to the Germans.

Gradually, as after the First World War, factories were cleared for civilian production. In April 1946, 42 factories were given clearance, making 600 so far in the British zone. At the same time, the British had to destroy some German industries which could have helped in reconstruction. One official minuted on the devastation wrought on German shipbuilding: 'we cannot go back on this now but it is a pity that this sort of apparently wanton destruction

[33] FO/371/55384, C C 6862, Soviet note 11 June 1946.
[34] FO/371/55384, C 6670/G.
[35] FO/371/55586, C 3216, Draft plan by Chancellor of the Duchy of Lancaster.

has to take place when food and materials are so short in the British zone.'[36] The trades unions and the local government in Hamburg protested strongly against what was going on and the *Burgermeister* resigned over the issue. The British view was that this was 'the first large scale example of what is to come and may be regarded as a test case'.[37] But, if this made the Foreign Office hesitate, the Admiralty argued vigorously that any German shipbuilding industry would always be a threat to Britain and to British shipbuilding.[38]

One group of British officials argued that it was 'desirable to ensure the substantial completion of necessary measures of industrial disarmament while public opinion in this country is prepared to support them'.[39] Any equipment of use to Britain should be seized to offset the costs of occupation. But there were equally vociferous proponents of the view that this would simply impoverish Germany and threaten Europe's recovery as a whole. In the meantime, the destruction went on. The great gantries at the Blohm and Voss works, where the battleship *Bismarck* had been built, were blown up, producing 11,000 tons of girders.[40] This was precisely what the French and Soviets wanted to see. They produced a 'General Statement of the Problem' which pointed out that German industry had been the second strongest in the world in 1938 and that it had actually increased in power during the war years. Indeed, on French calculations, it was 75 per cent higher than in 1939 despite allied bombing.[41] Their aim was to make Germany totally dependent on the outside world for strategic materials and thus unable to plan further aggression—a somewhat dubious ambition since Hitler had justified his expansionism by the need to acquire sources of raw materials.

The Soviets were in a satisfactory position because, if the zones were treated separately, they had to increase industrial production in their zone to provide enough coal and steel for their factories. On the other hand, the British had to make very substantial

---

[36] FO/371/55383, C 6597/g, minute by Patrick Dean, 17 June 1946.
[37] FO/371/55384, C 6944, Control Commission paper on Germany.
[38] FO/371/55384, C 6941, Admiralty letter 18 June 1946.
[39] FO/371/55384, C 6941, draft telegram from Control Commission.
[40] FO/371/55385, C 8904, 'Progress of demilitarization in the British zone of occupied Germany'.
[41] FO/371/64155, Report to the Council of Foreign Ministers, 'Liquidation of German War and Industrial Potential', Appendix C.

reductions and there was fierce debate between the allies about how much steel the Ruhr should be allowed to produce. At first the limit was 5.8 million tons, but the British quickly asked for this to be raised to 7.5 millions.[42] Food was particularly scarce, and the British had very limited ability to assist the Germans because they were asking the United States for food for their own people.

General Robertson, who had to deal with the issue of disarmament in the British zone, told the allied Co-ordinating Committee in January 1946, 'the British government would not agree to the premise that, if starvation, misery and slavery were the result of demilitarization, they would have to be accepted. No civilized nation was entitled to impose such terms and the way to world peace did not lie along this path.'[43] The Soviet representative, Sokolovsky, argued that, if Robertson had his way and Germany again produced 7.5 million tons of steel, all other countries would be threatened. He also claimed that the allies had no responsibility to prevent German starvation. General Clay followed a middle position, regarding Robertson's arguments as somewhat emotional and Sokolovsky's as exaggerated.

The same arguments were repeated throughout 1946 and 1947, with the Americans moving gradually towards the British position. In March 1947 the Soviet delegate to the Council of Foreign Ministers claimed that 'gigantic plants, created especially for purposes of aggression, as those of Hermann Goering, Krupp, Robert Bosch, I. G. Farben and others . . . remain intact in Western Germany.'[44] The British replied that all plants would be under government ownership and thus safe from misuse. However, they did not know how much to allow the plants to produce, as Germany was not being treated as an economic unit. What was needed to make planning possible were statistics on all types of production in the Soviet zone.

Given the economic conditions in Germany in 1946, destroying industry or sending factories abroad as reparations on any scale was unacceptable to the democracies; separating the Ruhr from the rest of Germany was a more practical proposition. Thus both the

[42] Truman, *Year of Decisions*, p. 233.
[43] *Foreign Relations of the United States 1947*, vol. 5, p. 486, Murphy to Acting Secretary of State, 18 January 1946.
[44] FO/371/64155, C 4399, statement by Soviet delegate to Council of Foreign Ministers, 11 March 1947.

British and the French toyed with the idea, though the British doubted whether they or the Americans would keep enough troops on the continent to garrison the area in the long run. French plans would have separated the Rhineland, Ruhr, and Westphalia from Germany; 50,000 allied troops would occupy the Ruhr and an international consortium would run the mines and industry there, while the mines in the Saar would be owned by the French themselves.[45] In the British view, the merit of this approach was that it was a 'clear cut, logical scheme . . . free of the type of compromise that proves [sic] so unsuccessful in the Versailles settlement'.[46] However, British economic advisers were very critical of such schemes, as they were of proposals to reduce German industrial capacity. In any case, the gradual separation of the Soviet zone changed attitudes. If Germany was to be divided by the Soviets then it was unwise to weaken it still further by separating the Ruhr. Furthermore, the democracies began to worry that the Soviets might succeed in enticing the people in the other zones to join their own. In other words, they began to worry more about German opinion than about offending the Soviets or about keeping Germany disarmed.[47]

LONG-TERM PLANNING

During the war itself, allied leaders could talk in largely theoretical terms about ways of weakening Germany and Japan to maintain peace. Once the war ended, the allies were catapulted into the day-to-day problems of feeding the defeated nations, destroying their military equipment, and sending their soldiers back to their homes. But officials were still concerned about the long-term problem of disarmament. In 1946 the British officials on the Control Commission for Germany prepared a paper on the organization required for long-term control of the country. The officers involved emphasized the need for a co-operative effort between the four zones, a good intelligence organization, and personnel with specialized knowledge. The control organization required would have to be separated from the allied garrisons. The British Army of the Rhine

---

[45] FO/371/55586, C 3216, 'The Settlement of Western Germany'.
[46] Ibid.
[47] FO/371/55586, C 3216, Troutbeck minute of 12 February 1946. See also Annan, *Changing Enemies*, ch. 10.

would be Britain's mobile reserve, while the force needed to keep Germany disarmed would have to be static.[48] Reaction in the British Foreign Office was mixed. One official commented, 'a peaceful Germany depends on a sensible allied policy and not on these sorts of control.' Others disagreed and thought that it was a choice between separating the Ruhr or long-term inspection of the type proposed.[49]

It was just about this time that Secretary Byrnes sent the British government his plan for disarmament treaties and said that he wanted to discuss it with Bevin at the forthcoming Foreign Ministers' conference in Paris.[50] Once the Soviets rejected Byrnes's plan, the whole situation became fluid once again. At the end of 1946 the economies of the British and American zones were merged in what can now be seen as a major step towards the gradual emergence of the Federal Republic of Germany in 1949. The Soviets attempted from June 1948 to May 1949 to squeeze the Western powers out of Berlin by blocking the access routes. Eastern Europe disappeared behind the Iron Curtain and the West established the North Atlantic Treaty Organization in 1949. By then the question had become one of how French resistance to the rearmament of Germany could be overcome. In 1950 the Western Chiefs of Staff symbolically approved the formation of gliding clubs in Germany. The British Air Ministry noted they 'would form a useful rallying point for aviation skill and experience'. The British High Commissioner was advised in October 1950 that the RAF looked on the clubs with approval: 'there is a tremendous potential of highly trained German technicians available, which would be given valuable training and experience and eventually provide a sound nucleus for a revived German air force.'[51]

Finally, in October 1954 the Federal Republic of Germany was permitted under the Paris agreements to re-establish its armed forces. The following year it joined NATO and began a steady military build-up to 66,000 men in 1956 and 270,000 four years later. It was still not allowed to have nuclear, chemical, or biological weapons. Nor was it permitted to have long-range missiles, strategic bombers, warships over 3,500 tons, or submarines over

[48] FO/371/55380, C 2396, 'Organisation for Long-Term Control of Demilitarisation of Germany'.
[49] Ibid. Comments by Franklin, Troutbeck, Harvey, and Burrows.
[50] FO/371/55381, C 4581/G.   [51] AIR/8/1482.

350 tons. The Western European Union carried out on-site inspection to ensure that the treaty's terms were fulfilled. Gradually the terms were modified. Restrictions on warship construction were lifted in 1980 and the Western European Union removed the other limitations on conventional weapons four years later.[52] On the other hand, Germany has reaffirmed its renunciation of nuclear, chemical, and biological weapons by its adherence to other international agreements.

It is likely that, if the allies had not fallen out and if they had kept Germany disarmed for forty years under the Byrnes Treaties, opposition to such discrimination would gradually have developed within Germany. There was some feeling in the FRG in the 1970s against the restrictions on the right to build large warships and even some opposition to signing the Nuclear Non-Proliferation Treaty.[53] However, because Germany was partitioned until October 1990, most resentment was felt about this division rather than about discriminatory disarmament measures. Not only did partition damage the economy but it also divided families, while the Paris agreement affected only the armed forces and defence industries.

In the united, disarmed Germany which Byrnes envisaged, the situation would probably have been very different. Nor would the German people have been much mollified by the growth of their industrial and economic power, and the influence that brought them in world councils. By the time Germany was reunited the FRG alone had become one of the world's Great Powers with a gross domestic product of 1,500 billion dollars, compared with 1,187 billion dollars for France and 986 billion dollars for Britain.[54] A united Germany would have been even wealthier. The popular argument is usually that this should be matched by military power, rather than that Germany had benefited economically from not being encouraged to have military ambitions to match its economic strength.

Admittedly there were always groups in the FRG opposed to

[52] *Western European Union, Information Report*, 38th Ordinary Session, Second Part, February 1993, p. 9.

[53] For opposition to the continuation of conventional restrictions see F. Tanner (ed.), *From Versailles to Baghdad* (United Nations Institute for Disarmament Research, 1992), p. 96.

[54] IISS, *Military Balance 1991–2*, pp. 55, 58, 75.

increased military spending, and large numbers of young men opposed conscription as conscientious objectors.[55] Thus the FRG continually spent a smaller proportion of its wealth on defence than either Britain or France, 3.3 per cent of its GNP in 1971 compared with 3.9 per cent for France and 5 per cent for Britain. This was a product of the domestic consensus, because there was no obvious external pressure on Bonn to keep expenditure low. There have also been strenuous German objections to exporting weapons to the Third World and using the armed forces outside German territory, even for UN peace-keeping. However, it was naturally far easier for Germans to argue for self-limitation than it would have been to defend the Byrnes Treaties. Limitation by others is inevitably and rightly regarded as a reflection of a lack of trust.

For the first decade after the Second World War, if the Cold War had not broken out, Germany had been maintained as a unit, and the Byrnes Treaties had been signed, the treaties would have kept Germany disarmed without much effort. But, as time went on, they would probably have provoked resentment inside Germany against discrimination and resentment in other states that Germany was not doing enough to maintain international order. If a prolonged attempt had been made after the war to destroy German industry in the interests of disarmament, this would have vastly increased German resentment and made the situation far more explosive. Disarmament of the defeated powers was one of the first priorities laid down by Churchill and Roosevelt, but in practice it rightly took second place to the prevention of starvation and the restoration of civilized conditions.

[55] For German views see 'Europe and defence: a Guardian survey', *Guardian*, 16 February 1987.

9

The Disarmament of Japan
after the Second World War

Allied leaders spent far less time during the Second World War worrying about how to reduce the power of Japan after its defeat than worrying about how to control Germany. The Germans were regarded by the allies as by far the greater danger, but the Japanese were nevertheless also to be disarmed. The prospects for this proving anything but ephemeral seemed even less encouraging than in the German case. Japanese soldiers had fought with particular heroism in the Second World War, frequently refusing to allow themselves to be captured alive. It was improbable that a people who had produced such soldiers would passively accept the disarmament of their country.

The likelihood of Japanese resistance to their demilitarization appeared to be increased by their behaviour in the inter-war period. In the 1920s Britain and the United States had pressed the Japanese government to accept the Washington Treaty system, limiting the size of the navies of the Great Powers. This was welcomed by the Japanese Finance Ministry but bitterly resented by most of the armed forces. One of the leading Japanese admirals said that the war against the United States began the moment the treaty was signed in February 1922.[1] He and others regarded it as just as much an example of forced disarmament as the restrictions imposed on Germany by the Treaty of Versailles, and in the 1930s they compelled the government to refuse to renew the treaty and instead to prepare for war.

[1] S. Asada in D. Borg and S. Okamoto, *Pearl Harbor as History* (Columbia University Press, New York and London, 1973), p. 235. On allied policy in Japan after the surrender see F. S. Dunn, *Peace-making and the Settlement with Japan* (Princeton University Press, 1960); H. B. Schonberger, *Aftermath of War: America and the Remaking of Japan, 1945–1952* (Kent University Press, Ohio, 1989); K. Kawai, *Japan's American Interlude* (University of Chicago Press, 1960); I. Nish, *Anglo-Japanese Alienation, 1919–1952* (Cambridge University Press, 1982), part 3.

US leaders were sufficiently well aware of the way this process was dominated by the Japanese armed forces to distinguish in 1945 between the Japanese military leaders and the people as a whole. But opinion in the United States was generally more hostile to Japan than to Germany. One account, published in 1944, argued, 'Japan is a different sort of enemy. Of Japan, we may find it necessary to dispose once and for all, so that danger from that source may not again trouble the civilized world.' The administration had to be strong enough to ignore such views.[2] On the Japanese side, the officials and statesmen who came to power after the surrender also frequently blamed their military leaders for the disaster. They believed that Japan would have to concentrate on economic reform rather than on rebuilding its military power, if the country were to recover its position in the international system. Thus there was a meeting of minds from 1945 to 1947 between the US occupiers and senior Japanese authorities.[3]

The Second World War broke the power of the old military elites in both Japan and Germany, and prevented them from opposing forced disarmament. So great was the trauma of defeat that the majority of the population in the two countries accepted the right of the allies to demobilize their forces. This made the demilitarization of the Axis powers quite different from the other cases discussed in this book, in which disarmament was bitterly resented and evaded by the vanquished states. Indeed, but for the Japanese and German cases, historians would argue that such resistance was an inevitable and natural human response to forced disarmament.

THE UNITED STATES AND THE DEMILITARIZATION OF JAPAN

Whereas the Americans, British, French, and Soviets shared power over Germany after its defeat, the United States could, to a large extent, formulate policy towards Japan on its own. The Soviets were not involved in the war against Tokyo until August 1945, and their influence was correspondingly reduced. Washington refused

---

[2] G. F. Eliot, *Hour of Triumph* (Reynal and Hitchcock, New York, 1944), p. 155. For the US administration's views see *The Memoirs of Harry S. Truman: Year of Decision 1945* (Hodder and Stoughton, London, 1955), p. 395. On other wartime attitudes see J. Dower, *War Without Mercy; Race and Power in the Pacific War* (Faber, London, 1986).

[3] See particularly Akio in Nish, *Anglo-Japanese Alienation*, part 3.

to allow them the separate occupation zone in Japan which they coveted. On their side, the Soviets refused to send troops to serve under a US commander.[4] To try to reduce Soviet resentment at their exclusion from real power, Byrnes established two committees on which they could be represented, the Far Eastern Commission in Washington and an Allied Council for Japan in Tokyo. However, the two bodies rapidly became locked in wrangles. They were, for example, unable to decide how to divide the reparations which the devastated and half-starved Japanese were supposed to pay. Their influence was marginal and the American occupation authorities treated them with contempt.[5]

US planners had been working for a number of years on policy towards Japan. In March 1944 they argued that the harshness of occupation policy should be increased in proportion to Japanese resistance. They were not in favour of trying the Japanese Emperor but of isolating him from his people and encouraging any anti-imperial feelings. They believed that the country would have to be occupied for an extended period to discourage the revival of militarism.[6] In May 1944 they proposed that Japan should not be partitioned but that its government should be suspended. In the first phase of occupation the country would be completely de-militarized. In the second phase the US would establish permanent bases there to prevent a revival of militarism. Finally, in the third phase, a Japanese government would be re-established when it could be relied upon to act peacefully.[7]

The initial post-surrender policy document given to General MacArthur, the Supreme Allied Commander, when he was *en route* to Tokyo laid down that 'Japan will be completely disarmed and demilitarized. The authority of the militarists and the influence of the military will be totally eliminated from her political, social, and economic life. Institutions expressive of the spirit of militarism and aggression will be vigorously suppressed.' Furthermore, the document continued, 'disarmament and demilitarization are the primary tasks of the military occupation and shall be carried out promptly and with determination.' The Japanese people were to be convinced

---

[4] T. W. Burkman (ed.), *The Occupation of Japan: The International Context* (MacArthur Memorial, Norfolk, Va, 1984), p. 19.

[5] FO/371/63692, F 15486.

[6] National Archives Washington, T 1221-2, CAC 120, 22 March 1944.

[7] *The Memoirs of Cordell Hull*, vol. 2 (Hodder and Stoughton, London, 1948), pp. 1598 ff.

that it was their military leaders who were responsible for their suffering.[8]

Demobilization was carried out as soon as the millions of Japanese soldiers could be brought back to Japan. Delays were caused by the size of the task involved and the shortage of transport. The British retained some of the soldiers for a while in Malaya to act as a labour force.[9] Such procrastination evoked protests from the Soviet representatives on the Far Eastern Commission. These in turn antagonized the Western countries, and the Americans eventually refused to give any more information about the repatriation process until the Soviets had told them what had happened to the Japanese army rounded up in Manchuria at the end of the war and carried off into Siberia.[10] The Soviets suspected that the British and Americans were retaining some Japanese military power for their own devices and refusing the radical economic and political transformation which they believed was necessary to prevent the re-emergence of militarism in Japan.[11] But these arguments showed more about the growth of the Cold War than about Japanese military power. The imperial forces had ceased to exist and former officers generally had little influence on the progress of events.

By October 1947 the American occupation forces had destroyed nearly 190,000 artillery pieces, 9,700 aircraft, and 2,393 tanks. Tens of thousands of pistols and swords had disappeared to the United States as souvenirs.[12] The Commonwealth Occupation Forces also reported that by May 1947 they had destroyed most of the Japanese military equipment found in their occupation zone, including 887 torpedoes, 400 incomplete torpedoes, 534 gun barrels, and 203 midget submarines. They had dumped 41,000 tons of munitions into the sea.[13] The process had been delayed by the difficulty of finding weapons, which were carefully camouflaged and spread among the islands to prevent their discovery by allied bombers. Nevertheless, with the help of large numbers of Japanese, the process was finally completed.

The Japanese attitude to disarmament was all of a piece with their failure to resist once their conventional armed forces had

[8] R. Buhite, *The Dynamics of World Power: A Documentary History of US Foreign Policy 1945–1973* (Chelsea House, New York, 1973), vol. 4, p. 10.
[9] FO/371/54381, F 9052 and 9976.
[10] FO/371/54282 F 11702, 'State of demobilization of Japanese armed forces'.
[11] Ibid
[12] FO/371/63795, F 14291.   [23] FO/371/63795, F 8212.

surrendered. As we have seen, after the French armed forces were defeated in 1940 a few Frenchmen fled abroad to continue the struggle under General de Gaulle. Some hoped for a time that the Vichy army would be able to assist the allies, while yet others set up resistance movements within France. There were similar guerrilla forces of greater or lesser size and determination in Yugoslavia, the Soviet Union, Poland, Malaya, and most of the other conquered territories. They brought down terrible reprisals on the heads of the civilian population but also did something to restore national morale and pride. Given that the Japanese armed forces had fought so much more effectively than the French, it was not unreasonable to expect the Japanese to continue the struggle as the French and others had done, but even more ferociously. Thus General MacArthur was given a 500,000-man occupation force. Within a month he was publicly declaring that this could soon be more than halved to 200,000 because there was no resistance to the American invaders, neither guerrilla warfare nor suicidal attacks nor effective assassination attempts. The British representative in the Far East reported in October 1945, 'in the present temper of the country I see no possibility of a reemergence of misgovernment or of an effective underground opposition in the foreseeable future.'[14]

Public opinion polls in the United States had shown support for savage reprisals against the defeated enemy; in June 1945 one poll found that a third of the US population was for hanging the Emperor and another third for putting him on trial. Popular hatred of Japan was such that, in December 1945, 22.7 per cent of Americans polled by *Fortune* magazine even expressed regret that more atomic bombs had not been dropped on Japanese territory.[15] Thus the Japanese had good cause for concern, despite reiterated claims by Churchill and other leaders that unconditional surrender 'does not mean that we stain our victorious arms by inhumanity or by mere lust for vengeance'.[16] US leaders declared that their policy was to democratize the country, and this sat ill with reprisals and retribution.

[14] For US views see Schonberger, *Aftermath of War*, p. 48. For British views see WO/203/5049.
[15] Dower, *War Without Mercy*, p. 54.
[16] W. Churchill, *The Second World War: The Hinge of Fate* (Reprint Society, London, 1953), p. 551.

US planners had discussed the possible application of Morgenthau's plan to Japan in April 1944.[17] This would have meant
reducing the country to handicraft industries and excluding it from
world trade. But the planners argued that, though this might have
been possible a hundred years before, the Japanese population had
grown from 30 to 75 millions and such numbers could not survive
in isolation. In any case future security would depend 'more and
more on how greatly Japanese attitudes, motivations, and policies
change and reduce the impetus towards war within Japan'. In the
meantime it was not unreasonable to destroy Japanese industries
which were not economically vital and which could be put to
military use, such as the aircraft industry. Any attempt to go further
and apply Morgenthau's ideas would be devastating.[18] The basic
good sense in this approach became more apparent as soon as the
occupation was established and the allies discovered just how close
the Japanese already were to mass starvation. When the Japanese
Ministry of Finance stated in October 1945 that 10 million would
die of famine in the next year, the British believed this to be an
exaggeration, but they did not dismiss the danger.[19]

THE NEW JAPANESE CONSTITUTION

From 1944 onwards US planners argued that the Japanese armed
forces would not just have to be reduced but that the country
would have to be completely demilitarized: 'Permission, such as
was granted to Germany after the last war, to retain the services in
capsule form would make extinguishment of Japanese military
traditions more difficult and would provide a nucleus for the
formation of a regular army, navy, and air force at a later date'.[20]
This became the conventional wisdom in the US administration
after the war and it was reflected in the new constitution drawn up
jointly by the Americans and Japanese. There is, however, dispute
about who took the initiative at the joint meetings to propose
Article 9 of the constitution which demilitarizes the country
in perpetuity. According to MacArthur, it was Prime Minister
Shidehara who suggested on 24 January 1946 that the constitution
should include a renunciation of war and MacArthur who wel-

[17] T 1221–3, CAC 194, 30 April 1944.
[18] Ibid.   [19] WO/203/5049.
[20] T 1221–2, CAC 194, 'Security policy vis-à-vis Japan', 30 April 1944.

comed the proposal. But the Japanese Prime Minister claimed in his memoirs that it was the American general who took the initiative. Moreover, the fact that the Japanese did not include such an idea in the draft constitution, which they passed to the Americans a week later, gives credence to the Japanese view.[21]

The constitution begins with a reference to war: 'we, the Japanese people . . . resolved that never again will we be visited by the horrors of war through the actions of government.' The theme is picked up again in Article 9, which echoes the Kellogg–Briand Pact of May 1928. This was familiar to many at that time because some of those Japanese leaders accused at the Tokyo war trials were alleged to have breached the pact. Thus Article 9 begins,

aspiring sincerely to an international peace based on justice and order, the Japanese people forever renounce war as a sovereign right of the nation and the threat or use of force as means of settling international disputes.

In order to accomplish the aim of the preceding paragraph, land, sea, and air forces, as well as other war potential, will never be maintained. The right of belligerency of the state will not be recognized.[22]

There was no argument between the government and the Americans about this Article and its implications, although it was modified by the Japanese Diet. One member, Asida Hitoshi, who later became Prime Minister, proposed the addition of the words 'aspiring to an international peace based on justice and order' and 'in order to accomplish the aim of the preceding paragraph'. Later he claimed that he inserted these phrases to justify the maintenance of some forces for the defence of Japan. After the acceptance of his amendments, he believed that the constitution allowed Japan to maintain self-defence forces, but he still argued later that it should be revised to make this clearer.[23]

The American authorities held, on the other hand, that Article 9 meant total disarmament. MacArthur stated forthrightly on 6 March 1947, 'by this undertaking and commitment Japan surrenders rights inherent in her own sovereignty and renders her future security and very survival subject to the good faith and

[21] J. K. Emmerson, *Arms, Yen and Power: The Japanese Dilemma* (Dunellen, New York, 1971), p. 50.
[22] Buhite, *Dynamics of World Power*, pp. 21 ff.
[23] Emmerson, *Arms, Yen and Power*, p. 52.

justice of the peace-loving peoples of the world.'[24] Reflecting this view, Prime Minister Yoshida asserted on 26 June, 'the provision of this draft concerning the renunciation of war does not directly deny the right of self-defence. However, since paragraph 2 of Article 9 does not recognize any military force whatsoever or the rights of belligerency of the state, both wars arising from the right of self-defence and the rights of belligerency have been renounced.'[25]

THE REVERSAL OF US POLICY

Ironically, by the time that the new constitution was passed, some members of the US administration were already thinking not of disarming the defeated but of rearming them to join in the struggle against communism. On 12 March 1947 the US President had already enunciated the 'Truman Doctrine', the promise to come to the assistance of states struggling against subversion. Within the US government the Policy Planning Staff, run by George Kennan, was calling for a united effort by the non-communist world to halt the expansion of communism. Kennan was increasingly anxious about plans to sign a peace treaty with Japan, which would lead to evacuation and to the abandonment of the country to its own devices.[26] In Kennan's view, 'the nature of the occupations policies pursued up to that time by General MacArthur's headquarters seemed on cursory examination to be such that, if they had been devised for the specific purpose of rendering Japanese society vulnerable to Communist political pressures and paving the way for a Communist takeover, they could scarcely have been other than they were.'[27] General MacArthur, not surprisingly, was unsympathetic to calls for a complete reversal of his policy. MacArthur dismissed the idea of a direct Soviet threat to Japan in a speech he made in March 1947. He thought it would be possible for the Japanese to have a small military establishment for their protection, but saw this as a retrograde step. Still reflecting the idealism of Cordell Hull's vision of the world, he believed it was preferable for the United Nations to assume responsibility for Japan's safety.[28]

[24] Emmerson, *Arms, Yen and Power*, p. 53.   [25] Ibid.
[26] G. Kennan, *Memoirs 1925-1950* (Hutchinson, London, 1968), p. 376.
[27] Ibid.
[28] See also Emmerson, *Arms, Yen and Power*, p. 66.

Nevertheless, there had always been military officers in the occupation who doubted the wisdom of the US demilitarization programme and reduced its effectiveness. One of the most prominent was General Charles Willoughby, MacArthur's close associate and head of intelligence. Willoughby was an admirer of Franco and Mussolini, and a fervent anti-communist. One of the histories of the period argues that Willoughby deliberately kept an embryonic Japanese general staff in existence by convening a group of senior Japanese officers for historical research. Local Assistance Bureaux of former soldiers were allowed by the Americans to reduce the suffering of discharged personnel but, in the course of their work, they also maintained a network of military contacts and kept open the possibility of re-establishing the army at a later date.[29]

In February 1948 George Kennan visited Japan and talked with MacArthur. Kennan believed that he had reached some agreement with the general, though he was increasingly anxious about what he saw in Tokyo. Kennan thought that MacArthur's radical agricultural and industrial reforms had caused confusion and that the occupation was a burden to the Japanese.[30] He also argued that too many Japanese had been purged because of their association with previous regimes. On his return to Washington, Kennan urged the end of reform legislation and greater emphasis on economic recovery.[31] On his side, MacArthur opposed the idea of re-establishing the Japanese armed forces, partly because he believed such a move would slow the pace of economic recovery. He remained doubtful of the need for the Japanese to protect themselves against invasion, but then Kennan's main fear was subversion, not invasion. MacArthur evidently regarded this too as exaggerated.[32] Thus he rejected the National Security Council's November 1948 proposal that Japan should recruit 150,000 policemen. It was not until after the outbreak of the Korean War in June 1950 that he reversed his policy and on 8 July called for the formation of a National Police Reserve of 75,000.[33]

By then, pressure in Washington for a reversal of policy was anyway becoming irresistible. John Foster Dulles, who was acting as an adviser on Japanese issues to the Secretary of State, was a

---

[29] M. Harries and S. Harries, *Sheathing the Sword: The Demilitarization of Japan* (Heinemann, London, 1987), pp. 220 ff.
[30] Kennan, *Memoirs*, pp. 391 ff.   [31] Ibid.
[32] Emmerson, *Arms, Yen and Power*, p. 66.   [33] Ibid.

determined advocate of negotiating a peace treaty with Japan and of re-establishing its armed forces: 'far distant from us and close to the Soviet Union, the US would assume an almost impossible burden in attempting its defence without any help from the Japanese themselves.'[34] Dulles expected strong opposition to rearmament from the Japanese public and from neighbouring states, but he felt this could be reduced by beginning with a strengthened police and coastal patrol force. US officials also rightly expected the Japanese economy to benefit from the Korean War, and this would reduce the burden presented by a resumed defence effort.[35]

The Joint Chiefs of Staff, chaired by Omar Bradley, also weighed into the debate. As though the Japanese had been disarmed for fifty years, Bradley argued, 'no sovereign state can forever avoid its responsibilities for its own security by relying upon an aura of goodwill among others when peaceful conditions are so seriously threatened as they are today. A military vacuum is a short-lived anomaly.'[36] The Joint Chiefs had suddenly discovered that Japan had an 'inalienable right' to possess its own armed forces, though this had certainly not been much in evidence when the Byrnes plan had been under discussion. They insisted that any peace treaty must avoid implying that Tokyo had somehow abandoned this right. On its side, the State Department was against inserting clauses into the treaty which implied either that the US would withdraw from Japan or that the Japanese would rearm. However, by September 1950 the Secretaries of State and Defence were able to write a joint memorandum to the President, which stated flatly that the peace treaty 'must not contain any prohibition, direct or implicit, now or in the future, of Japan's inalienable right to self-defense in case of external attack'.[37]

With the US so determined to alter its relationship to Japan, the Japanese themselves were forced to change policy. Prime Minister Yoshida was initially unenthusiastic but eventually signed peace and security treaties which gave Washington the right to maintain bases in his country. This was resented by many Japanese, who wanted US bases withdrawn altogether or confined to islands such

---

[34] *Foreign Relations of the United States 1950*, vol. 6, Dulles to Nitze, 20 July 1950.

[35] *FRUS 1950*, vol. 6, 1265, memorandum by R. A. Fearey, 8 August 1950.

[36] FRUS 1950, vol. 6, p. 1278, Bradley memorandum of 22 August 1950.

[37] *FRUS 1950*, vol. 6, p. 1297, memorandum for the President, 7 September 1950.

as Okinawa. The Soviets protested that the Americans were not allowed by the wartime agreements to sign separate peace treaties with the defeated states, and asked whether the Japanese were contemplating raising their own armed forces. Washington replied that, since 'irresponsible militarism' had not been driven from the world, it was reasonable for Japan to participate with the United States in individual and collective self-defence.[38]

The Japanese also formed a National Police Reserve, later renamed the Self-Defence Force. A convenient myth was developed that this was permitted under Article 9 of the constitution, even if armed forces as such were prohibited. By 1954 the Self-Defence Force numbered 146,000 and it steadily increased to 206,000 in 1960 and 266,000 in 1973. At the same time, the defence burden remained less than 1 per cent of gross national product because of the mighty growth of the Japanese economy. Even in absolute terms, Japanese defence spending was low. In 1972 Japan was spending 26 dollars a head on defence compared with 125 in Britain and 399 in the United States.[39] From 1945 to 1950 Japan was unusual in maintaining no armed forces of its own and genuinely keeping to Article 9. From 1950 to the present it has been unusual in devoting such a small part of its gross national product to defence and in maintaining the transparent pretence that armed forces equipped with some of the most advanced weapons in the world are somehow different because they have a different title.

THE JAPANESE VIEW OF DEFENCE AND DISARMAMENT

The discrediting of the Japanese military elite would not have been enough to allow Japan to be peacefully disarmed in 1945 had public attitudes not also changed fundamentally. After all, the Prussian army was discredited in 1806 and the French in 1940, but the Prussians and French still tried to evade the restrictions which the victors imposed upon them. No doubt the US planners were right to assume that it was easier to verify that a defeated country was abiding by the peace terms if it were totally demilitarized than if its armed forces were merely limited. But this was not the reason for Japanese behaviour. Commentators have argued that

[38] Buhite, *Dynamics of World Power*, p. 49.
[39] IISS *Military Balance 1973–5*, p. 75 and *Military Balance 1975–6*, p. 81.

Japan was different because, 'so deep, so all-consuming became the hatred of war and to preparations for war that twenty-five years after the nation's surrender, pacifism still motivated the great majority of the Japanese people.'[40] This is an exaggeration; Japanese public opinion did not become pacifist overnight in 1945. Three factors changed: first, those who had been hostile to the aggressive policy of the armed forces in the 1930s could now express that hostility freely; secondly, the Japanese elite turned to economic rather than military development; thirdly, the mass of Japanese became not pacifist but deeply hostile to ultra-nationalism.

Thus the public was not as opposed to rearmament as is often suggested. According to the polls conducted by the *Yomiuri* newspaper in December 1950, 43.8 per cent were in favour of rearmament, 38.7 per cent hostile, and 17.5 per cent undecided. The percentage in favour rose during the Korean War to 58 per cent in October 1951, the undecided remained roughly constant, and the percentage hostile fell to 24.9. There were some fluctuations but 54 per cent were still in favour in January 1954, though the number against had grown again to 39 per cent and the undecided had fallen to 7 per cent.[41] Because of the nature of Japanese politics, Japanese leaders would have liked to develop a consensus over the issue. That was not achieved, but the majority of the electorate was never opposed to rearmament, only to militarism and aggression.

The onset of the Cold War snuffed out the experiment in forced disarmament foreshadowed in allied wartime plans and enshrined in the Japanese Constitution and the abortive Byrnes Treaty. The experiment might just have worked for a time because of the discrediting of the Japanese armed forces and the change in the attitudes of the Japanese elite and general public. If the Cold War had not broken out at all, then Japan would only have been allowed riot police and a customs force. Any deliberate and significant evasion of the constitution would quickly have become obvious because of the total nature of the disarmament imposed. If the Cold War had merely been delayed for a few more years, it would

---

[40] Emmerson, *Arms, Yen and Power*, p. 40.
[41] N. Ike, *Japanese Politics* (Eyre and Spottiswoode, London, 1958), p. 232. For later Japanese views on defence see Defence Agency, *Defense of Japan*, translated by the *Japan Times*, 1986 edn, p. 338; 1987 edn, pp. 190 ff.; 1988 edn, pp. 194 ff.; 1989 edn, pp. 198 ff.

have been more difficult to remilitarize Japan in the face of the Byrnes Treaty on its disarmament. To MacArthur this would have been a resounding success, to Charles Willoughby and George Kennan it came to seem ever more ill-advised. Rarely has the old adage about yesterday's enemy becoming today's friend been more appropriate.

What must surprise the historian is the way US officials could not only change policy to suit their convenience in the altered strategic circumstances but transform their basic premises, apparently without any embarrassment or self-consciousness. The US documents do not make clear whether Bradley's discovery of an 'inalienable right to self defense' was ever challenged, yet this was exactly what Churchill, Roosevelt, Byrnes, and the other Western policy-makers would have denied from 1939 to 1947. Indeed, if they had not ridiculed the notion of such a right, they would have said precisely that it was alienable and that the Axis powers had lost it because of their aggressive policies. The same unselfconscious transformation in Western attitudes was visible in the changed attitude to the Japanese Constitution. This was intended as a major barrier to the revival of militarism and, had it been the Japanese themselves who circumvented it by renaming their re-created armed forces, no doubt there would have been plenty of Americans to protest against such 'Jesuitical casuistry'.

Of course, it might be argued that the beliefs held by Willoughby and later by Bradley fit into the general pattern, under which it has been victorious soldiers from Wellington through Foch and Robertson who have sometimes voiced scepticism about the advantages and durability of forced disarmament measures. 1945 was exceptional in that it is difficult to find examples of soldiers who openly criticized allied disarmament policy at that time. Their doubts were hidden because of the enormity of Nazi crimes, the massacres perpetrated by the Japanese army in China, Malaya, and elsewhere, and by the extent of the destruction and bitterness caused by the war. It was hardly surprising that General MacArthur and others should cling for as long as possible to any measure which might prevent the recurrence of such a holocaust. The Cold War simply encouraged some military men to voice the doubts which had been there all the time, hidden from the public and perhaps even from themselves.

Within three short years, forced disarmament had changed from being the panacea in Churchill's policy to an irrelevant obstruction to Western strategic policy and an irritating anachronism.

10

The Disarmament of Iraq
1991–1995

The attempt to disarm Iraq after its defeat by UN forces in 1991 was the first major example of enforced disarmament since the destruction of the Axis armies in 1945. This was a typical example of the sort of forced disarmament which follows a limited war. It was tactically offensive but strategically defensive because it was part of a general struggle by the US and its allies to maintain the status quo and prevent the spread of weapons of mass destruction. Nevertheless, the Baghdad government resisted with all the means at its disposal. As with Germany after the First World War, Iraq had been defeated but not overrun. Thus the anti-Iraqi coalition led by the United States tried to persuade the government in Baghdad to co-operate by threats, by economic sanctions, and by military incursions. On its side the Iraqi government resisted allied pressure, just as Germany had done in the 1920s, by procrastination, by subterfuge, by pressure on allied inspectors, and by presenting itself as the victim of persecution.

The contrasts between Iraq's position and Germany's are nevertheless very clear. Even disarmed and defeated, Germany was one of the world's Great Powers; indeed, that was the root of the problem. Iraq's power rests only on its military capability which is, in turn, bought by the proceeds from its oil exports. When these are cut off, its offensive strength ebbs rapidly. The allied powers tried to curtail every aspect of Germany's military power in the 1920s; in the 1990s the UN only attempted to restrict specific Iraqi capabilities. In the intervening seventy years, technology had also changed dramatically so that the UN coalition had more power to enforce its will and far greater ability to publicize its cause. Thus the chances of success were much higher in the 1990s, though the programme of enforced disarmament still depended upon the perseverance and cohesion of the coalition which supported it.

GENESIS OF THE DISARMAMENT PROGRAMME

In August 1990 Iraq seized the wealthy Gulf emirate of Kuwait. The Iraqis had long claimed Kuwaiti territory yet, ironically, during their protracted and bitter struggle against Iran in the 1980s, Baghdad had become deeply in debt to the Kuwaiti government.[1] Thus the annexation of Kuwait achieved both financial and territorial objectives. Conversely, the international community was faced not only with the disappearance of one of the major oil producers but with the first example since the Second World War of the annexation of a sovereign state.[2] To liberate Kuwait, a coalition blessed by the UN and led by the United States gradually built up forces in Saudi Arabia. When the Iraqis had still refused to withdraw from Kuwait by February 1991, key targets in Baghdad itself were destroyed by allied air forces and its armed forces entrenched around Kuwait were bombed and then overrun by the coalition's armies. There were many in the West who wanted UN forces to advance on Baghdad and remove the Iraqi President, Saddam Hussein. However, allied leaders argued that they had no mandate to do so and that the coalition would not hold together if its forces moved too far into Iraqi territory.

The UN Security Council decided that, if the Iraqi government was going to survive, it should at least be made to abide by the arms control treaties it had previously signed. The UN's terms for ending the war were laid down in Resolution 687 of 3 April 1991. The preamble to this resolution makes clear why the British and Americans pressed the Council to insist on the partial disarmament of Iraq.[3] First, Baghdad had threatened to use chemical weapons against allied forces, despite the fact that it was a party to the 1925 Geneva Protocol which prohibits the use of asphyxiating and poisonous gases. Nor was the threat an empty one, since the Iraqis had used such weapons both in their war against Iran in the 1980s

[1] J. K. Cooley, 'Pre-Gulf War diplomacy', *Survival*, March–April 1991. Some of the most useful material on the disarmament of Iraq has come from the UN Institute for Disarmament Research. See particularly *Research Paper* no. 11, *The Implications of IAEA Inspections under Security Council Resolution 687* (UN, 1992); *Research Paper* no. 12, *Security Council Resolution 687 of 3 April 1991* (UN, 1992), and Fred Tanner (ed.), *From Versailles to Baghdad: Post-War Armament Control of Defeated States* (UN, 1992).
[2] Goa, East Timor, and large areas of Palestine have all been annexed, but none had been a sovereign state or a member of the UN.
[3] *Research Paper* no. 12, p. 63.

and against rebels among their own Kurdish people.[4] Secondly, there were rumours that the Iraqis were developing biological weapons, even though they had signed the 1972 Convention which bans the production of such weapons, and their use is also prohibited by the Geneva Protocol.[5]

Thirdly, there were fears that Iraq was trying to produce nuclear weapons, despite the fact that it was a party to the Nuclear Non-Proliferation Treaty (NPT). The Israelis had destroyed an Iraqi nuclear reactor in 1981, claiming that Saddam Hussein planned to use it to produce fissile material for nuclear weapons. At the time there had been a tendency to dismiss the Israeli contention, because many believed that Menachem Begin's government in Tel Aviv was more concerned to secure electoral advantage than the disarmament of Iraq.[6] Iraq's small declared nuclear facilities were inspected by the International Atomic Energy Agency (IAEA) to ensure that they had purely civilian uses. However, as the years went by, disquieting reports appeared, suggesting that not all facilities had been declared. In 1982 an Iraqi scientist who sought asylum in Canada claimed to have evidence of Iraqi plans to produce nuclear bombs. Eight years later Iraqi agents were caught allegedly smuggling triggers for nuclear weapons through Heathrow airport.[7]

During the Gulf War, Baghdad had fired Scud missiles at Saudi Arabia and Israel. Saddam Hussein's cynical motive for the attack on the Israelis was to provoke them to retaliate. This would have severely embarrassed the Saudi, Egyptian, Syrian, and Kuwaiti governments, which supported the action against Iraq but could not be seen to be involved in an alliance with Israel. Washington managed to prevent Israeli reprisals against Iraq during the war, partly by supplying Israel with Patriot missiles which could be used

---

[4] 'US accuses Iraqis of making mustard gas for use in Gulf battles', *The Times*, 8 March 1984; 'West "outraged" as UN clears Iraq of massacring Kurds', *The Times*, 16 March 1989.

[5] 'Iraq "developing typhoid, cholera and anthrax weapons"', *The Times*, 19 January 1989; 'Saddam piled up anthrax', *The Times*, 6 July 1995.

[6] 'Thatcher condemns Israel for its unprovoked attack', *The Times*, 10 June 1981 and 'Air strike puts bite into election campaigning', *The Times*, 11 June 1981. For a more recent critical appraisal of the Israeli action see D. G. Boudreau, 'The bombing of the Osirak reactor', *International Journal of World Peace*, June 1993.

[7] 'Iraq "aims to have nuclear bombs"', *Guardian*, 28 January 1982; 'Iraqi expelled after nuclear trigger plot', *The Times*, 29 March 1990. But see also 'Exporters jailed for Iraq deal appeal against conviction', *The Times*, 21 May 1994.

to intercept some of the Scuds. However, it may be that the US had to give some commitment to Israel that it would remove the Scud missiles after the war and prevent the Iraqis being armed in the future with weapons of mass destruction.

Thus it was hardly surprising that Resolution 687 put so much emphasis on destroying Iraqi chemical weapons and missiles, and halting any plans that it had to produce nuclear and biological weapons. Saddam Hussein had shown that he was not only an aggressor but that he was prepared to ignore any agreement which was not backed by force. His transgressions threatened efforts by the international community to inhibit the spread of missiles and of weapons of mass destruction. Thus his defeat provided an exceptional opportunity to bolster the various non-proliferation regimes and to demonstrate that agreements could not be breached with impunity.

THE POLITICAL IMPLICATIONS

Victorious states have to decide whether they are prepared for the political disadvantages of imposing disarmament on the defeated. In this case, the coalition was hardly concerned about any deterioration in its relations with Saddam Hussein. There were only two political impediments to its action. First, the Arab countries were sensitive to the idea of a coalition led by the US bullying a fellow Arab nation. The Yemeni delegation may have voiced common Arab views when it denounced Resolution 687 in the Security Council on the grounds that it was unjust to disarm the defeated.[8] Subsequently, when the US used or threatened to use force to make Iraq disarm, various Arab nations distanced themselves from American actions. From the outside it is impossible to tell whether this was mainly to placate their peoples and avoid seeming to be Western 'stooges' or whether Arab leaders really objected to allied actions.

The second reason for caution was that the allies did not want to destroy Iraq and allow Iran to become relatively even more powerful in the Gulf region. The Iranian government was no more friendly than Saddam Hussein either to the West or to the conservative Arab states. They also feared that the rebellious Shiites in

---

[8] *Research Paper* no. 12, p. 3.

the south of Iraq might actually want to become part of Iran and thus add to its population of 53 millions who already dwarfed the 18 million Iraqis and 8.5 million Saudis. In the north of Iraq the Kurds had struggled for decades to form a new state incorporating the Kurdish areas of Turkey and Iran. Together, the reluctance either to weaken Turkey or to destroy Iraq goes far to show why the allies did not overrun Iraq in the first place and why they hesitated to give full backing to secessionist movements of Kurds and Shiite rebels.[9]

Resolution 687 was designed to weaken the Iraqi government, not to destroy the Iraqi state. The Baghdad government was to renounce chemical, biological, and nuclear weapons together with missiles with a greater range than 150 kilometres. Iraq was left with what remained of its very substantial conventional arsenal after the war. *The Military Balance*, produced by the International Institute for Strategic Studies in 1990, credited Iraq with 5,500 main battle tanks and 512 combat aircraft. By 1993–4 the Institute believed that Baghdad still had some 2,200 tanks, about 130 fighter ground attack aircraft, and 180 fighters.[10] Under Article 24 of Resolution 687 the UN proclaimed a continuing embargo on all arms supplies to Iraq yet, without spares, sophisticated weapons such as aircraft were unlikely to operate for very long. Thus Iraqi forces would gradually be weakened but not prohibited altogether.

VERIFICATION

If Iraq were to be partially disarmed, the UN was the only institution which could legitimize and oversee the process. The war had been fought under UN auspices, even if the US had made certain that the UN exerted no operational control. The end of the Cold War had also revived interest in the UN, and there was a great deal of optimism in the early 1990s that it would come to play an ever more important international role. On the other hand, the UN headquarters itself had no experience of verifying an arms control agreement and no intelligence organization. It would therefore

[9] 'US cool over proposal for Kurds' haven', *Independent*, 10 April 1991. For an examination of Iran's position see S. Chubin, 'Iran and regional security in the Gulf', *Survival*, Autumn 1992.

[10] IISS, *Military Balance 1989–1990*, p. 101 and *Military Balance 1993–4*, p. 116. For the UN arms embargo see S/25930, 'Chairman of the Security Council Committee established by Resolution 661 (1990)', 11 June 1993.

obviously rely heavily on the United States and to a lesser extent on the information and experience of other coalition members.

Resolution 687 called on the Secretary General to establish a Special Commission to 'carry out immediate on-site inspection of Iraq's biological, chemical and missile capabilities'. UNSCOM, as it came to be known, was also to destroy any of the Iraqi weapons which came under the UN prohibition. The Secretary General was to work with the IAEA, which was given far more sweeping powers than it had under the NPT to inspect Iraq's nuclear capabilities, to destroy any equipment which might be related to the production of nuclear weapons, and to ensure future Iraqi compliance with the treaty. All the banned weapons were to be destroyed within forty-five days of the establishment by the Security Council of the Special Commission. Such a timetable was completely unrealistic, given the size of the Iraqi arsenal of chemical weapons, the lack of recent experience with forced disarmament, the need to set up a new agency, and the attitude of the Iraqis.

Baghdad obstructed and delayed the UN's inspectors as much as possible. Already by 26 June 1991, Rolf Ekeus, the Swedish diplomat who had been appointed chairman of the Special Commission, complained that Iraq was hiding equipment suspected of being part of a nuclear weapons programme. On 15 August 1991 the Security Council passed Resolution 707 condemning Iraqi recalcitrance. In the strongest language, the Council demanded that Iraq abide by its general treaty obligations and that it should thus allow 'the Special Commission, the IAEA and their inspection teams immediate, unconditional and unrestricted access to all areas, facilities, equipment, records and means of transportation which they wish to inspect'.[11]

Such demands were not going to be met without continuing pressure and threats. Apart from hiding their nuclear programme, the Iraqis had not declared their full range of chemical weapons and they admitted later that they had unilaterally destroyed many of these weapons, even though they were obliged under Resolution 687 to leave this task to the UN. They also admitted that they had minimized the number of Scud missiles in service by claiming that they had fired sixty-seven more missiles against Iran than was in fact the case. The Commission suspected that many missiles were

---

[11] *Research Paper* no. 12, p. 68, Resolution 707 of 15 August 1991, para. 3.11.

hidden and that the Iraqis might modify shorter-range missiles so that they could reach the ranges banned by the agreement. Furthermore, the Iraqi government failed to declare the machine tools made by the British-based firm of Matrix Churchill, which the IAEA wanted to examine, and refused to admit to other aspects of its nuclear programme.[12]

Despite such resistance, the UN became increasingly aware of the extent of Iraqi weapons development. The nuclear programme, which was code-named Petrochemical 3, had absorbed tens of billions of dollars and employed 20,000 workers on thirty sites. One research team was run by Dr Jaffar Dhia Jaffar, who had been educated at Birmingham University and Imperial College, London. Dr Jaffar and his team had experimented for some years with calutrons to separate uranium 235 from 238. This was an antiquated separation system used by Dr Ernest Lawrence during the Second World War and dismissed by Western experts because it was considered both expensive and slow. However, the Iraqis had incorporated new technology and made considerable progress with the system. They were constructing two large factories, each to hold ninety to a hundred calutrons, which would have given them the ability to separate substantial quantities of weapons-grade uranium. Another team had investigated the much more modern gas centrifuge system for separating weapons-grade uranium, with parts bought in the Federal Republic of Germany, Switzerland, the US, and Sweden. Although progress here had been much slower, the far-reaching nature of Iraqi ambitions was shown by the discovery that they had also begun investigating Lithium-6, an isotope used only in the production of hydrogen bombs.[13]

Despite all this effort, Iraq had still not produced an atomic weapon; on the other hand, it had one of the largest stockpiles of chemical weapons in the world. Some were already loaded into rockets at Khamisiyah, where the Commission blew up 389 filled and 36 partially filled weapons. Some chemical weapons had been

[12] Security Council S/24108, 'Note by the Secretary General', 16 June 1992, Appendix 11; S/25982, 'Report by the Director General of the IAEA, 10 June 1992 on the 19th IAEA On-Site Inspection in Iraq'.
[13] 'Seized papers show Iraq tried to build nuclear missiles', *The Times*, 5 October 1991; 'UN poised to adopt sweeping nuclear search rights in Iraq', *The Times*, 12 October 1991. See also D. Fischer, *Towards 1995; The Prospects for Ending the Proliferation of Nuclear Weapons* (UNIDIR and Dartmouth, Aldershot, 1993), pp. 48 ff.

destroyed during the fighting but, after short-notice inspections at
a number of sites, the Commission concluded that the majority was
stockpiled at the Muthanna arsenal. Some were mustard gases of
the type used in the First World War, and some were the much
more toxic nerve agents. The deactivation of these weapons was
hazardous both to those carrying it out and to the environment.
Fortunately, the Iraqis were as helpful in this process as they were
obstinate in their opposition to inspection.[14]

What is impressive is how similar some of Iraq's methods of
hampering the UN inspectors were to those used by the Germans
seventy years before. The Germans invented ludicrous civilian uses
for their flame-throwers and other weapons; the Iraqis suddenly
discovered a high regard for academic freedom and protested that
inspection of university departments would infringe academic independence and upset the students. Like the Germans, the Iraqis
wanted advance notice of inspections and tried to limit the size of
the inspecting team and the duration of the visit. Inspectors' hotel
rooms were ransacked and documents stolen; mobs were encouraged to demonstrate and threaten the UN teams. Light bulbs replaced bottles as the most favoured missile to hurl at the inspectors,
and threats were frequent in both cases. Iraqi soldiers fired over the
heads of the IAEA team which first discovered the calutrons. In
March 1994 the Iraqis ambushed two UN guards and damaged the
helicopter which took them to hospital. Rumours spread that there
was a reward of a thousand dollars for any guards killed.[15]
The Germans and Hungarians convicted their fellow citizens who
passed information to allied inspectors; Iraqi intelligence passed
notes to the UN inspectors purporting to come from spies, in the
hope that these would mislead and confuse them.

The psychological warfare employed by the Germans and Iraqis
was also similar. The kaiser's bust presided over the entrance to the
gloomy Hotel Adlon where the allied inspectors stayed in Berlin.

[14] Security Council S/24108, 'Note by the Secretary General', 16 June 1992,
Appendix 11.
[15] For the March 1994 attacks see *Arms Control and Disarmament Quarterly
Review*, no. 33, April 1994 (Foreign and Commonwealth Office, London), p. 23.
For the earlier history see Security Council, S/25620, 'State of the Implementation
of the Plan for the Ongoing Monitoring and Verification of Iraq's Compliance
with Relevant Parts of Section C of Security Council Resolution 715 (1991)'; S/
25960, 'Report of the Executive Chairman of the UN Special Commission',
16 June 1993. G. Milhollin, 'The Iraqi Bomb', *New Yorker*, 1 February 1993;
'When an inspector calls the shots', *The Times*, 30 July 1992.

The lobby of the dimly lit Sheraton Hotel in Baghdad was dominated by a picture of a crucified dove dripping blood and labelled 'UN', and by a massive portrait of Saddam Hussein. Admittedly, the Iraqis missed some tricks. There seems to have been no attempt to starve the UN inspectors into submission, but there were cases where Iraqis tipped plates of food into the inspectors' laps.[16]

The Iraqis frequently accused UN inspectors of being CIA agents. Such claims were given plausibility because UNSCOM had to seek US assistance. Washington deployed a U2 high-flying reconnaissance aircraft to help with the inspection effort. The Iraqis made a formal complaint to the UN each time that it passed over their territory and said that the plane was being used for 'despicable criminal purposes'.[17] The US also supplied satellite photographs, and it was to the Americans that an Iraqi expert allegedly defected, bringing information about calutrons and other covert nuclear facilities in the north of the country. He also gave guidance on where in Baghdad the inspectors would need to look for details of the Iraqi nuclear programme.

The task of the inspectors was made immensely easier and safer as a result of modern means of communication. Allied inspectors were isolated and thus vulnerable in Germany in the 1920s. The inspectors in Iraq were in constant communication with the outside world. When Iraqi police and soldiers surrounded a team of forty-four IAEA inspectors, led by an American, David Kay, in their bus in a Baghdad car park in September 1991, millions watched the course of events on television.[18] Because of media coverage, the inspectors and their backers in New York, Washington, and Vienna had a great deal more support for their efforts than was the case for allied inspectors in the 1920s. Modern methods of communication also meant that copies of the documents the inspectors seized could be beamed to UNSCOM headquarters before they were retaken by the Iraqis. Of course, mobs could still have wounded or even killed the inspectors, but retribution was also more certain than it had been seventy years before. In the cruise missile the United States had a weapon against which the Iraqis could not retaliate. Because

[16] Milhollin, 'The Iraqi Bomb'.
[17] 'When an inspector calls the shots', *The Times*, 30 July 1992; S/24108, Appendix 1, para. 25 ff. and S/25620.
[18] 'Hurd demands release of UN inspectors' and 'UN team sits it out in car park', *The Times*, 26 September 1991; 'A deadly game of chicken', *Time*, 7 October 1991, p. 40.

of its accuracy, individual ministries or buildings could be destroyed in a very controlled response to Iraqi obstruction.[19]

On their side the Iraqis frequently wakened the inspectors with threatening telephone calls in the middle of the night. The invention of the 'bug' or listening device made it unsafe for the inspectors to discuss and co-ordinate their plans in many buildings inside Iraq, as the allied inspectors had been able to do in Germany in the 1920s.[20] All this inevitably played on the nerves of the inspectors, while Iraqi propaganda agencies tried to convince the Arab world that the country was the victim of Western aggression.

Each Iraqi concession had to be achieved by implicit or explicit threats.[21] Early in 1992 the US administration leaked plans to bomb the country if prevarications did not cease, though Presidents Mubarak of Egypt and Assad of Syria both protested against such a move. Baghdad responded to UN pressures by making additional declarations about its chemical and missile programmes, and declaring its readiness to agree to the destruction of related buildings and equipment.[22] In July the level of tension rose again. The Commission had become suspicious of the activities of the Ministry of Agriculture in Baghdad to which its inspectors, led by an American, Karen Jansen, were refused access. For seventeen days the inspectors sat outside the building while demonstrators marched around them shouting anti-Western slogans and pelting them with vegetables. UN vehicles were daubed with paint and had their tyres slashed. Tensions increased when two UN guards were wounded by a car bomb in the Kurdish part of Iraq. Finally, the inspectors returned to their hotel after an Iraqi tried to attack one of them with a skewer. They were subsequently withdrawn to Bahrain.[23] Washington again threatened to use force, but in the end it was the Commission which compromised. On 26 July Rolf Ekeus agreed with Iraq's ambassador at the UN that only inspectors from certain countries acceptable to Iraq—Germany, Finland, Russia,

[19] P. Towle, 'The Post Nuclear World: The New Ethics of War', *European Security Analyst*, June 1993.
[20] Milhollin, 'The Iraqi Bomb'. On Germany in the 1920s see J. H. Morgan, *Assize of Arms* (Methuen, London, 1945).
[21] For US threats see 'Pentagon draws up plan to bomb Iraq', *The Times*, 20 March 1992.
[22] For UN reports see S/24108, p. 4, para. 10.
[23] S/25960, Report of the Executive Committee of the Special Commission, 16 June 1993; 'Saddam defiant' and 'US threatens Iraqis with force after UN inspector attacked', *The Times*, 23 July 1992.

Sweden, and Switzerland—would examine the Ministry of Agriculture. By then the inspection was carried out simply to uphold the UN's right of access since Achim Biermann, the German leader of the inspection team, believed that any incriminating documents had already been removed.[24]

On 2 August, two years after the invasion of Kuwait, Iraqi newspapers reiterated their country's claims to the emirate. At the same time, an unidentified gunman shot at a Czech guard working for the UN. Coincidentally, the US was sending some 5,000 troops to the region for joint manoeuvres with the Kuwaiti armed forces. Fearing another conflict, an inspection team led by Nikita Smidovich from Russia abruptly cancelled a visit to the Iraqi Ministry of Military Industrialization in case they were seized as hostages.[25] Later the French, British, and Americans increased pressure on the Iraqi government by banning Iraqi military aircraft from attacking the Shiite rebels in the south. The Iraqis responded by bringing Sam 2 and 3 missiles into this 'air exclusion zone' and threatening the allied aircraft which were enforcing it. Baghdad removed the Sams only after another confrontation and exchange of threats. Afterwards it tried to recover face by halting the flights of UN aircraft which brought the teams of inspectors into Iraq.[26]

George Bush, who was then in the last days of his presidency, decided to take action. On 13 January 1993 a first wave of forty American and British bombers attacked Iraqi missile sites in the south of the country. On 17 January, forty Tomahawk cruise missiles and thousands of pounds of laser-guided bombs hit Iraqi targets. The cruise missiles from the US warships *Hewit*, *Stamp*, and *Cowpens* destroyed buildings at the former nuclear centre outside Baghdad. These had already been examined at least sixteen times by IAEA inspectors, who had overseen the destruction of most of the equipment there. The slight possibility remained that some of the twelve workshops used to make moulds might have had nuclear applications, though the demonstrative importance of the attack was clearly much greater than its immediate effect on

[24] 'Baghdad still defiant as arms monitors gain access', *The Times*, 29 July 1992.
[25] 'Mirage and reality', *The Times*, 4 August 1992 and 'Arabs hesitate over Western move to close Iraqi air space', *The Times*, 19 August 1992.
[26] 'Pentagon initially failed to grasp threat from Sams', *The Times*, 9 January 1993; 'Saddam bans UN plane in fresh challenge to West', *The Times*, 11 January 1993.

Iraqi military programmes.[27] Unfortunately, a stray missile hit the
Al-Rashid Hotel in the centre of Baghdad, killing two women and
injuring fifteen other people. Another missile killed one woman,
wounded several others, and destroyed homes in a different part of
the city. Many Arab countries distanced themselves from US policy,
and Roland Dumas, the French Foreign Minister, also argued in
public that the attack on 17 January was disproportionate to Iraqi
'offences'.[28]

Either to avoid further attacks or to improve relations with
President Clinton, who was inaugurated on 20 January 1993, Iraq
then approved the entry of fifty-two UN inspectors, under an
American leader, into Baghdad to monitor the destruction of its
chemical weapons. For once, the inspectors were actually helped at
the airport by Iraqi staff and passed quickly through customs.[29]
Despite this unprecedented level of co-operation, further friction
was inevitable.[30] In June the Iraqis refused to allow inspectors to fly
over Baghdad or to destroy equipment and materials which
UNSCOM said could be used to make chemical weapons. Initially,
they also refused to allow the UN to install monitoring cameras on
their territory. These were designed to make sure that the missile
test sites at al-Azimand and al-Rafah near Baghdad were not used
to test long-range missiles.[31]

Again the US threatened to attack Iraqi missile sites. This caused
panic buying in Baghdad, a rise of 20 per cent in food prices, and a
corresponding fall in the value of the Iraqi dinar against the dollar.
The Western press was briefed with information that the Americans had sixteen warships in the Red Sea and Gulf area, some
armed with Tomahawk cruise missiles, together with about
250 American, British, and French aircraft based in neighbouring
states.[32] Nevertheless, the Iraqis were determined not to appear

[27] 'UN destroyed key equipment before air raids took place', *The Times*,
18 January 1993.
[28] 'Paris breaks ranks with allies over Iraq raids', *The Times*, 21 January 1993.
[29] 'Iraq greets UN team as Saddam wins propaganda points', *The Times*,
22 January 1993; 'Iraq hands over list of nuclear suppliers to UN inspectors', *The
Times*, 26 January 1993.
[30] 'US aircraft attacks missile battery in northern Iraq', *The Times*, 23 January
1993.
[31] S/25960, 'Report of the Executive Chairman of the Special Commission',
6 June 1993; 'Iraqis braced for showdown after UN team pulls out', *The Times*, 6
July 1993; 'UN questions Iraq over missile sites', *The Times*, 27 July 1993.
[32] 'Formidable arsenal ready to strike Baghdad test sites', *The Times*, 13 July
1993; 'Iraq told not to "play with fire"', *The Times*, 14 July 1993.

intimidated. They knew that Arab leaders had criticized American threats to use force and that the French were also hostile to further attacks. Three UN officials who tried to seal the Iraqi missile sites had to leave in mid-July, following the failure of their mission. It was not until the end of the month that Baghdad backed down, while claiming that it had emerged with its head held high and dignity preserved. President Saddam Hussein's press secretary, Abdul Jabbar Mohsen, took the opportunity to brand UN inspectors as 'scoundrels and lowly people' and appealed to the Iraqis to insult them at every opportunity.[33]

Despite such rhetoric, IAEA inspectors believed that the Iraqi nuclear weapons programme had been brought to a halt. Bob Kelley, leader of one IAEA team, told the press in July 1993, 'the nuclear weapons programme that existed in Iraq before the war is finished, damaged, devastated' and with it billions of dollars' worth of equipment. Chemical weapons had been located and the Scud missiles, which the Iraqis had declared, were destroyed. Most important of all, the Iraqis finally agreed to the UN's plan for long-term monitoring in the country to prove that production of banned weapons had not been restarted.[34]

Inspection of nuclear facilities now depended on regular environmental monitoring much more than on the discovery of incriminating documents, which had played such an important part in the early stages. On their nineteenth visit to Iraq in April 1993, for example, IAEA inspectors took surface water samples from some fifteen different sites. Such methods had already exposed Iraqi efforts to cover up their nuclear weapons programme, and the intention was to take samples from each site twice a year so that any changes would be noticed. The IAEA also visited or revisited eighteen Iraqi factories or research centres; they found that the Al Furat centre, which the Iraqis had intended to use for centrifuge manufacture, was being turned into an office complex. They used radiation detection equipment to check that the Al Qaim phosphate

[33] 'Baghdad claims victory over UN', *The Times*, 21 July 1993; 'Iraqis to accept UN arms monitors', *The Times*, 23 July 1993; 'UN sets up cameras at missile site in Iraq', *Daily Telegraph*, 28 July 1993.

[34] 'UN low-level flights monitor Iraq arms', *Independent*, 18 September 1993; 'Baghdad's UN-Project dismantled', *Daily Telegraph*, 1 July 1993; 'UN weapons team gives Iraq all-clear', *The Times*, 1 November 1993; 'Baghdad bows to UN arms demands', *The Times*, 27 November 1993. On long-term monitoring see *Arms Control and Disarmament Quarterly Review*, no. 32, January 1994, p. 50.

factory was not being employed to separate uranium from phosphates, and they visited the Ur aluminium factory to make sure that it was producing windows and foil rather than weapons.[35] Such methods were slow and painstaking rather than dramatic, but essential if Iraq was to be kept disarmed.

Some dramatic revelations were still to come. Rumours of an Iraqi biological weapons programme had continued to reach the inspectors. However, it was not until August 1995 that hard evidence became available. At that time Saddam Hussein's son-in-law, General Hussein Kamel, fled to Jordan. The Iraqi government then tried to blame him for the biological weapons programme by leaving 147 boxes of documents at a chicken farm he owned outside Baghdad, and then taking Rolf Ekeus to the farm. The documents allegedly showed that the programme had begun in 1988. By the time of the Gulf War, Iraq had loaded biological weapons containing anthrax, aflatoxin, and botulinum into bombs, artillery shells, and missiles. UN press briefing suggested that such weapons had represented a far more immediate menace than the nuclear programme, and that US threats to retaliate had alone deterred Baghdad from waging biological warfare.[36]

WEAKNESSES IN THE ALLIED POSITION

In the 1920s the allies weakened their position *vis-à-vis* Germany by the multiplicity of their aims. The demand for reparations and the changes in Germany's frontiers reduced allied determination to enforce disarmament because they made the Germans seem to be the victims of allied persecution. In the 1990s, UN efforts to protect Kurds in the north of Iraq and Shiite tribesmen in the south from the government in Baghdad reduced the cohesion of the anti-Iraqi coalition. Allied intervention in Germany in the 1920s (in the Rhineland, on the border with Poland, and in the Ruhr) excited German nationalism, just as UN operations in north and south Iraq angered many Iraqis and other Arabs who were not necessarily sympathetic to Saddam Hussein.

Resolution 687 also stipulated that Iraq should pay compensation for 'any direct loss, damage, including environmental damage

---

[35] *Research Paper* no. 12, p. 66; S/25970, 'Note by President of the Security Council', 18 June 1993.
[36] 'Iraq's germ war secrets found at farm', *Independent*, 5 September 1995.

and the depletion of natural resources, or injury to foreign governments, national and corporations, as a result of Iraq's unlawful invasion and occupation of Kuwait'.[37] Yet it was clear that the Iraqis would not be able to pay for any damages or for the Special Commission until they had begun to export oil. Such exports were prohibited after their original occupation of Kuwait in 1990, but in Resolution 706 of August 1991 the Security Council offered Iraq a compromise. Some oil could be exported and the money received from its sale would go into a special account to be used in part for paying reparations and the cost of the Commission.[38] Iraq rejected the terms. The result was that the country's main trade was virtually halted for several years, with devastating consequences for the ordinary Iraqi.

On 20 April 1993 Iraq sent a letter to the UN, outlining the effects of the economic blockade on infant mortality. According to the Iraqi figures, 61,442 children under the age of 5 had died between August 1990 and August 1992 as a result of UN sanctions. In the over 5 age-group mortality was 1,833 per month in 1990, 4,872 in 1991, and 6,363 in 1992. In 1992 17.5 per cent of newborn children were underweight compared with 10.8 per cent in 1991 and 4.5 per cent in 1990.[39] The Iraqis sent another letter to the UN the following month, arguing that cholera, typhoid, and dysentery had all increased as a result of the embargo.[40]

The deteriorating state of Iraqi health was confirmed from other sources. Appealing for increased UN aid for the Iraqi people in October 1995, the head of the UN's World Food Programme in Baghdad reported that famine in central and southern Iraq was worse than in the Sudan and that 4 million people were short of food. Children were particularly badly hit, a fact supported by a letter to the *Lancet* in December 1995. The letter, from researchers who worked in Iraq in August 1995 under the auspices of the Food and Agriculture Organization, suggested that more than 560,000

[37] *United Nations Security Council Resolutions Relating to the Situation between Iraq and Kuwait* (UN Department of Public Information, December 1991), p. 24, paras 16–18 of Resolution 687.

[38] Ibid., p. 28. See also 'UN report describes catastrophe in Iraq', *Independent*, 22 March 1991.

[39] S/25657, 'Letter dated 20 April 1993 from the Permanent Representative of Iraq'.

[40] S/25775, 'Letter dated 11 May 1993 from the Permanent Representative of Iraq.

children had died because of the sanctions.[41] The allies could argue both that the reports were exaggerated and that, in any case, President Hussein could change the situation whenever he wanted by exporting oil under the terms dictated by the UN. He, rather than the Security Council, was therefore responsible for any increase in infant mortality. They could also point out that recent revelations about Iraqi biological weapons showed that they were still hiding their military activities. But the impact of sanctions on ordinary civilians raised fundamental questions about the methods which the UN should employ to enforce disarmament. Economic sanctions were unlikely to be effective against a dictator like Saddam Hussein because they were a threat to his prestige and position, and they did not touch Hussein himself, his family, or his entourage.

There is a finite, though undefined, limit to the amount of suffering the public is willing to overlook in the cause of disarmament. Different constituencies will have different limits. In the 1920s the United States was more sympathetic to Germany than Britain and Italy were prepared to be. Britain and Italy were more sympathetic than Belgium and France. In the 1990s Jordan was most sympathetic to Iraq's position; Britain and America took the toughest stance; Russia and China were most ambiguous. China was opposed to any interference in the internal affairs of states, fearing to give any legitimacy to foreign interference in support of Chinese human-rights activists. But the Chinese also hesitated to antagonize Washington and thus they voted for Resolution 687 and subsequent measures against Iraq. Gorbachev and Yeltsin loyally supported the disarmament of Iraq, despite vocal criticism in Russia of attacks on a former ally. But both the Russian Communist and nationalist parties, such as the Liberal Democrats led by Vladimir Zhirinovsky, said that policy would be changed if they ever came to power. This represents a much greater long-term threat to the cohesion of the anti-Iraqi coalition than criticisms of its actions by the Arab states.[42]

---

[41] 'Health of Baghdad's children', *Lancet*, 2 December 1995, p. 1485; 'Sanctions push Iraq to disaster', *Guardian*, 18 October 1995. Fortunately there were some signs in 1996 that Iraq was willing to compromise on the issue. See 'Saddam yields to UN's terms in oil-for-food deal', *The Times*, 21 May 1996.

[42] 'Zhirinovsky warns west to keep out', *The Times*, 21 December 1993.

Despite all their difficulties, the Special Commission and the IAEA had achieved many of the UN's objectives by the end of 1993. They had destroyed large numbers of Iraqi chemical weapons and some Scud missiles. They had also demolished or forced the Iraqis to destroy equipment for producing fissile material and for carrying out research into nuclear weapons. Iraq had agreed to a continuing programme of inspection and the Special Commission built a permanent headquarters in Baghdad, thereby demonstrating its commitment to a very lengthy programme. Members of the coalition continued to finance UNSCOM operations. Washington supplied vital reconnaissance equipment and Germany loaned the transport aircraft needed. Allied determination was maintained for the time being, although long-term financing still depended upon an Iraqi agreement to export oil on the terms laid down by the UN.[43]

If the Security Council showed a surprising degree of coherence over Iraq, Saddam Hussein demonstrated the resistance which even a weak but determined state can put up to forced disarmament. Iraq's only strengths were its armed forces and its oil industry, and both had been severely damaged. Large areas of the country were in the hands of rebels. All the Great Powers voted for the disarmament of Iraq, and the country was regarded as a pariah even in the Middle East, yet Saddam Hussein could only be made to co-operate by an oil embargo and frequent military threats from a superpower.

Germany in the 1920s and Iraq in the 1990s used a combination of psychological warfare, mob violence, and passive resistance against allied inspectors. The campaigners hoped that they could exhaust the patience and determination of the 'government' forces. However, it is debatable whether such methods can be decisive. The inspectors' life in Germany was certainly unpleasant, but that was not the reason for their withdrawal. After the Locarno Conference, the British became ever more anxious to improve relations with Berlin. More important, they were unwilling to go to war to make Germany disarm, and the Weimar government was well aware of this. It was only a matter of time, therefore, before the allies' 'bluff' was called. For the moment, there is no sign that the US will follow the British example, and the Iraqis cannot therefore dismiss the possibility that the treaties will be enforced. On the

[43] S/25982.

contrary, Iraqi obstruction perpetuates its pariah status and has made the hostile coalition more determined.

The international community was very fortunate that Iraq attacked Kuwait in 1990 rather than five or ten years earlier. In 1980 the Soviet Union would have vetoed a Security Council resolution calling for military action to liberate Kuwait or for Iraq's subsequent disarmament. Admittedly, Moscow would have been placed in a very difficult situation if Iraqi breaches of the NPT had become known. On the one hand, Iraq was one of the Soviet's few allies and a major market for its tanks, military aircraft, and guns; on the other hand, the Soviet Union was always a loyal supporter of the NPT. It would probably have tried to put quiet diplomatic pressure on the Iraqis to halt their programme, but this would not have made Saddam Hussein desist. Similarly, had Iraq not conquered Kuwait, the Western countries led by the United States would have been reluctant to attack Iraq simply to compel it to abide by the NPT, not least because there was a strong tendency to exaggerate Iraqi military power and the number of casualties any war would bring.[44]

The military technological balance was also quite peculiarly propitious for UN actions in the early 1990s. The development of cruise missiles and other precision-guided munitions gave the international community a discriminatory weapon which it had never possessed before, and against which the Iraqis found it impossible to retaliate effectively. The end of the Cold War meant that the superpowers had aircraft and satellites which they could spare for reconnaissance over Iraq. They also had weapons specialists who could be seconded to UN teams.

The threats to UNSCOM are long-term ones. A Middle Eastern 'Locarno' would be most likely to occur if there were a dramatic change in the composition of the Russian government or if the US public turned against the whole enterprise, perhaps because of the sufferings caused by the economic sanctions against Baghdad. The continued disarmament of Iraq depends just as much on American resolution and the backing of the Security Council as the neutralization of the Black Sea depended upon Anglo-French co-operation in the 1860s or the disarmament of Germany depended upon Anglo-French willpower in the 1920s. While Saddam Hussein

[44] P. Towle, *Pundits and Patriots: Lessons from the Gulf War* (Institute for European Defence and Strategic Studies, London, 1991).

remains President, his determination to acquire nuclear weapons must be assumed. Another government with less far-reaching international ambitions might quite possibly take a different view. In this respect the disarmament of Iraq differs from the demilitarization of Dunkirk in the eighteenth century or of the Black Sea in the 1860s. In those cases it was clear that any French or Russian government would want to denounce the disarmament clauses imposed upon it. But, fortunately, not all governments capable of producing nuclear weapons actually want to do so; many realize that, if they initiated a nuclear programme, this would only set off a nuclear arms race with their neighbours, and nuclear weapons are quite peculiarly expensive to make and difficult to use effectively.

Thus the issue is whether the consensus among the permanent members of the Security Council will outlast Saddam Hussein or whether, as with the break up of the Anglo-French coalition in 1870 or in the 1920s, the Security Council will be blocked and the defeated government will be able to overturn the peace settlement and rearm.

11

Enforced Disarmament without War?
The Control of North Korean
Nuclear Weapons

As we have seen, there have been times where the disparity in power has been great enough for a state or group of states to compel a weaker country to disarm without going to war; such a disparity led to the temporary submission of Carthage before the Third Punic War and the forced disarmament of the Czechs in 1938. The Cuban missile crisis of 1962 and the Libyan chemical weapons crisis of 1989 also offer some analogies with these earlier situations.

Naturally such cases are rare. Weaker powers frequently hope that stronger neighbours will not carry out their threats to attack them if they refuse to disarm or that, if such attacks do take place, they will receive assistance from allied or friendly states. Dictators may believe that their power and prestige demands that they refuse to bow to threats of war. In democracies, public opinion may force governments to resist threats, even when the chances of success in war are slight. Thus the Finns resisted for a time the full might of the Soviet Union in the Winter War of 1939–40; in that case they lost the 'Mannerheim' line of fortifications, just as the Czechs had lost their defences but, unlike the Czechs, the Finns suffered very heavy casualties in the process. Of course they might argue that, in the long run, their sacrifices were not in vain; after 1945 they were treated with much more respect by the Soviets than other East European states which had not resisted Soviet power.

In the early 1990s the international community tried to compel North Korea either to prove that it was not developing nuclear weapons or to cease such development. As so often, the aim was strategically defensive, that is, to prevent further countries developing nuclear weapons. Aborting any North Korean programme was regarded by Washington and Seoul as particularly important, given the prevailing tensions in North Asia, the possibility that other states in the region would follow Pyongyang's example, and the unpredictable nature of the North Korean regime. The ease with which Iraq had begun the development of nuclear weapons in secret had increased anxieties and made the US and its allies more determined to impose their will. However, the ability of the Iraqis to delay international inspection, even after they had been defeated in a war, underlined the difficulty of forcing the undefeated North Koreans to accept external diktats without the open use of force.

BACKGROUND

In 1985 the North Korean government signed an agreement with Moscow under which the Soviets would continue to supply technical and other assistance for the North Korean civil nuclear programme. On its side, to demonstrate that it was interested purely in the civil applications of nuclear technology, Pyongyang adhered to the NPT. Under the treaty, it promised to sign a 'safeguards agreement' which would allow the IAEA to inspect its nuclear facilities to ensure that it was not producing nuclear weapons. However, it refused to sign the agreement until January 1992. Before then IAEA inspectors were allowed to monitor a small Soviet-supplied nuclear reactor, but the organization knew nothing about the rest of the North Korean programme as the country was even more hermetically sealed off from the outside world than the Soviet Union had been since the 1930s.[1]

The United States, on the other hand, was increasingly concerned about the North Korean programme. It believed that, when the programme was complete, North Korea would be able to produce some thirty nuclear weapons a year. It was also aware that North Korea was not only extending the range of Soviet-designed Scud missiles but developing other missiles with a range of 4,000–5,000 kilometres. Given the inaccuracy of these weapons, the US believed that they could only be intended for use with nuclear warheads.

With the backing of the United States and Russia, the IAEA tried

---

[1] For the general political background in the Korean peninsula see Y. W. Kihl, *Politics and Policies in Divided Korea* (Westview Press, Boulder, Colo., 1984); R. N. Clough, *Embattled Korea* (Westview Press, Boulder, Colo., 1987).

to persuade North Korea to open its nuclear facilities to inspection. The Koreans' prolonged refusal to accept this was a sign, but not by itself an absolute proof, that Pyongyang had tried at some stage or other to produce nuclear weapons. Alarm was increased because satellite reconnaissance revealed the presence of nuclear facilities north of the capital which the US intelligence community believed resembled a storage plant for enriched nuclear material.

MOTIVATION

Western and South Korean analysts produced a number of reasons why North Korea might want nuclear weapons, though, in the absence of North Korean justifications, these had to be purely deductive. First of all, it would hardly have been surprising if the North Koreans had felt threatened by US nuclear weapons both during the Korean War and afterwards. Washington had indeed considered using nuclear weapons during the war and had desisted, partly out of fear that they would have insufficient military impact.[2] Secondly, South Korea planned a nuclear weapons programme in the 1970s and, given the bitter hostility between the two Koreas, this, together with growing South Korean conventional military power, may have encouraged the North Korean project. In the event, the United States was able to persuade Seoul to abandon its nuclear weapons programme. The South Koreans were threatened with the loss of all assistance over nuclear technology and with the cessation of US military aid. Since US forces have been stationed in South Korea ever since the Korean War, this provided Washington with a good deal of leverage. The government in Seoul knew that it would lose more than it would gain from developing its own nuclear force.[3]

North Korea might also have developed nuclear weapons to balance Seoul's economic and political strength. In the 1960s and 1970s the two Koreas were locked in a competition to see which

[2] D. Calingaert, 'Nuclear Weapons and the Korean war', *Journal of Strategic Studies*, June 1988.

[3] On the South Korean nuclear programme see Y.-S. Ha, *Nuclear Proliferation World Order and Korea* (Seoul National University Press, 1983); on continued South Korean nuclear ambitions see 'Unified Korea should have nuclear weapons', *Korea Newsreview*, 31 October 1992 and H.-S. Wang and S. Rabson, 'South Korea and the Bomb; a not-so-new story', *Brown Journal of World Affairs*, Spring 1994, pp. 321 ff.

could develop diplomatic links with the greater number of countries. However, as the southern economy grew ever stronger and eventually began to dwarf its northern counterpart, so countries found that their interests were served by forming links with Seoul rather than Pyongyang. Even China exchanged ambassadors with South Korea, and two-way trade between the two countries grew to 5.8 billion dollars in the first nine months of 1992.

Fear that it was developing nuclear weapons increased North Korean prestige and made Washington and other capitals take an interest in its policies. North Korean exports were negligible and it was culturally isolated. Foreign tourists were few and the hotels in North Korea were primitive compared with the luxurious 'palaces' in the South. Media interest focused on the South, particularly after the Olympic Games were held in Seoul in September 1988. The North Koreans may have hoped to offset all these setbacks by threatening to develop nuclear weapons. Certainly they spoke about the nuclear option as 'the dam which makes the water flow'.

In any conflict with the South the northern government could expect little outside support. During the Korean War it had been armed by the Soviet Union, and its forces had been assisted by Soviet military advisers. Soviet help was not enough to protect North Korea against defeat by General MacArthur's forces, and its army was saved in the winter of 1950 only by massive Chinese intervention. However, by 1993 the Soviet Union had collapsed, and neither China nor Russia was likely to assist Pyongyang militarily. Yeltsin told the South Korean President in June 1994 that his government would disregard its military obligations under the 1961 Soviet–North Korean Treaty.[4] Thus the North Korean government may have seen nuclear weapons as a way of defending the country without Chinese and Soviet aid. The Koreans may also have hoped that the threat to develop nuclear weapons would persuade the United States to reduce its military presence in South Korea and particularly to end the extensive military exercises code-named 'Team Spirit', which US and South Korean troops had undertaken in the spring of each year since 1976.

Such a rich menu of possible motives made it easy to explain why North Korea might want nuclear weapons, but it did not help Western governments decide how to respond when Pyongyang

[4] 'Yeltsin pledges press on North Korea: military treaty with North Korea a dead letter', *Korean Newsreview*, 4 June 1994.

showed itself unable or unwilling to prove that it was not developing nuclear weapons, thereby causing a series of crises between North Korea and the international community led by the United States. If defensive concerns were fundamental the US could make concessions, but such appeasement either did not reduce North Korean suspicions nor persuaded it, for some time, that it could keep asking for more. Pyongyang's delaying tactics might equally be explained by its continuing need to enhance its prestige and decrease its isolation. Again, the longer it maintained its weapons programme the more concessions it could squeeze from Washington and Seoul. But its procrastination could equally be explained by divisions within the North Korean government, by unwillingness to admit, when exposed, that it had lied about its nuclear programme, and by a determination not to appear to be forced to change its policy.

THE CRISES

In April 1991 the Soviet Union warned that it would cease to provide technical assistance for the North's civil nuclear programme unless Pyongyang signed the safeguards agreement. The South Korean Defence Minister, Lee Jong Koo, also warned that Seoul might attack the North Korean facilities with commandos.[5] Pyongyang then announced that it would sign the agreement only if US bases in the South were also inspected to show that they were 'nuclear free'. Eight months later the US declared that it was withdrawing all nuclear weapons from South Korea. The North might therefore feel that its nuclear weapons programme—or the threat of such a programme—had already begun to pay dividends. In fact, the withdrawal of tactical nuclear weapons from South Korea was part of a general policy of returning these weapons from foreign bases to the United States, though it fitted well with efforts to placate Pyongyang.[6]

At that time and subsequently, North Korean policy vacillated

[5] 'Nuclear warning to Pyongyang', *The Times*, 16 April 1991. See also 'Yeltsin promises to pressure N.K. to stop development of Nuke arms', *Korea Newsreview*, 28 November 1992.

[6] 'Nuclear exit', *The Times*, 12 December 1991; 'ROK pushes for mutual UN-checks', *Korea Newsreview*, 6 June 1992. See also *Information Service on The Unification Question on the Korean Peninsula* (National Unification Board, Republic of Korea, 11 April 1994), hereafter *Information Service*.

unpredictably between defiance and détente, and it was impossible to tell whether this was part of a deliberate policy to confuse foreign governments, caused by uncertainty over how to interpret and respond to outside events, or the result of power struggles within the North Korean government. In November 1991 Pyongyang dismissed Seoul's claim that it would no longer have US nuclear weapons on its territory as 'insignificant'. Yet in mid-December North and South Korea signed a reconciliation and non-aggression agreement.[7] This was followed immediately by a joint declaration by the two governments on denuclearization, under which the peninsula was to be freed from nuclear weapons.

President Bush then visited Seoul and offered to forego the Team Spirit exercises in 1992, if the North accepted inspection. Again Pyongyang could feel that it had made a substantial gain. The South Korean armed forces were openly upset by the ending of the exercise, which they regarded as essential if a future North Korean attack were to be resisted. On its side, North Korea made a major concession by ratifying the safeguards agreement, but the IAEA then became aware of the extent of its programme. Pyongyang admitted to having 90 grammes of plutonium and that it had conducted one reprocessing operation. IAEA examination of the plutonium and the nuclear waste proved that there had, in fact, been four reprocessing operations from 1989 to 1992. US satellite photographs also showed that the North Koreans were trying to disguise the storage buildings which had apparently been designed to hold nuclear waste.[8]

The situation deteriorated at the beginning of February 1993, when the IAEA pressed for special inspections to remove the suspicions which had now been aroused. Pyongyang refused to allow the Agency to make the examinations requested at Yong-byon, 60 miles north of the capital.[9] It may be that the northern government had underestimated the technical sophistication of the IAEA system and had believed that it could hide its reprocessing from the inspectors. As a result, it signed the safeguards agreement then drew back when its lies were beginning to be exposed. To save

---

[7] 'Korea's threat alarms US', *The Times*, 11 November 1991.

[8] 'Bush prepared to cancel manoeuvres', *The Times*, 7 January 1992; *Information Service*, p. 41. On military attitudes to Team Spirit see 'Korea, US military hope for continuing Team Spirit', *Korea Newsreview*, 27 March 1993.

[9] For a summary of the position to 1994 see *Programme for Promoting Nuclear Non-Proliferation Newsbrief*, University of Southampton, no. 25, 1994.

face, in March Pyongyang gave notice of its intention to withdraw from the NPT, closed its borders to all outsiders, and issued a war alert. Houses had to cover their windows as the capital was blacked out. At the same time, the US and South Korea decided that the North had not made enough concessions to justify abandoning the 1993 Team Spirit exercises. The US Ambassador in Seoul said later that this decision probably increased Pyongyang's intransigence.[10]

The US might have immediately pressed for UN sanctions against North Korea, but many commentators were rightly pessimistic about the efficacy of economic sanctions against a dictatorship. Moreover, unlike Iraq, which really did suffer when sanctions were imposed, North Korea was largely isolated from world trade. Its chief partner was China, and the Chinese Foreign Minister warned that Beijing was opposed to sanctions.[11] China had itself only adhered to the NPT in 1992, and it took the view that the confrontation with the North should be ended by negotiation rather than by economic sanctions.

Under the terms of Article X of the NPT, a state wishing to withdraw has to give three months' notice to all treaty parties and to the Security Council. It also has to explain to them what 'extraordinary events' connected with the subject-matter of the treaty 'jeopardized its supreme interests' and led it to withdraw. The IAEA and the NPT parties were now faced with an acute dilemma. Plainly, the treaty would be completely undermined if parties could gain the benefits provided by the NPT and then denounce it whenever it became convenient to do so. The legal situation was analogous to the one which had arisen when Russia had denounced the demilitarization of the Black Sea in 1870. In that case St Petersburg had subsequently been persuaded to agree to the Declaration of London, stating that parties could not unilaterally denounce treaties to which they were party. Current law is determined by the Vienna Convention on the Law of Treaties. Article 54 of the Vienna Convention states that a party may withdraw from a

[10] 'Koreans renege on nuclear treaty', *The Times*, 13 March 1993; 'North issues war alert and closes borders', *The Times*, 16 March 1993; 'Seoul may seek US help as North declares "semi-war"', *The Times*, 17 March 1993. For US Ambassador Gregg's opinions see the press interview he gave subsequently, which was reported by Reuters and reprinted in the IAEA daily press summary 191 of 22 July 1994.
[11] 'Peking joins anti-nuclear pact', *The Times*, 10 March 1993; 'Pyongyang sanctions opposed', *The Times*, 24 March 1993; 'Kim, Jiang agree to cooperate closely on North Korean nuclear problem', *Korea Newsreview*, 2 April 1994.

treaty in conformity with its provisions or with the consent of all the parties. Implicit in Article X of the NPT is the notion that the parties or the Security Council have to decide whether to accept the justification advanced by a state for withdrawal from the treaty, but the article is certainly unclear.[12]

On 1 April 1993 the IAEA's Board of Governors found North Korea in breach of the safeguards agreement and voted to refer the question to the Security Council, with China and Libya voting against and India, Pakistan, Syria, and Vietnam abstaining. Pressed by China, the United States offered high-level talks with Pyongyang to try to resolve the issue. This represented a major concession by Washington, since Pyongyang had long demanded bilateral discussions to increase its prestige and exclude the South Koreans. The talks were said to have made sufficient progress by the middle of June, when North Korea's withdrawal from the treaty was to become effective, for Pyongyang to announce that it was suspending its decision.[13]

However, the relaxation of tensions proved only temporary. In October the batteries and film for the IAEA cameras monitoring the North Korean nuclear installations ran out and Pyongyang refused to allow them to be renewed. In December the North offered to give the IAEA some access to its nuclear sites, but not to the installation at Yongbyon which the IAEA regarded as particularly suspicious. It also rejected the offer by Boutros-Ghali, the UN Secretary General, to mediate in the dispute. At the same time a CIA report was leaked to the press, arguing that North Korea had already produced enough plutonium for one or two nuclear bombs. This was challenged by the US State Department, which argued that it was too pessimistic.[14] A few days later Pyongyang headed

[12] For the 'Declaration of London' see M. Hurst (ed.), *Key Treaties of the Great Powers* (David and Charles, Newton Abbot, 1972), vol. 2, p. 459. For the Vienna Convention see T. B. Millar (ed.), *Current International Treaties* (Croom Helm, London, 1984), pp. 10 ff. For the NPT and PTBT see SIPRI *Arms Control: A Survey and Appraisal of Multilateral Agreements* (Taylor and Francis, London, 1978), pp. 77, 88.

[13] 'Atomic powers warn North Korea to abide by arms treaty' and 'Dangerous game', *The Times*, 2 April 1993; 'Pyongyang suspends treaty withdrawal', *The Times*, 12 June 1993; 'Pyongyang takes small step to nuclear deal', *The Times*, 21 July 1993.

[14] 'Blow for US in sanctions fight against North Korea', *Daily Telegraph*, 28 December 1993; 'CIA says Pyongyang has nuclear bomb', *The Times*, 27 December 1993.

off a declaration by the IAEA that it was in breach of its international obligations by offering to allow further inspections.

These went ahead in March 1994, though again it seemed as though Pyongyang had grossly underestimated the Agency's efficiency or was simply responding to external pressures without any coherent policy. The seven inspectors found that seals placed earlier on equipment had been damaged, and they were not allowed to map gamma radiation or take samples they needed from the Yongbyon establishment. Faced with this evidence of cheating, the US cancelled one meeting that its officials were scheduled to have with the North Korean negotiators. It also announced that it would go ahead with Team Spirit exercises and deploy Patriot missiles to South Korea.[15] The North denounced this as an aggressive move, although in fact the ground-to-air missiles could not be used offensively and were sent to the South as some protection against North Korean Scud missiles. The crisis worsened in May, when the North Koreans removed fuel rods from one of their reactors without allowing the IAEA to inspect the process and thus assess whether some of the fuel had been removed previously to make nuclear weapons. The rods contained enough plutonium on their own to produce four or five bombs. South Korea placed its forces on full alert and the US argued that economic sanctions should be imposed by the Security Council to 'punish' North Korea for its actions. However, before this could occur, Pyongyang responded by withdrawing from the IAEA and mobilizing its army.[16]

Once again the crisis was defused at the last moment. In mid-June 1994 former President Jimmie Carter visited Pyongyang, just as the US was poised to ask the Security Council to impose some economic sanctions on North Korea. During the visit, Kim Il Sung offered to hold a summit conference with the South Korean Presid-

[15] 'Pyongyang backs nuclear checks', *The Times*, 6 January 1994; 'Korea talks grind to a halt despite Seoul concession', *The Times*, 4 March 1994; 'Pyongyang curbs nuclear inspectors', *The Times*, 16 March 1994; 'Pyongyang claims US missile move brings war nearer', *The Times*, 23 March 1994; 'Seoul to receive Patriot missiles', *Korea Newsreview*, 26 March 1994, p. 7.

[16] 'Washington presses for sanctions on Pyongyang', *The Times*, 21 March 1994; 'Team Spirit rescheduled for November', *Korea Newsreview*, 30 April 1994;. 'On the brink with North Korea', *New York Times*, 19 May 1994;. 'Koreans defy UN on reactor fuel tally', *The Times*, 28 May 1994; 'UN Council urges North Korea to preserve Atom-fuel evidence', *New York Times*, 31 May 1994; 'North Koreans talk of war and decide to quit nuclear agency', *The Times*, 14 June 1994.

ent and to freeze the North Korean nuclear programme. The news was greeted with euphoria in Seoul but with muted enthusiasm in Washington, where it was regarded as another delaying tactic. The administration told the North Koreans that a freeze would have to be continuously monitored by on-site IAEA inspection, that reprocessing would have to cease, and that work on new nuclear facilities would have to be halted. Pyongyang accepted the US terms, even though they went far beyond the NPT itself. The readiness to compromise with ex-President Carter would suggest that North Korean leaders were mainly concerned about prestige and were prepared to compromise when treated with sufficient respect. However, the outcome may have turned on changes within the North Korean government.

On 8 July Kim Il Sung died and this introduced further uncertainties. The North Korean leader was expected to be succeeded by his son, Kim Jong Il, who was regarded in the West as more aggressive than his father. Yet in August 1994 Pyongyang assured US negotiators it would remain an NPT party and forgo reprocessing spent fuel rods, if the US supplied it with modern nuclear reactors and moved towards establishing diplomatic relations with the North Korean government. In October an 'agreed framework' was reached between US and North Korean negotiators. North Korea would abandon its current plans for gas graphite reactors, which were regarded as particularly suitable for producing material for nuclear weapons. In their place the international community would for a time provide heavy oil for North Korea's conventional power stations. It would also supply two large light-water reactors. The North Koreans hoped that these would be produced by Russia or by any other country except South Korea, presumably because they resented any dependence on Seoul or suggestions that the southern regime was superior to their own. However, US negotiators found that Seoul alone was prepared to bear the main burden of financing the provision of light-water reactors, which the South Korean authorities estimated would cost 4 billion dollars. A Korean Energy Development Organization (KEDO) was to be set up to oversee the whole process and the US negotiators sought additional financial help from Japan, Europe, and the Middle East.[17]

[17] For South Korean attitudes to the crisis see 'No imminent war threat on Korean peninsula', *Korea Newsreview*, 18 June 1994. For the death of Kim Il Sung see 'Death of a dictator', *Sunday Telegraph*, 10 July 1994; 'Kim Il Sung',

THE THREAT OF WAR

In the crises between 1992 and 1994, both Korean and US spokesmen discussed the possibility of war breaking out. William Perry, the US Defense Secretary, said in April 1994 that the US had the capacity to destroy North Korean nuclear facilities in a pre-emptive strike. However, he admitted that an attack on the facilities might start a general war and emphasized US determination to avoid this. At the same time Anthony Lake, the National Security Adviser, told reporters that the US would be victorious if war came. Similarly, the South Korean Defence Minister, Rhee Byoung Tae, predicted in March 1994 that the North would suffer 'only miserable defeat' in a war with the Western allies, while a North Korean official said that Seoul would become 'a sea of flame when war broke out'.[18]

Both the South Korean and the US governments wished to avoid war if at all possible, while convincing North Korea that they were determined to oppose any breach of the NPT. Yet public opinion in neither country was in any way prepared for war. The US people had shown considerable doubts about going to war against Iraq in 1991, despite the clear evidence of Iraqi aggression. The Clinton administration wanted to concentrate its attention on improving the US economy, from which it had already been distracted by other international crises in Bosnia and Somalia. The South Korean government under Kim Young-Sam was the first to be freely elected in the country without the interference of the army. The new government was primarily interested in maintaining economic growth and strengthening democratic institutions. It wanted cooperation with Pyongyang, not confrontation, and certainly not war.

The Times, 11 July 1994; 'North Korea keeps door open as son of Kim takes over', *The Times*, 14 July 1994. For the August 1994 agreement see 'Geneva talks may yield N-transparency', *Korea Newsreview*, 20 August 1994. After extensive negotiations, the Korean Peninsula Energy Development Organization and North Korea signed an agreement on 15 December 1995 under which the organization would build the two new reactors in North Korea and train North Koreans to operate them. Pyongyang would pay for the reactors over the twenty years after they were completed. 'KEDO, North Korea sign N-reactor accord', *Korea Newsreview*, 23 December 1995.

[18] 'CIA chief warns on Korean war', *The Times*, 2 December 1993; 'Pyongyang hits at patriot build-up', *The Times*, 29 March 1994; 'South's military forces outclass North's', *Korea Newsreview*, 2 April 1994.

As far as elite opinion was concerned, there was a marked contrast between Washington and Seoul. US newspapers and Congressmen sometimes suggested that a military strike on North Korean nuclear facilities was possible and might be necessary. South Korean newspapers, by contrast, implied that an attack was most unlikely, even in June 1994 when tension was at its height. Yet, paradoxically, when agreement was reached in October it was bitterly criticized for a time in South Korea. Because the North had not committed itself to being sufficiently open, even members of the ruling party called for changes in the personnel of the South Korean foreign ministry. The US wanted to end the crisis and forget about North Korea; the South Koreans would have been prepared to continue to put pressure on Pyongyang, despite their determination to avoid an open conflict. Seoul saw the issue primarily in terms of inter-Korean relations, Washington in terms of nuclear proliferation.[19]

On their side the North Koreans probably felt victimized by the international community, which did not apply similar pressure on other countries that had developed or considered developing nuclear weapons. President de Klerk of South Africa admitted in March 1993 that his country had produced six nuclear weapons, although it had subsequently decided to dismantle them. Israel, India, and Pakistan were suspected of having secretly developed nuclear weapons, yet none was the subject of the sort of concerted pressure which was brought to bear on North Korea. The US could, of course, argue that the legal position was different. Until 1991, when South Africa adhered to the NPT, none of these four countries was a party to the NPT and thus they had no legal commitment to abandon nuclear weapons. If North Korea had developed nuclear weapons, it had done so while it was a party to the NPT. North Korean actions put it legally on a level with Iraq, not with Israel, India, or Pakistan.

Washington and its allies regarded North Korea with particular suspicion. On 9 October 1983 three North Korean officers tried to

[19] 'No imminent war threat on Korean peninsula', *Korea Newsreview*, 18 June 1994, but note the interview which President King Young-sam gave to the press in June 1994 in which he said, 'I will stop the North from developing nuclear weapons by all means.' See 'Cooperation for Peace on the Korean Peninsula affirmed', *Korea Newsreview*, 11 June 1994, p. 4. On Korean disappointment with the deal see 'Kim seen to be haunted by US–N.K. deal', *Korea Newsreview*, 22 October 1994.

assassinate President Chun and other members of the South Korean cabinet when they were on a state visit to Burma. Seventeen South Koreans were killed, including four cabinet ministers.[20] Four years later, apparently in order to upset the Olympic Games in Seoul, two North Korean agents put a bomb on a South Korean airliner, which destroyed it over the Indian Ocean. In both cases one or more of the North Korean agents were captured, so there could be no doubt about the official nature of the plots. Given such a record, it was hardly surprising that the international community regarded the prospect of North Korean nuclear weapons with alarm. Some US policy-makers and commentators believed that a conventional war should be risked in the early 1990s to avoid a nuclear confrontation five years later. But their views were in the minority and this was probably obvious to decision-makers in Pyongyang.

THE CUBAN MISSILE CRISIS

There are some similarities between the North Korean crisis and the Cuban missile crisis of 1962. In the earlier case the Soviet leader, Nikita Khrushchev, decided to place intermediate and medium-range ballistic missiles on the island of Cuba.[21] The SS4 missiles had a range of 1,020 nautical miles and the SS5s about 2,200. The Soviets had considerable numbers of these missiles but few ICBMs which could reach the United States from the Soviet Union itself. Placing missiles in Cuba would thus balance the large US ICBM force. It would also protect Cuba from a US invasion. The Kennedy administration had already supported one abortive invasion by Cuban exiles in April 1961. Washington's hostility to Cuba's radical government was intense and it was involved in a number of plots to assassinate the Cuban leader, Fidel Castro.[22] Placing Soviet missiles in Cuba would protect the island behind Moscow's nuclear 'umbrella'.

Khrushchev needed to deploy the missiles in Cuba before the US either detected them or decided how it was going to respond. Washington would be cautious about attempting to destroy a fully operational nuclear missile force within easy range of much of the

[20] Clough, *Embattled Korea*, p. 182.
[21] *Khrushchev Remembers* (Little Brown, New York, 1971), p. 491.
[22] J. Ranelagh, *The Agency: The Rise and Decline of the CIA* (Sceptre, Cambridge, 1987).

most populated part of the country. In the event, however, intelligence reports of the arrival of the missiles were confirmed by US reconnaissance aircraft before the missiles were activated. Militarily the Soviets were then in a very weak position. According to the IISS, the US had 294 ICBMs, 144 SLBMs (submarine launched missiles), and 600 bombers. On the other hand, the Soviets only had 75 ICBMs, a few SLBMs, and 190 inferior bombers.[23]

Furthermore, the US had total conventional military superiority in the Caribbean. Thus the Soviets could only respond effectively to any US military action by an attack on Berlin or some other area where the West was at a disadvantage. The Soviets might have doubted that the US would attack the missiles, but this would have been a mistake. President Kennedy was under intense pressure from the Joint Chiefs of Staff and from many of his civilian advisers to use force. By 23 October the B52 force was on airborne alert, the older B47s had been dispersed, and the ICBM missiles were at readiness. At the same time the US 'quarantined' Cuba with its warships to prevent any further Soviet missiles reaching the islands.[24]

In 1962 the Kennedy administration managed to convince Soviet leaders that they were not bluffing. The two governments then struck an unequal bargain. The Soviets agreed to withdraw the SS4 and SS5, while the US promised not to attack the Cuban government. It also secretly agreed to withdraw its Jupiter missiles from Turkey. The agreement was one-sided because the Soviets failed in their ambition to balance the US ICBMs, and the outcome was generally regarded as a victory for the United States and a humiliation for Moscow. Had the Jupiter deal not been secret, the arrangement would have looked much more like a normal arms-control agreement rather than an example of forced disarmament. The crisis probably helped to bring about Khrushchev's fall in 1964 and spur the very heavy Soviet programme of warship and missile construction, which meant that the Soviets overtook the US in the number of their ICBMs in 1970 and in SLBMs in 1974. Forced disarmament worked for a time, but it was arguably disadvantageous in the long run.[25]

[23] IISS *Military Balance 1975–1976*, p. 73.

[24] K. R. Tidman, *The Operations Evaluation Group* (Naval Institute Press, Annapolis, Md., 1984), pp. 233 ff.

[25] On the crisis itself see D. A. Welch and J. G. Blight, 'An introduction to the ExComm transcripts', *International Security*, Winter 1987–8.

In the 1990s the US enjoyed total nuclear superiority over North Korea. This would have been the case even in the unlikely eventuality of China coming to Pyongyang's support. But such superiority was irrelevant, since the US would not use its nuclear weapons except to respond to a North Korean nuclear attack. In conventional terms, the local balance in the Korean peninsula looked more tempting from Pyongyang's point of view, as Table 6 shows.[26]

Table 6   Conventional balance between North Korea, South Korea, and the USA.

	North Korea	South Korea	USA
Troops	1,127,000	633,000	34,830
Tanks, etc.	3,700	1,800	100
Aircraft	780	600	230

However, the bald statistics hid great discrepancies in the nature of the weapons deployed. US and South Korean tanks and aircraft were several generations more modern than their North Korean equivalents. During the crises the US introduced new helicopters into the peninsula and new radars to assist artillery to attack enemy batteries. The quality of the troops was more difficult to compare. North and South Koreans acquired a formidable reputation in Vietnam. US forces are at their best when fighting conventional wars, and the figures ignore the 400,000 additional troops which General Luck, the US Commander in South Korea, promised would be sent in the event of a war. US weaknesses were economic and political, not military. A full-scale war would further damage the US economy *vis-à-vis* its Asian rivals, and it was by no means clear that the US people were prepared to incur very heavy casualties while the memories of the Vietnam War were still so fresh.

In 1962 the US had not been scarred by the Vietnam War and its economy was unchallenged. Cuba was close to the US itself and the US people believed that their vital interests were at stake there. Furthermore, Washington did not need to listen to Caribbean opinion in 1962; in the early 1990s any war would be fought on Korean soil and thus the South Korean government and its opposition to a 'pre-emptive strike' could not be ignored. Consequently,

[26] 'If the shooting starts who will win?', *Time*, 4 April 1994, pp. 19 ff.

Pyongyang took risks on the assumption that Washington would not attack. Khrushchev rightly decided that he could not make that gamble once the US was alerted to the presence of his missiles in Cuba.

THE LIBYAN CRISIS OF 1989

Another crisis which offered some parallels and contrasts with the confrontation with North Korea in the early 1990s was the US–Libyan confrontation in 1989. In January 1989 Washington alleged that Libya was building a factory to produce chemical weapons at Rabta, 40 miles south of Tripoli. Western firms were involved in the Libyan project, although they may not have known that the new plant was to produce chemical weapons.[27] President Reagan speculated in an interview with ABC television that the US might attack the factory, although US spokesmen subsequently tried to play down the immediacy of such an action. George Bush, the President-elect, said that the US would consider such options only if other methods failed.[28] Nevertheless, the ambiguity in the US position might have increased Libyan anxieties.

US threats against Libya were credible because the US had attacked Tripoli and Benghazi in April 1986. It had been criticized at that time, particularly in the Arab world, but such opposition would not have prevented Washington launching another strike if it had decided to do so.[29] There was also no way that Libya could retaliate against the USA except via terrorism, and terrorist attacks would only bring further US reprisals. The situation in the Korean Peninsula was very different. There was uncertainty about whether the US armed forces could actually destroy North Korean nuclear facilities in airborne or missile attacks. Even if a US attack were successful, North Korea could respond either with Scud missiles or by a ground attack against South Korea. Thus the US had always treated North Korea much more cautiously than Libya. It failed to retaliate when the North Koreans seized a US intelligence ship in January 1968 and when they killed two US officers in the demilitarized zone between the two countries in August 1976. The North

---

[27] 'US and allies in full exchange of intelligence', *The Times*, 5 January 1989.

[28] 'US embarrassed by Reagan revelation on military strike', *The Times*, 24 December 1988.

[29] 'Armed intervention on chemical works rejected by Reagan', *The Times*, 6 January 1989.

Koreans were naturally more likely to predict future US behaviour on the basis of Washington's habitual caution towards themselves than on the more assertive line the US had taken in the 1962 and 1989 crises.

The US could also deny the Libyans the equipment they needed for the Rabta plant, if it could persuade its allies to co-operate. To a large extent, this meant 'leaning on' West Germany, since some thirty West German firms were alleged to be involved in the Libyan project. Correspondents called the resulting confrontation 'the worst diplomatic row with Bonn in postwar history' with Chancellor Kohl accusing Washington of treating his country 'like a banana republic'. But overt pressure worked in the way that diplomatic pressure on West Germany had not succeeded in doing up to that time.[30] There was no similar way that the US could interrupt the North Korean nuclear programme, because the North Koreans had already been given the technology by the Soviets and their programme was independent of outside assistance. Again, the parallel illustrates the strength of the North Korean position and the weakness of the American one.

Without knowing Pyongyang's aims and motives it is impossible to say what objectives, if any, the North Korean government gave up under international pressure between 1991 and 1994. If its objectives were to increase its international prestige and importance, to gain diplomatic recognition and economic assistance, and to reduce the US military (and particularly nuclear) presence in South Korea, then its strategy worked admirably. Washington intended to enforce the disarmament of North Korea, but the North Koreans could claim that it was Washington and Seoul which were coerced into disarmament. If, on the other hand, Pyongyang's objective really was to become a nuclear weapon state then it was Pyongyang which accepted disarmament, at least for a time.

Even if this was the case, it is impossible to say how much was achieved by threats and how much by incentives. What one can say is that the incentives offered were very considerable, including

---

[30] 'Bonn investigates blocked Libyan export deals', *The Times*, 11 January 1989; 'Bonn MPs demand full account of German role', *The Times*, 19 January 1989; 'US wins time to toughen chemical arms controls', *The Times*, 21 January 1989; 'Firms are raided as Germany steps up Rabta investigation', *The Times*, 26 January 1989.

4 billion dollars' worth of nuclear equipment, the establishment of diplomatic relations between Washington and Pyongyang, and the abandonment of efforts to arraign Pyongyang for its past policies. On the other hand, it was hard for the Clinton administration to make credible threats to attack North Korean nuclear facilities because of the very obvious state of public opinion in South Korea and, whatever individual commentators and Congressmen may have said, in the USA itself. Washington's difficulties were compounded by the nature of the target for such threats. Pyongyang was not likely to be weakened by the doubts which assailed the Czech democrats in 1938; indeed, there could hardly be a greater contrast than that between the democratic government of President Benes and the granite-faced totalitarianism of Kim Il Sung. The Western states opposed the North Korean acquisition of nuclear weapons partly at least because they feared the 'irrational' nature of the regime. But this very quality weakened their ability to coerce the North Koreans. Pyongyang could resist for several years because of Western fears of the government's 'irrational' nature, because the West's nuclear superiority was largely irrelevant and it was clear that Western and South Korean publics wanted, above all, to avoid a conventional war.

The Soviet Union's overall power was incomparably greater in 1962 than North Korea's thirty years later. Its legal position was also stronger since there was no agreement to keep nuclear weapons out of Cuba, while North Korea was an NPT party. Yet, paradoxically, Kim Il Sung had a better hand and played his cards much more effectively than Khrushchev had done in the Cuban missile crisis. He thus made certain that any deal would be seen to be far less favourable to the US than the agreement struck in 1962. If the arrangement with North Korea in October 1994 was a case of enforced disarmament, Pyongyang had camouflaged it very effectively.

Conclusion

THE LIMITATIONS

Has the effort involved in forcing another state to disarm and keeping it disarmed ever been worthwhile for the victors, or has it simply exacerbated tensions between the nations without preserving the imbalance of power caused by war?

For Napoleon, Hitler, and other dictators, forced disarmament was an interim measure while they decided whether to destroy defeated states completely. Both Napoleon and Hitler used the weapons and money seized from their defeated enemies in their continued drive for expansion. The effort involved in forcing their enemies to disarm was not great, and they may even have enjoyed the bitterness and humiliation felt by the defeated governments and peoples. However, such feelings increased the determination of the vanquished states to join in an attack on the dominant power when opportunity arose, and to impose the most vindictive terms after its defeat. Prussian and Austrian armies fought against Napoleon in 1814 and 1815; French armies rejoined the allies towards the end of the Second World War. The Prussians in 1815 and the French in 1945 were among the least forgiving of the victors.

Victorious democracies have forced their enemies to disarm in order to justify the losses their own people have suffered and to try to preserve their security. But such efforts have usually increased the bitterness of the vanquished, and their anger and frustration have grown as the years have passed. Nor were these political disadvantages always offset by undeniable military gains; despite the effort put into disarming Germany in the 1920s, the French still had good reason to feel the latent menace represented by Germany's industrial might and demographic strength.

Surrendering weapons is a symbol of defeat, an acknowledgement of submission and vulnerability. Defeat is usually followed by acrimonious disputes within the vanquished states, among the military leaders or between soldiers, statesmen, and civilians about responsibility for their predicament. The bitterness of the defeated forces is dramatically increased if they have to submit to intrusive inspection of their arsenals and barracks. The more they resist, the more demanding the inspectors are likely to be. Unless the vanquished accept that their defeat was morally justified, as many Germans did after 1945, forced disarmament will always increase their resentment.

Alongside its political disadvantages, forced disarmament can damage the environment. The demilitarization of Dunkirk in the eighteenth century threatened the health of the inhabitants and the ecosystem of the surrounding area. Dunkirk may have been exceptional for its period, but the problem became potentially more serious as weapons technology advanced. The allied policy of dropping thousands of tons of chemical weapons into the sea at the end of the Second World War continues to cause anxiety, fifty years later. The UN has taken far greater care of the environment during the disarmament of Iraq, but this increased the duration and cost of the operation. The easiest way to destroy high explosive is often to detonate or burn it. The cheapest way to demobilize tanks is to drive them into the sea, but the environmental consequences can be serious.

THE ADVANTAGES

For those states defeated by aggressive dictators, it is better to be disarmed than to be absorbed entirely into their empires or destroyed by ethnic cleansing. Prussia was in a better position under Napoleon than Spain, the Netherlands, or Saxony. Vichy France was favoured compared with the Nazi repression of Poland, Serbia, or Bohemia. For the dictators it was sometimes beneficial to weaken but not to destroy an enemy completely. Until the last two years of his empire, Prussia gave Napoleon less trouble than Spain. Indeed, the Prussians actually fought on his side against Russia in 1812. Some Frenchmen volunteered to fight for the Nazis in the Second World War, while the Poles, Czechs, and Dutch remained sunk in bitter resentment against their conquerors.[1]

---

[1] For an account by one French volunteer see G. Sajer, *The Forgotten Soldier* (Sphere Books, London, 1977).

As far as victorious democracies are concerned, after a limited war there is usually little or no animus among the victorious public against the vanquished peoples. In a total and prolonged war, public passions naturally become more inflamed as the destruction increases and the casualties mount. Stories of war crimes are often spread by the media, so that the struggle becomes one between peoples as well as governments. After a localized war, victors' demands are usually designed to achieve restricted, tactical objectives, such as the demilitarization of the Black Sea in 1856. Support for such measures is normally confined to the educated elite. After a total war, the general public expects governments to press for more far-reaching measures of disarmament. Peace treaties have to be tailored to suit both strategic objectives and public demands.

Forced disarmament is a relatively harmless response to these public pressures. Victors are bound to try to make the most of their achievements. Even if democratic statesmen acknowledged privately that their country's military success was ephemeral, they would have to meet public demands to compensate for the losses incurred. Relatives of those who have made the ultimate sacrifice will quite reasonably be infuriated by any suggestion that they achieved only a temporary gain. In victorious democracies forced disarmament can be seen as a channel for public feelings which might otherwise find outlets in demands for revenge—much more extensive war crime trials, purges of those who supported the enemy government, and massive reparations. If the public can be convinced that at least hostile armies have been rendered harmless for the foreseeable future, their anger and frustration may be assuaged. Otherwise their wrath may be turned on helpless enemy people or on their own leaders. Forced disarmament may embitter the vanquished, but some of the alternatives would give far more reason for their hatred and resentment.

In this respect, forced disarmament fulfils the same role as the ritual signs of defeat performed by animals of the same species once one has overcome another. Such rituals were described by Konrad Lorenz in his study of aggression. The defeated wolf turns his head away from the victor, exposing the unprotected side of his neck; the stag bares his flank and the jackdaw the vulnerable base of the skull.[2] Among humans, forced disarmament 'buys time'

[2] K. Lorenz, *On Agression* (University Paperback, London, 1967), pp. 113 ff.

while the victors' aggressive instincts subside and while they begin to sympathize with the state to which defeat has reduced the enemy peoples.

Despite the bitterness it produces in the defeated army, many would accept the arguments in favour of the destruction of enemy weapons in the moment of victory. This is much less destabilizing than allowing them to be sold and spread broadcast across the world. For a time after a war, forced disarmament may even be accepted by some of the vanquished, particularly in an age of total warfare. Most people will be relieved that the fighting has stopped, that incessant demands for money and recruits have ended, that their lives have been spared, and that normal everyday ways of life can gradually be restored. The Athenians may have wept to see their fleets burnt and their walls demolished, but they rejoiced that their city and their lives had been spared. The Carthaginians were prepared to accept demilitarization; it was the threatened destruction of their city which drove them to a last desperate effort to resist Roman demands. Some Germans actually co-operated in destroying their own weapons in 1919, as indeed they and the Japanese did in 1946. While the period of contrition, relief, and exhaustion lasts, forced disarmament has fewer disadvantages than advantages.

THE RAMIFICATIONS OF FORCED DISARMAMENT

The physical destruction of enemy weapons will give the victors some breathing-space, even if no attempt is made to prevent the enemy rearming at a later date. How much time will be gained depends largely upon the nature of the weapons. The walls of ancient cities and the ships of traditional fleets were good targets for immediate measures of forced disarmament because they took time and effort to rebuild—although not as much time as the victors hoped. Hand-held weapons, armour, and catapults could be more quickly replicated. Today ships, aircraft, tanks, and nuclear weapons take at least a decade to develop and produce. This period can be reduced if machine tools and drawings of weapons have survived the defeat. The survival of the scientists and work-force involved is even more important in the long run. They can be temporarily dispersed by the victors but, protected by humanitarian law and sentiment, they can reconvene as soon as the victorious armies have withdrawn.

Some commentators have suggested that defeated states can actually benefit because the victors prohibit existing and thus obsolete weapons, leaving the vanquished free to experiment with new equipment.[3] Some also say that such measures force the defeated army to improve their tactics and training to compensate for the limitations imposed on them, but it is difficult to find examples which support this general line of argument. The military reformers had already begun trying to modernize the Prussian army after its defeat by Napoleon and before the French Emperor imposed legal limits on its size. Napoleon's edicts made the reformers' task much harder rather than easier. Some have suggested that allied limitations on the German armed forces after the First World War encouraged them to experiment with tanks, missiles, and aircraft, and thus were indirectly responsible for the success of German *Blitzkrieg* tactics against France and the smaller European powers in 1940. But the Treaty of Versailles banned the Germans from having military aircraft and tanks. It thus made it much more difficult for the Germans to experiment with such weapons in the 1920s. It was the determination to learn from and undo the defeat, combined with the efficiency of the German staff and Hitler's determination to overturn the whole Versailles system, which was at the root of German military success at the start of the Second World War, not the disarmament measures imposed at Versailles.

Other commentators have argued that forced disarmament may benefit the economy of a defeated state by preventing it from 'wasting' money on defence and armaments. This argument was particularly fashionable when the German and Japanese economies were growing very rapidly in the 1960s and 1970s. However, it seems much less persuasive in the 1990s, when Taiwan, South Korea, and China have far more dynamic economies than Germany and Japan and yet spend highly on defence. Taiwan and China each spent 5 per cent of their GNP on defence in 1994, while South Korea spent 3.6 per cent, yet the Taiwanese economy grew by 6.1 per cent, the Chinese by 11.8, and the South Korean by 8.6. Japan, which spent 1 per cent on defence, grew by 0.6 per cent. Deep-rooted factors were responsible for the economic success of Ger-

[3] See, for example, the obituary of Arthur Rudolph, the Nazi missile designer, in *The Times*, 4 January 1996. The obituarist argued that Rudolph was able to work on missiles in Germany precisely because they were not limited by the Treaty of Versailles.

many and Japan in the 1960s, rather than the level of their defence spending.[4]

If the vanquished gain no obvious military and economic advantages from enforced disarmament, victors may hope that limited forced disarmament measures will be easier for the vanquished to accept than more far-reaching measures. This seems logical but it is difficult to prove. All forced disarmament measures are regarded as humiliating and an infringement of sovereignty. Peoples only accept them, as many Germans did in 1945, when they see no alternative, or on the very rare occasions when they are actually disgusted with their past and see their own disarmament as justified. In other circumstances a limited measure may cause equal resentment but be more difficult to enforce, because it does not reduce the totality of the defeated state's power. On the other hand, limited measures emerge from limited victories, and a state achieving a partial victory may well decide that it is still worth trying to enforce some measure of disarmament, even if it angers the defeated nation and will prove only temporary.

At the other extreme, unconditional surrender followed by complete demilitarization—as envisaged for Germany and Japan after 1945—obviously makes it impossible for a beaten enemy to rearm in secret to the extent necessary to threaten the victors. But such demilitarization will gradually break down without permanent, far-reaching, and intrusive inspection. If they insist that the vanquished should honour the letter of the agreement, the inspectors will be accused of worrying about trivia and bringing the whole process into disrepute. Allied inspectors in Germany in the 1920s were concerned about the production of replica weapons and sporting rifles. It is also notable how the German police in the 1920s and the Japanese in the early 1950s came to resemble armies. To avoid a multitude of such problems, the optimum solution—as in Iraq today—may be to prohibit only the most menacing of the enemy's weapons.

Nuclear, chemical, and biological weapons occupy a category of their own, because the general inhibitions and treaties against using and even possessing them have gradually increased. Iraq, like the vast majority of states, had already agreed before the Gulf War not to acquire nuclear weapons and not to use or to threaten to use

---

[4] IISS, *Military Balance 1995–1996*, pp. 264 ff.

chemical weapons. Postwar enforcement has largely been concerned with making the Iraqis abide by their promises. This separ-
ates the issue from other post-bellum enforcement actions, where
disarmament has from the beginning been imposed rather than
voluntary. Any eighteenth-century French government was going
to be hostile to the demilitarization of Dunkirk, any nineteenth-
century Russian government was going to try to end the neutralization of the Black Sea, any German government in the 1920s was
likely to press for the revision of many aspects of the Versailles
Treaty. But, unless the NPT system breaks down completely, an
Iraqi government might one day agree to uphold the treaty without
external pressure to do so. Forced disarmament may thus be replaced by voluntary moves and have more lasting results than in
the other cases studied.

A thorough attempt to destroy a state's military potential, rather
than just to compel it to abandon specific weapons, would involve
the destruction of the enemy economy and profoundly damage its
people. This is reflected in Roman plans for Carthage before the
Third Punic War, in the fate of Dunkirk in the eighteenth century,
and in the debate over the Morgenthau plan in the Second World
War. The port of Dunkirk was an ideal haven both for an invasion
force and for merchant and fishing vessels. The one could not be
destroyed without devastating the other. Virtually any modern
industry can be converted to supply military equipment. In a
national emergency, the speed of such a transformation often
surprises those responsible for implementing it. Glass-manufactur-
ing companies can make gun sights, chemical industries could
produce explosives or poisonous gases, shoe factories may turn out
army boots. Only frequent and intrusive inspection can warn that
this is taking place; only force or the threat of force can prevent it.

Given enemy determination to rearm, prolonged forced disarmament depends upon the struggle between the will-power of the
victors and the vanquished. In the 1920s and 1930s the German
determination to rearm was ultimately stronger than the French
determination to resist this process. The French government had to
consider the conflicting views of its own people, its armed forces,
and its allies. In the end the French would have to fight in order to
preserve the Versailles system; their willingness to do so was sapped
by the losses in the First World War, by the difficulties encountered
in the occupation of the Ruhr, and by the failure of the British and

Americans to give them support. The German government and people were united by their determination to reconstitute their strength and to undo the Treaty of Versailles. Gustav Stresemann and Adolf Hitler employed very different methods, but they both wanted to overthrow the Treaty of Versailles and restore German strength.

It is sometimes better for the victorious statesmen to recognize that their achievements cannot be prolonged indefinitely. They may then force the defeated nation to disarm for a specific and relatively limited period. This avoided the humiliation faced by British governments in 1870 and 1935, when they had to admit that peace treaties were being breached by former enemies, that they were unwilling to go to war to enforce them and that the achievements of the previous war were being undone. Of course, in the moment of victory governments would be criticized for having asked their people to sacrifice their lives when the fruits of victory were admitted to be so temporary. At such moments, when the enemy has been vilified and its war crimes emphasized, it is hard for governments to tell their people, or even to imagine themselves, that the present lull is temporary and that they may even need the assistance of former enemies in struggles against their current allies. Yet this was the case within a few years of even the bitterest of wars, as both the Soviet and Western peoples were reminded after 1945.

Usually it was civilian statesmen rather than their military commanders who were responsible for introducing disarmament measures into peace treaties. It was Alexander and Metternich who espoused them in 1815 and Wellington who moderated their demands; it was Lloyd George, Wilson, and Clemenceau who insisted on the forced disarmament of Germany in 1919, and Foch, Robertson, and other soldiers who voiced their doubts; it was the same statesmen who wanted to limit Hungary, Bulgaria, and Austria to tiny forces and General Bliss who pointed out the disadvantages of such severe measures; it was Churchill, Roosevelt, and Stalin who backed forced disarmament in 1945, and sometimes individual allied officers like General Willoughby who opposed it. Military commanders have been more aware than their civilian counterparts of the inherent difficulties of finding hidden weapons, of altering the balance of power by what are often limited measures, and of enforcing disarmament over a long period. In some cases they have foreseen the need to use the defeated forces for their own purposes and sympathized with the defeated army, which has expended so much blood and demonstrated so much skill and courage to no avail. Scipio and Hannibal found much to talk about when they went over the Second Punic War together in their retirement; Roddie and Bingham liked their German counterparts in the 1920s, while Morgan, the civilian lawyer in uniform, took a much more vengeful stance.

To democratic politicians, the political problems involved in peace-making are only too obvious; the military problems involved in forced disarmament appear more easily surmountable because weapons and troops are tangible, can be counted, and thus apparently controlled. To civilians in general it often seems both natural and necessary to force defeated enemies to give up their arms. Enemy states cannot be trusted and yet, in modern times, victory for democratic Western states fortunately cannot be made permanent by killing or enslaving enemy peoples. Thus forced disarmament is a *via media* between the unthinkable means of genocide or ethnic cleansing and the goal of perfect security. It causes little controversy between civilian leaders, even when allies can agree on few other war aims—as in the Second World War.

RESISTANCE AND CO-OPERATION

Disarmament has been imposed both upon declining and rising powers. France in 1713, Russia in 1739, Germany in 1919, Germany and Japan in 1945 were all rising powers. Poland in the eighteenth century, France in 1815 and 1940, Russia in 1917, Austria and Hungary in 1919 were all declining powers. Growth or decline in a state's power is the result of deep economic, demographic, political, and geographical problems which forced disarmament cannot control. Common sense would suggest that forced disarmament is less likely to be successful when imposed on rising rather than on declining powers. But this is difficult to prove, and the decline may be more obvious to historians than to the leaders of defeated powers who resisted disarmament measures or to the victors who imposed them. Weak powers may resist out of ignorance of the odds against them, out of desperation, as Poland did in the eighteenth century, or out of pride. Whatever the weakness of modern Iraq to Western eyes, this has not stopped

Saddam Hussein vigorously contesting UN efforts to disarm his country.

Thus neither the 'common-sense' notion that limited measures of disarmament will be resisted less strongly than more far-reaching ones, nor that weak or declining powers will oppose forced disarmament less vigorously than rising ones is fully confirmed by the evidence. Nor is this as surprising as it appears at first sight. As a contemporary strategist has pointed out, strategy is the realm of paradox rather than of logic or common sense.[5] The quickest way of ending a campaign may not be a direct attack on an enemy but a circuitous and unexpected one. So again the quickest way for a vanquished nation to rearm may be for it to accept its disarmament willingly and openly.

Defeated nations have three basic options when ordered to disarm: to resist, to wait upon events, or to co-operate. Which they choose depends partly upon the depth of anger against the treaties and the fear among the defeated people of the measures the victors might take if thwarted. Germany in the 1920s and Iraq in the 1990s chose the first option and waged a form of guerrilla warfare against the inspectors, including evasion, threats, mob attacks, and propaganda. In these two cases public bitterness against the treaties was high, while fear of the allies was limited. Such instances have been rare; in Dunkirk in the eighteenth century, in the Black Sea ports after the Crimean War, in Austria and Bulgaria between the two World Wars, and in Japan and Germany after 1945, the inspectors were apparently left to carry out their duties unmolested.

Where it has occurred, resistance has been ineffective, as it is doubtful whether the inspectors were withdrawn from Germany more quickly because of these tactics and, at the time of writing, the UNSCOM inspectors show no signs of leaving Iraq. Harassment prolongs the war psychology and the victors' inclination to see the vanquished as their enemies. However, it may be necessary for the restoration of the pride of the defeated nation, even if it actually postpones the moment when it will be allowed to re-enter international society and disarmament will cease to be imposed. A second option for the defeated is to wait, in the way Russia bided its time after 1856, until the victorious coalition is weakened or

[5] E. N. Luttwak, *Strategy: The Logic of War and Peace* (Belknap Press of Harvard University Cambridge, Mass., 1987), part 1.

divided, as eventually it must be, and then to denounce the treaties. This will produce a crisis, but the erstwhile victors may be in no position to resist. This strategy is more likely to be successful than harassment, but it will be less satisfying to the defeated peoples.

Finally the vanquished may opt to co-operate with the victors and recognize the international 'pecking order' established, if only temporarily, by the war. This is what Austria did in 1809 and Germany and Japan decided to do after 1945. Very often this is the quickest way to be readmitted to the international system, as it encourages the victors to co-opt their former enemies into their alliances. But it means that the defeated may have to fight alongside their conquerors against their former allies, something which embittered Prussian patriots in the Napoleonic period, and which even the Vichy government refused to Hitler's Nazi regime.[6]

The defeated nations which were co-opted into alliances were quickly rearmed after the Second World War: Hungary, the German Democratic Republic, and Bulgaria by the Warsaw Pact; Italy, the Federal Republic of Germany, and Japan by the Western allies. Those nations which remained neutral endured more far-reaching measures of forced disarmament for a longer period. By the postwar treaties, Finland was prevented from having missiles. The negotiators no doubt had strategic missiles of the V-2 type in mind, but the treaties still inhibited the Finns for many years from buying anti-tank and anti-aircraft missiles. The British had wanted Finnish armaments limited in 1946 because they expected Finland to be absorbed into the Soviet alliance system. Later they were more accommodating towards the Finns when they bought British equipment, but London's attitudes still restricted Helsinki's freedom of choice. Austrian defence forces were also hampered by international agreement. Vienna's requests for treaty amendments so that it could buy battlefield missiles were bitterly denounced in the Soviet press during the 1960s and 1970s.[7]

THE LITERATURE OF PEACE-MAKING

There would be a greater chance of deciding what can reasonably be expected of forced disarmament if, after the immediate postwar

[6] For Prussian reactions see P. Paret, *Clausewitz and the State* (Clarendon Press, Oxford, 1976), pp. 214 ff.

[7] F. Tanner (ed.), *From Versailles to Baghdad: Post-War Armament Control of Defeated States* (United Nations, New York, 1992), chs. 4 and 7.

passions had faded, there had been more extensive discussion of the whole process of peace-making. Unfortunately, far more attention has been devoted by soldiers over the centuries to fighting wars and by diplomats and statesmen to preventing wars through conflict resolution than to postwar peace conferences. Statesmen actually involved in peace conferences have been primarily concerned in their memoirs with defending their decisions rather than formulating strategic advice. Relatively few statesmen and diplomats have examined the general handicaps faced after great wars: the popular expectations which cannot be satisfied, the hostilities which cannot be assuaged, the losses and damage which can never be made good, the brutal choices between weakening the enemies or trusting to their good intentions, knowing that in most cases they will never forgive or forget the humiliation of defeat.

The best-known histories of previous peace conferences have been published just after the end of wars. The publication dates speak for themselves: Sir Charles Webster's collection of documents on the Vienna Congress was published in 1921, Harold Nicolson's study of the Congress of Vienna appeared in 1946, and William O. Shanahan's assessment of the disarmament of the Prussian army came out the previous year. But by then it was too late for harried statesmen and diplomats to pay attention to their conclusions. Moreover, conclusions need to be reiterated in peacetime or they will be forgotten; Churchill and Roosevelt knew in 1945 that reparations could not easily be squeezed from vanquished nations but, by the 1990s, allied statesmen were again trying to compel the Iraqis to 'pay for' the damage they had caused.

Because of the relative paucity of the literature, the strategy of peace-making is still ill-formulated. National leaders often speak and behave at peace conferences as if the problems they encounter are unique rather than perennial ones for those in their position: Clemenceau, Wilson, and Lloyd George arguing in Paris over reparations, war guilt, and the fate of the German armed forces; Eden, Molotov, and Hull discussing in Moscow whether Germany should be partitioned; Churchill, Roosevelt, and Stalin arguing at Teheran over how many Germans should be put to the sword. The nature of the debates had changed since the eighteenth century because democratic statesmen were more restricted in their options, but these discussions still echoed peace-makers' talk down the ages, from the time when the Thebans and Spartans disputed whether the city of Athens should be destroyed forever.

Forced disarmament has suffered from analytical neglect along-side other aspects of peace-making. Statesmen resort to such meas-ures partly to justify their support for the war and partly in a genuine attempt to prolong the imbalance of power created by their victory. They try to influence the future behaviour of a defeated state by both altering its constitution and diminishing its power. In 1815, 1919, and 1945 the victorious powers insisted that new governments should be installed in the defeated nations. Napoleon, Kaiser Wilhelm, and Hitler were each to be driven from power or killed and replaced by more sympathetic leaders. But in none of these cases were the allies satisfied that this gave them enough security. The new governments might be forced from office by their discontented peoples or they might be tempted themselves to rebuild their country's strength, hence they had to sign treaties accepting the reduction in their military power, even though this might reduce their credibility with their own people. Castlereagh, Wellington, and Alexander might say that the struggle had been against Napoleon and not against the French people as a whole, but they knew that this was a convenient myth to reduce the ferocity of the settlement. Thus forced disarmament and the instal-lation of a friendly government were not as contradictory as they appeared to the defeated peoples.

Forced disarmament is clearly no panacea, but it is equally clearly a perennial aspect of peace-making. Its importance is in-creasing, not only because other measures for reducing the power of a defeated enemy have become unthinkable, but also because wars become ever more costly and destructive. Military leaders may be sceptical of its efficacy and advisability. Political analysts may not consider it worth examination, but it will recur after each great war in which one side is decisively defeated and democratic statesmen seek something more than the negative objective of defeating enemy forces and restoring the status quo. They and their people will wish, however ineffectively, to prolong the achieve-ments of victory. Questioning the value of forced disarmament may come to be synonymous for liberal democracies with question-ing the value of war itself.

APPENDIX

Selected Articles from Treaties relating to Enforced Disarmament

Treaty between King Henri II and Queen Elizabeth I
Signed at Cateau-Cambresis, 2 April 1559
Article 15
The port of Eyemouth in Scotland, and all buildings erected by the French, the Scottish or the English, in violation of the treaty of Boulogne, shall be demolished within three months from the date of this treaty.

Premier traité d'amitié entre le Czar, Pierre I, et les Turcs
Signed at Pruth 10/12 July 1711.
Article I
Que la Forteresse d'Azoph sera rendue a l'Empire Ottoman, dans l'état ou elle étoit, lorsqu'elle fut prise, avec toutes les Terres et Juridictions qui en dependent.
Article II
Que les trois Forteresses de Tychan, Kaminiek, et du nouveau Fort construit près de Samar seront démolies, et le canon du dit dernier Fort avec toutes les munitions remis à l'Empire: Et qu'il ne sera jamais permis de rebâtir d'autres Forts dans les dits trois endroits.

Traité de paix et d'amitié entre la Porte Ottoman et Sa Majesté Czarienne
Signed at Constantinople 5/12 avril 1712.
Article IV
Comme la Ville d'Asoph est située à l'extrémité de l'Empire Ottoman et que la Forteresse de Circaski est sur les Confins de la Muscovie comme Place frontière, de sorte que si l'on bâtissoit quelques nouveaux Forts entre les deux, cela ne manqueroit pas de causer quelque mécontentement et quelque jalousie, on est convenu, pour l'éviter, qu'il ne sera point bâti de nouveaux Forts entre ces Places frontières ni d'une part, ni de l'autre. En outra cela, que dans l'espace de quatre Mois, à compter du jour de la signature de la présente Convention, tout Fort ou quelque Place que ce soit, ayant l'air de Forteresse, située entre les deux susdites Places

frontières sur le Territoire de la dernière, pour la conservation de Magasin de Tagharrock, sera détruite jusqu'aux fondemens . . .

Treaty of Peace and Friendship between the Most Serene and Most Potent Princess Anne . . . and the Most Serene and Most Potent Prince Louis

Signed at Utrecht 31 March/12 April 1713
Article IX
The most Christian King shall take care that all the fortifications of the city of Dunkirk shall be razed, that the harbour be filled up, and that the sluices or moles which serve to cleanse the harbour be levelled, and that at the said king's own expence, within the space of five months after the conditions of peace are concluded and signed; that is to say, the fortifications towards the sea within the space of two months, and those towards the land, together with the said banks, within three months; on this express condition also, that the said fortifications, harbour, moles or sluices, be never repaired again.

Definitive Treaty of Peace and Friendship between France and Great Britain

Signed at Versailles, 3 September 1783
Article XVII
Le Roi de la Grande Bretagne voulant donner à sa Majesté très Chrétienne une prévue sincère de réconciliation et d'amitié, et contribuer à rendre solide la paix rétablie entre leurs dites Majestés, consent a l'abrogation et suppression de tous les articles relatifs à Dunkerque, a compter du traité de paix conclu à Utrecht en 1713, inclusivement jusquà ce jour.

Treaties between France and Prussia

Signed at Paris 8 September 1808
Separate Articles
Article 1.
S.M. le Roi de Prusse, voulant éviter tout ce qui pourrait donner de l'ombrage à la France, prend l'engagement de n'entretenir pendant 10 ans, a compter du 1er Janvier 1809, que le nombre de troupes ci-dessous specifie, savoir:
10 Régiments d'infanterie formant un effectif de 22,000 hommes.
8 Régiments de cavalerie ou 32 escadrons formant au plus un effectif de 8,000 hommes.
Un corps d'artilleurs mineurs et sapeurs au plus de 6,000
Non compris la Garde du Roi évaluée infanterie et cavalerie au plus 6,000

Total 42,000 hommes

Article 2.
Les dix ans apres, S.M. le Roi de Prusse rentrera dans le droit commun et entretiendra le nombre de troupes qui lui paraîtra convenable suivant les circonstances.
Article 3.
Il ne sera fait, pendant ces dix ans, aucunne levée extraordinaire de milice ou de gardes bougeoises, ni aucun rassemblent tendant à augmenter la force ci-dessus spécifiée.
Article 4.
S.M. le Roi de Prusse s'engage à ne conserver à son service aucun sujet appartenant aux provinces qu'il a cédées.
Article 5.
En retour le la garantie stipules dans le Traité de ce jour, et comme caution d'alliance contractée avec la France S.M. le Roi de Prusse promet de faire cause commune avec S.M. l'Empereur des Français si la guerre vient à se déclarer entre lui et l'Autriche, et dans ce cas, de mettre à sa disposition une division de 16,000 hommes, tant infanterie que cavalerie et artillerie. Le présent engagement durera dix années ...
Article 6.
Les présent articles séparés seront ratifiés et les ratifications en seront échangées dans le même delas que celles des Traités de ce jour.

Military Convention between Austria and France

Signed at Vienna 27 October 1809
Separate Articles
Article 2
S.M. l'Empereur d'Autriche, d'après la diminution de ses possessions, et empressée d'éloigner tout ce qui pourrait faire naître l'inquiétude et la défiance entre les deux Etats, ainsi que de manifester ses dispositions politiques, s'engage à réduire les cadres de ses troupes de manière que le nombre total des troupes de toutes armes et de tout genre ne s'élève pas au-dessus de 150,000 hommes, pendant la durée de la guerre maritime.

Protocol of Conference between Great Britain, Austria, Prussia and Russia, respecting the Territorial Arrangements and Defensive System of the Germanic Confederation

Signed at Paris 3 November 1815
Article I
Considering that His Majesty the King of the Low Countries ought to participate in a just proportion in the advantages resulting from the present arrangement with France, and considering that state of his Frontiers on the side of that country, it is agreed, that the Districts which formed part of the Belgic Provinces, of the Bishopric of Liège and the

Duchy of Bouillon, as well as the towns of Philippeville and Marienburg, with their Territories, which France is to cede to the Allies, shall be assigned to His Majesty the King of the Low Countries to be united to his dominions.

His Majesty the King of the Low Countries shall receive, moreover, out of that part of the French contribution which is destined towards strengthening the line of Defence of the States bordering upon France, the sum of 60,000,000 Francs, which shall be laid out in fortifying the Frontiers of the Low Countries in conformity with the plans and regulations which the Powers shall settle in this respect.

Article II

The districts which, by the new Treaty with France, will be detached from the French territory in the department of the Sarre and the Moselle, including the fortress of Sarre-Louis, shall be united to the dominions of the King of Prussia.

Article III

The territories which France is to cede in the department of the Lower Rhine, including the Town and Fortress of Landau, shall be united to those possessions on the left bank of the Rhine which devolve to His Imperial and Royal Apostolic Majesty by the Final Act of the Congress of Vienna. His Majesty may dispose of his possessions on the left bank of the Rhine, in the territorial arrangements with Bavaria and other States of the Germanic Confederation . . .

Article V

In order that His Majesty the King of Sardinia may participate in a just proportion, in the advantages resulting from the present arrangements with France, it is agreed, that the portion of Savoy which remained to France in virtue of the Treaty of Paris of 30 May, 1814, shall be united to the dominions of His Said Majesty with the exception of the Commune of St Julian, which shall be given to the Canton of Geneva . . .

His Majesty the King of Sardinia shall receive, moreover, out of that part of the French contribution which is destined for the strengthening of the line of Defence of the States bordering upon France, the sum of 10,000,000 Franks, which is to be laid out in fortifying his frontiers, in conformity with the plans and regulations which the Powers shall settle in this respect.

It is likewise agreed that, in consideration of the advantages which His Sardinian Majesty will derive from these dispositions, both in the extension and means for defending his territory, that part of the pecuniary Indemnity payable by France, to which His said Majesty might lay claim, shall serve towards putting the indemnities of Austria and Prussia on the level of a just proportion . . .

Article VII

... In consideration of the arrangements above specified the Four Powers insure to His Majesty the King of Bavaria the following advantages:–
a. An amount proportional to the part of the French contributions intended to reinforce the defensive line of the frontier States ...
d. the right to garrison the fortified town of Landau, which will be one of the fortresses of the Germanic Confederation ...

General Treaty of Peace between Great Britain, Austria, France, Prussia, Russia, Sardinia, and Turkey

Signed at Paris, 30 March 1856
Article XI
The Black Sea is Neutralized; its Waters and its Ports, thrown open to the Mercantile Marine of every Nation, are formally and in perpetuity interdicted to the Flag of War, either of the Powers possessing its coasts, or of any other Power ...
Article XII
... In order to afford to the Commercial and Maritime interests of every Nation the security which is desired, Russia and the Sublime Porte will admit Consuls into their Ports situated upon the Coast of the Black Sea in conformity with the principles of International Law.

Convention between Russia and Turkey, limiting their Naval Force in the Black Sea

Signed at Paris, 30 March 1856
Article I
The High Contracting Parties mutually engage not to have in the Black Sea any other Vessels of War than those of which the number, the force, and the dimensions are hereinafter stipulated.
Article II
The High Contracting Parties reserve to themselves each to maintain in that Sea 6 steam-vessels of 50 metres in length at the line of flotation, of a tonnage of 800 tons at the maximum, and 4 light steam or sailing vessels of a tonnage which shall not exceed 200 tons each.

The Peace of Brest-Litovsk — The Treaty of Peace Between Russia and Germany, Austria–Hungary, Bulgaria, and Turkey

Signed at Brest Litovsk, 3 March 1918
Article IV
As soon as a general peace is concluded and Russian demobilization is carried out completely, Germany will evacuate the territory lying to the east of the line designated in paragraph 1 of Article III ...

Article V
Russia will, without delay, carry out the full demobilization of her army
inclusive of those units recently organized by the present Government.
Furthermore Russia will either bring her warships into Russian ports and
there detain them until the day of the conclusion of a general peace, or
disarm them forthwith . . .

Limitation of the Armaments of Germany in Accordance with the
Military, Naval and Air Clauses of the Treaty of Versailles

Signed at Versailles, 28 June 1919
In order to render possible the initiation of a general limitation of the
armaments of all nations, Germany undertakes strictly to observe the
military, naval and air clauses which follow.

Article 160
1. By a date which must not be later than March 31st 1920, the German
Army must not comprise more than seven divisions of infantry and three
divisions of cavalry.
The total number of effectives in the Army of the States constituting
Germany must not exceed one hundred thousand men, including officers
and establishments of depots. The Army shall be devoted exclusively to
the maintenance of order within the territory and to the control of the
frontiers.
The total effective strength of officers, including the personnel of staffs,
whatever their composition, must not exceed four thousand . . .
The number and strength of the units of infantry, artillery, engineers,
technical services and troops . . . constitute maxima which must not be
exceeded.
The following units may each have their own depot
              An Infantry regiment;
              A Cavalry regiment;
              A regiment of Field Artillery;
              A battalion of Pioneers.
3. The divisions must not be grouped under more than two army corps
headquarters staffs.
The maintenance or formation of forces differently grouped or of other
organizations for the command of troops or for preparation for war is
forbidden.
The Great German General Staff and all similar organizations shall be
dissolved and may not be reconstituted in any form.
The officers or persons in the position of officers, in the Ministries of War
in the different States in Germany and in the Administrations attached to
them, must not exceed three hundred in number and are included in the

maximum strength of four thousand laid down in the third sub-paragraph of paragraph (1) of this article.

Article 162
The number of employees or officials of the German States, such as Customs officers, forest guards and coastguards, shall not exceed that of the employees or officials functioning in these capacities in 1913.

The number of gendarmes and employees or officials of the local or municipal police may only be increased to an extent corresponding to the increase of population since 1913 in the districts or municipalities in which they are employed.

These employees and officials may not be assembled for military training.

Article 164
Up to the time at which Germany is admitted as a Member of the League of Nations, the German Army must not possess an armament greater than the amounts fixed . . . with the exception of an optional increase not exceeding one-twenty-fifth part for small arms and one-fiftieth part for guns, which shall be exclusively used to provide for such eventual replacements as may be necessary.

Germany agrees that, after she has become a Member of the League of Nations, the armaments fixed . . . shall remain in force until they are modified by the Council of the League. Furthermore, she hereby agrees strictly to observe the decisions of the Council of the League on this subject.

Article 166
At the date of March 31st, 1920, the stock of munitions which the German Army may have at its disposal shall not exceed the amounts fixed in Table No. 3. annexed to this section [not reproduced].

Within the same period the German Government will store these stocks at points to be notified to the Governments of the Principal Allied and Associated Powers . . .

Article 167
The number and calibre of the guns constituting at the date of the coming into force of the present Treaty the armament of the fortified works, fortresses, and any land or coast forts which Germany is allowed to retain must be notified immediately by the German Government to the Governments of the Principal Allied and Associated Powers, and will constitute maximum amounts which may not be exceeded.

Within two months from the coming into force of the present Treaty, the maximum stock of ammunition for these guns will be reduced to and maintained at the following uniform rates: fifteen hundred rounds per piece for those the calibre of which is 10.5 cm. and under; five hundred rounds per piece for those of higher calibre.

Article 168

The manufacture of arms, munitions, or any war material shall only be carried out in factories or works the location of which shall be communicated to and approved by the Governments of the Principal Allied and Associated Powers, and the number of which they retain the right to restrict.

Article 170

Importation into Germany of arms, munitions, and war material of every kind shall be strictly prohibited.

The same applies to the manufacture for, and export to, foreign countries of arms, munitions, and war materials of every kind.

Article 171

The use of asphyxiating, poisonous or other gases and all analogous liquids, materials, or devices being prohibited, their manufacture and importation are strictly forbidden in Germany.

The same applies to materials specially intended for the manufacture, storage and use of the said products or devices.

The manufacture and the importation into Germany of armoured cars, tanks and all similar constructions suitable for use in war are also prohibited.

Article 173

Universal compulsory military service shall be abolished in Germany.

The German Army may only be constituted and recruited by means of voluntary enlistment.

Article 174

The period of enlistment for non-commissioned officers and privates must be twelve consecutive years.

The number of men discharged for any reason before the expiration of their term of enlistment must not exceed in any year five per cent of the total effectives fixed by the present Treaty.

Article 175

The officers who are retained in the Army must undertake the obligation to serve in it up to the age of forty-five years at least.

Officers newly appointed must undertake to serve on the active list for twenty-five consecutive years at least.

Officers who have previously belonged to any formations whatever of the Army, and who are not retained in the units allowed to be maintained, must not take part in any military exercise whether theoretical or practical, and will not be under any military obligations whatever.

The number of officers discharged for any reason before the expiration of their term of service must not exceed in any year five per cent of the total effectives of officers provided for in the present Treaty.

Article 176

On the expiration of two months from the coming into force of the present Treaty, there must only exist in Germany the number of military schools which is absolutely indispensable for the recruitment of the officers of the units allowed. These schools will be exclusively intended for the recruitment of officers of each arm, in the proportion of one school per arm.

The number of students admitted to attend the courses of the said schools will be strictly in proportion to the vacancies to be filled in the cadres of officers. The students and the cadres will be reckoned in the effectives fixed by the present Treaty.

Article 177

Educational establishments, the universities, societies of discharged soldiers, shooting or touring clubs and, generally speaking, associations of every description, whatever be the age of their members, must not occupy themselves with any military matters.

In particular, they will be forbidden to instruct or exercise their members, or to allow them to be instructed or exercised, in the profession or use of arms . . .

Article 178

All measures of mobilization or appertaining to mobilization are forbidden.

In no case must formations, administrative services or general staffs include supplementary cadres.

Article 179

Germany agrees from the coming into force of the present Treaty not to accredit nor to send to any foreign country any military, naval, or air mission nor to allow any such mission to leave her territory, and Germany, further, agrees to take appropriate measures to prevent German nationals from leaving her territory to become enrolled in the Army, Navy, or Air Services of any foreign Power . . .

The present provision does not however affect the right of France to recruit for the Foreign Legion in accordance with French military laws and regulations.

Article 180

All fortified works, fortresses, and field works situated in German territory to the west of a line drawn fifty kilometres to the east of the Rhine shall be disarmed and dismantled.

The construction of any new fortification, whatever its nature and importance, is forbidden in the zone referred to in the first paragraph of the present article.

The system of fortified works of the southern and eastern frontiers of Germany shall be maintained in its existing state.

Article 181
After the expiration of a period of two months from coming into force of the present Treaty, the German forces in commission must not exceed:

    6 battleships of the Deutschland or Lothringen type
    6 light cruisers
    12 destroyers
    12 torpedo-boats

or an equal number of ships constructed to replace them as provided in Article 190.
No submarines are to be included.
All other warships, except where there is provision in the present Treaty, must be placed in reserve or devoted to commercial purposes.

Article 183
After the expiration of a period of two months from the coming into force of the present Treaty, the total personnel of the German Navy, including the manning of the fleet, coast defences, signal stations, administration and other land services, must not exceed fifteen thousand, including officers and men of all grades and corps.
The total strength of officers and warrant officers must not exceed fifteen hundred . . .

Article 190
Germany is forbidden to construct or acquire any warships other than those intended to replace the units in commission provided for in Article 181 of the present Treaty.
The warships intended for replacement purposes as above shall not exceed the following displacement:

    Armoured ships 10,000 tons
    Light cruisers 6,000 tons
    Destroyers 800 tons
    Torpedo-boats 200 tons

Except where a ship has been lost, units of the different classes shall only be replaced at the end of a period of twenty years in the case of battleships and cruisers, and fifteen years in the case of destroyers and torpedo-boats, counting from the launching of the ship.

Article 191
The construction of acquisition of any submarine, even for commercial purposes, shall be forbidden in Germany.

Article 194
The personnel of the German Navy shall be recruited entirely by voluntary engagements entered into for a minimum period of twenty-five consecutive years for officers and warrant officers; twelve consecutive years for petty officers and men.
The number engaged to replace those discharged for any reason before the

expiration of the term of service must not exceed five per cent per annum of the totals laid down in this Section (Article 183).

The personnel discharged from the Navy must not receive any kind of naval or military training or undertake any further service in the Navy or Army . . .

Article 198

The armed forces of Germany must not include any military or naval air forces.

Limitation of the Armaments of Austria in accordance with the Military, Naval, and Air Clauses of the Treaty of Saint-German-En-Laye

Signed at Saint-German-en-Laye, 10 September 1919.

Article 119

Universal compulsory service will be abolished in Austria. The Austrian Army will in future only be constituted and recruited by means of voluntary enlistment.

Article 120

The total number of military forces in the Austrian Army shall not exceed 30,000 men, including officers and depot troops.

Subject to the following limitations, the formations composing the Austrian Army shall be fixed in accordance with the wishes of Austria:

1. the effectives of units must be fixed between the maximum and minimum figures shown in table IV [not included].

2. the proportion of officers, including the personnel of staffs and special services, shall not exceed one-twentieth of the total effectives with the colours, and that of non-commissioned officers shall not exceed one-fifteenth of the total effectives with the colours.

3. the number of machine-guns, guns and howitzers shall not exceed per thousand men of the total effectives with the effectives of those fixed in table V [not included].

The Austrian Army shall be devoted exclusively to the maintenance of order within the territory of Austria and to the control of her frontiers.

Article 122

All measures of mobilization or appertaining to mobilization are forbidden.

In no cases must formations, administrative services or staffs include supplementary cadres.

The carrying out of preparatory measures with a view to requisitioning animals or other means of military transport is forbidden.

Article 123

The number of gendarmes, Customs officers, foresters, members of the local or municipal police or other like officials may not exceed the number of men employed in a similar capacity in 1913 within the boundaries of Austria as fixed by the Treaty . . .

Article 125

All officers must be regulars. Officers now serving who are retained in the Army must undertake the obligation to serve in it up to the age of 40 years at least. Officers now serving who do not join the new Army will be released from all military obligations; they must not take part in any military exercises, whether theoretical or practical.

Officers newly appointed must undertake to serve on the active list for 20 consecutive years at least.

The number of officers discharged for any reason before the expiration of their term of service must not exceed in any year one-twentieth of the total of officers provided for in Article 120. If this proportion is unavoidably exceeded, the resulting shortage must not be made good by fresh appointments.

Article 126

The period of enlistment for non-commissioned officers and privates must be for a total period of not less than 12 consecutive years, including at least 6 years with the colours . . .

Article 128

Educational establishments . . . as well as all sporting and other clubs must not occupy themselves with any military matters.

Article 132

The manufacture of arms, munitions and war material shall only be carried on in one single factory, which shall be controlled by and belong to the State, and whose output must be strictly limited to the manufacture of such arms, munitions and war material as is necessary for the military forces and armaments referred to . . .

The manufacture of sporting weapons is not forbidden, provided that sporting weapons manufactured in Austria taking ball cartridge are not of the same calibre as that of military weapons used in any European army.

Article 134

The importation into Austria of arms, munitions and war material of all kinds is strictly forbidden.

The manufacture for foreign countries and the exportation of arms, munitions and war material is also forbidden.

Article 135

The use of flame-throwers, asphyxiating, poisonous or other gases, and all similar liquids, materials or devices being prohibited, their manufacture and importation are strictly forbidden in Austria . . .

The manufacture and importation into Austria of armoured cars, tanks or any similar machines suitable for use in war are equally forbidden.

Article 136
Austria will have the right to maintain on the Danube for the use of the river police three patrol boats.
Article 140
The construction or acquisition of any submarine, even for commercial purposes, shall be forbidden in Austria.
Article 144
The armed forces of Austria must not include any military or naval air forces.

[The Treaties of Neuilly of 27 November 1919 and of Trianon of 4 June 1920, which limited the armed forces of Bulgaria and Hungary respectively, followed the pattern of the Treaty of Saint-Germain with appropriate alterations for force levels.]

The Franco-German Armistice 1940

Signed in the forest of Compiègne on 22 June 1940
Article I
The French Government orders the cessation of hostilities against the German Reich in France as well as in its possessions, colonies, and protectorates, and at sea. It orders those French troops that are already surrounded by the German troops to lay down their arms immediately.
Article III
In the occupied area the German Reich has all the rights of an occupying Power . . . The French Government engages to facilitate in every way the regulations relating to the exercise of these rights . . .
Article IV
French armed forces on land, on the sea, and in the air are to be demobilized and disarmed in a period still to be set, but the troops necessary to maintain order within the country are excepted. Germany and Italy will fix their strength and their armaments.
The French armed forces in the territory to be occupied by Germany are to be withdrawn into territory not to be occupied and demobilized. Before being withdrawn into the unoccupied zone these troops will leave their weapons and equipment at the places where they are on the entry into force of the present agreement. They will be responsible for the due delivery of the equipment and arms to the German troops.
Article V
As a guarantee of the execution of the terms of the armistice it is stipulated that there shall be handed over in good condition all guns, tanks, anti-tank guns, military aircraft, all means of transport and ammunition of French units which are still resisting and which at the time this agreement

becomes effective are in the territory not to be occupied. The German armistice commission will decide the extent of these deliveries . . .

Article VI

The arms, munitions and war equipment of every type, remaining in unoccupied French territory, in so far as it is not left at the disposal of the French Government for the arming of authorized French formations, must be stored or put in safe keeping under German or Italian control . . . The manufacture of new war material in the unoccupied territory is to be stopped immediately.

Article VIII

The French navy (except for that part of it which is to be left at the disposal of the French Government for the protection of French interests in the colonial empire) will be concentrated in ports to be designated, and will be demobilized and disarmed under the control of Germany and Italy respectively. The peacetime stations of ships should decide the designation of ports.

The German Government solemnly declares to the French Government that it does not intend to use the French war fleet which is in harbours under German control for its purposes in war, with the exception of units necessary for the purpose of guarding the coast and sweeping for mines. It further solemnly and expressly declares that it does not intend to bring up any demands respecting the French war fleet at the conclusion of peace.

All warships outside France are to be recalled to France, with the exception of that portion of the French war fleet which shall be designated to represent French interests in the colonial empire.

Article X

The French Government pledges not to undertake any hostile action against the German Reich with any portion of its remaining armed forces or in any other manner.

The French Government will also prevent members of its armed forces from leaving the country and prevent armaments of any sort, including ships, planes, etc., being taken to England or any other place abroad. The French Government will forbid French citizens to fight against Germany in the service of the States with which the German Reich is at war. French citizens who violate this provision will be treated by German troops as insurgents.

Article XVIII

The French Government will bear the costs of maintenance of German occupation troops on French soil.

Article XX

French troops in German prison camps will remain prisoners of war until the conclusion of peace.

Article XXIV
This agreement is valid until the conclusion of a peace treaty. The German Government may terminate this agreement at any time with immediate effect if the French Government fails to fulfil the obligations it assumes under the agreement.

Redraft of the Treaty for the Disarmament and Demilitarization of Germany

January 1947
The Governments of the United States of America, the Union of Soviet Socialist Republics, the United Kingdom of Great Britain and Northern Ireland and the French Republic . . . being determined that . . . the disarmament and demilitarization of Germany shall be enforced so long as the peace and security of the world may require . . . have agreed as follows.

Article I
(A) All German armed forces, including land, air, anti-aircraft, and naval forces, all organizations auxiliary to the foregoing, and all para-military organizations in any form or guise shall be and shall remain completely disarmed, demobilized, and disbanded.
(B) The German War Ministries, the General Staff, and the staffs of all para-military organizations shall be and shall remain disbanded.
(C) No German military or para-military organization in any form or guise shall be permitted in Germany. All activity of any organization, group of persons or individuals which teaches the theory, principles, technique or mechanics of war or prepares the participants for war shall be prohibited.
(D) German nationals shall not be permitted to leave Germany to become enrolled in the armed forces of any foreign power, or to be attached to such armed forces for the purpose of assisting in the military, naval, or air training thereof, or otherwise to perform services in aid of the training or equipping of such armed forces . . .
(E) The German government and German nationals shall be forbidden:
(1) to manufacture or produce in Germany or to import into Germany materials which are specifically and exclusively designed for war purposes, or fissionable materials except as authorized under international agreement;
(2) to conduct fundamental or applied scientific research of a wholly or primarily military nature, in particular with reference to materials referred to under (E) (1) of this Article;
(3) to plan, design, construct, utilize or operate military installations for any purpose.

(F) Except to the extent authorized by the Allied Control Authorities, the German Government and German nationals shall be forbidden:
(1) to operate any civil aircraft from, into, or over the territory of Germany; to manufacture, import, and utilize civil aircraft, aircraft engines, aircraft parts and aircraft supplies; to train aviation personnel; or to engage in any kind of aviation activity . . .
Article II
(A) The enforcement of the provisions of Article I shall be ensured by means hereinafter set forth.
(B) The contracting parties shall within 6 months of the entry into force of the present treaty, establish an Inspectorate which, through its officers and agents, shall conduct in all parts of German territory such inspections, enquiries and investigations as may be necessary to determine whether the provisions of this treaty are being observed . . .
(D) Before the Allied Control Council ceases to be the supreme authority for Germany, the Contracting Parties shall . . .
(2) Establish a Commission of Control. The Commission shall take action upon the affirmative vote of a majority of its members. The Inspectorate shall be placed under the authority of the Commission of Control, to which it shall then report immediately upon the termination of the supreme authority in Germany of the Allied Control Council.
(E) The Commission of Control
(1) shall keep the contracting parties informed of the results of inspection, enquiries and investigations, and of any action which they may take in connexion with any violation of this treaty . . .
(3) Shall submit a report to the contracting parties whenever, in the opinion of the representatives on the Commission of one or more of the contracting parties, there is reason to believe that a violation of the provisions of Article I or of paragraph (d) . . . has occurred or is about to occur . . .
(F) Upon receipt of a report and recommendations from the Commission of Control, the Contracting Parties will promptly consult together and take such prompt action, including action by land, air and sea forces, as may be necessary to ensure the immediate cessation or prevention of the violation of the provisions of Article I. Such action will be taken on agreement of three or more of the Contracting Parties. Action under this Article shall not be taken by less than three of the Contracting Parties . . .
Article VII
(C) The present treaty shall remain in force for a period of 40 years from the date of its coming into force unless before the expiration of that period all the Contracting Parties shall agree that sufficient guarantees against aggression on the part of Germany are otherwise provided. Failing such agreement on their part, the Contracting Parties agree to consult together

six months before the date of expiration of the present treaty for the purpose of determining whether the interests of international peace and security require its renewal, with or without modification, or whether the German people have so far progressed in the reconstruction of their life on a democratic and peaceful basis that the continued imposition of the prohibitions and controls defined herein is no longer necessary.

United Nations Security Council Resolution 687

New York, 3 April 1991

The Security Council . . . Conscious also of the statements by Iraq threatening to use weapons in violation of its obligations under the Geneva Protocol for the Prohibition of the Use in War of Asphyxiating, Poisonous or other Gases, and of Bacteriological Methods of Warfare, signed at Geneva on 17 June 1925, and of its prior use of chemical weapons and affirming that grave consequences would follow any further use by Iraq of such weapons,

Recalling that Iraq has subscribed to the Declaration adopted by all States participating in the Conference of States Parties to the 1925 Geneva Protocol and Other Interested States, held at Paris from 7 to 11 January 1989, establishing the objective of universal elimination of chemical and biological weapons,

Recalling further that Iraq has signed the Convention on the Prohibition of the Development and Production and Stockpiling of Bacteriological (Biological) and Toxin Weapons and on their Destruction, of 10 April 1972 . . .

Aware of the use by Iraq of ballistic missiles in unprovoked attacks and therefore of the need to take specific measures in regard to such missiles located in Iraq,

Concerned by the reports in the hands of Member States that Iraq has attempted to acquire materials for a nuclear-weapons programme contrary to its obligations under the Treaty on the Non-Proliferation of Nuclear Weapons of 1 July 1968 . . .

Recalling the objective of the establishment of a nuclear-weapons-free zone in the region of the Middle East . . .

Conscious also of the objective of achieving balanced and comprehensive control of armaments in the region . . .

7. Invites Iraq to reaffirm unconditionally its obligations under the Geneva Protocol . . . and to ratify the Convention on the Prohibition of the Development, Production and Stockpiling of Bacteriological (Biological) and Toxin Weapons . . .

8. Decides that Iraq shall unconditionally accept the destruction, removal or rendering harmless, under international supervision, of:

a) all chemical and biological weapons and all stocks of agents and all

related subsystems and components and all research, development, support and manufacturing facilities;
b) all ballistic missiles with a range greater than 150 kilometres and related major parts, and repair and production facilities;
9. Decides, for the implementation of paragraph 8 above, the following:
a) Iraq shall submit to the Secretary-General, within fifteen days of the adoption of this resolution, a declaration of the locations, amounts and types of all items specified in paragraph 8 and agree to urgent, on-site inspection as specified below;
b) the Secretary-General, in consultation with the appropriate Governments and, where appropriate, with the Director General of the World Health Organization (WHO), within 45 days of the passage of this resolution, shall develop, and submit to the Council for approval, a plan calling for the completion of the following acts within 45 days of such approval:
I) the forming of a Special Commission which shall carry out immediate on-site inspection of Iraq's biological, chemical and missile capabilities, based on Iraq's declarations and the designation of any additional locations by the Special Commission itself:
II) the yielding by Iraq of possession to the Special Commission for destruction, removal or rendering harmless, taking into account the requirements of public safety, of all items specified under paragraph 8(a) above . . . and the destruction by Iraq, under supervision of the Special Commission, of all its missile capabilities including launchers as specified under paragraph 8(b) above;
III) the provision by the Special Commission of the assistance and co-operation to the Director General of the International Atomic Energy Agency (IAEA) required in paragraphs 12 and 13 below:
10. Decides that Iraq shall unconditionally undertake not to use, develop, construct or acquire any of the items specified in paragraphs 8 and 9 above and requests the Secretary-General, in consultation with the Special Commission, to develop a plan for the future ongoing monitoring and verification of Iraq's compliance with this paragraph to be submitted to the Council for approval within 120 days of the passage of this resolution;
11. Invites Iraq to reaffirm unconditionally its obligations under the Treaty on the Non-Proliferation of Nuclear Weapons, of 1 July 1968;
12. Decides that Iraq shall unconditionally agree not to acquire or develop nuclear weapons or nuclear-weapons-usable material or any subsystems or components or any such research, development, support or manufacturing facilities related to the above . . .
13. Requests the Director-General of the International Atomic Energy Agency (IAEA) through the Secretary-General . . . to carry out immediate on-site inspection of Iraq's nuclear capabilities based on Iraq's declara-

tions and the designation of any additional locations by the Special Commission . . . to develop a plan for submission to the Security Council within 45 days calling for the destruction, removal or rendering harmless as appropriate of all items listed . . . above.

14. Takes note that the actions to be taken by Iraq . . . represent steps towards the goal of establishing in the Middle East a zone free from weapons of mass destruction and all missiles for their delivery and the objective of a global ban on chemical weapons . . .

Bibliography

PUBLISHED TREATIES AND DOCUMENTS

French

Costes, A. *La Délégation Française auprès de la Commission Allemande d'Armistice* (Imprimerie Nationale, Paris, 1947–57).

Editeur des Archives Diplomatiques, *Le Congrès de Vienna et les traités de 1815* (Amyot, Paris, n.d.).

Koch, M. de and Schoell, F. *Histoire abrégée des traités de paix entre les puissances de l'Europe* (Gide Fils, Paris, 1817).

Mantoux, P. *Les Délibérations du Conseil des Quatre* (Centre National de la Recherche Scientifique, Paris, 1955).

United States

Documents on Disarmament 1945–1959 (Department of State, Washington, 1960).

Foreign Relations of the United States, 13 vols (US Government Printing Office, Washington, 1942–7).

Great Britain

Hurst, M. *Key Treaties of the Great Powers* (David and Charles, Newton Abbot, 1972).

Librarian and Keeper of the Papers of the Foreign Office, *Treaties &c. Between Turkey and Foreign Powers 1535–1855* (London, 1855).

Medlicott, W. N., Dakin, D., and Lambert, M. E. *Documents on British Foreign Policy 1919–1939*, 56 vols in 4 series (HMSO, London, 1946–).

Oppen, B. R. von. *Documents on Germany under Occupation* (Royal Institute of International Affairs, Oxford University Press, London, 1955).

Parry, C. *Consolidated Treaty Series* (Oceana, Dobbs Ferry, NY, 1969).

Stevenson, J. *Calendar of State Papers, Foreign Series of the Reign of Elizabeth* (Reprinted by Kraus Reprints, Liechenstein, 1966).

Temperley, H. and Penson, L. M. *Foundations of British Foreign Policy from Pitt to Salisbury* (Cambridge University Press, 1938).

Turnbull, W. *Calendar of State Papers Foreign Series of the Reign of Edward VI 1547–1553* (Longman Green, London, 1861).

Webster, C. K. *British Diplomacy 1813–1815, Select Documents* (G. Bell, London, 1921).

General

League of Nations Armaments Year-book (Geneva, 1932).
Martens, G. F. *Traités de l'Europe* (Librairie de Dieleriel, Gottingue, 1817).
Security Council Documents: S/24108, S/25620, S/25657, S/25775, S/25930, S/25960, S/25970, S/25982.
United National Institute for Disarmament Research, *Security Council Resolution 687 of 3 April 1991 in the Gulf Affair: Problems of Restoring and Safeguarding Peace.*
United Nations Security Council Resolutions Relating to the Situation Between Iraq and Kuwait, UN Department of Information, December 1991.

AUTOBIOGRAPHIES, LETTERS, DIARIES, ETC.

D'Abernon, Viscount. *An Ambassador of Peace* (Hodder and Stoughton, London, 1929).
Baudouin, P. *The Private Diaries of Paul Baudouin*, trans. Sir Charles Petrie (Eyre and Spottiswoode, London, 1948).
Beust, F. F., Count von. *The Memoirs of Count Beust* (Remington, London, 1887).
Bright, J. *The Diaries of John Bright*, ed. R. A. J. Walling (Cassell, London, 1930).
Byrnes, J. F. *Speaking Frankly* (Heinemann, London, n.d.).
Cadogan, A. *The Diaries of Sir Andrew Cadogan, 1938–1945*, ed. D. Dilks (Cassell, London, 1971).
Castlereagh, R. S., Viscount. *Correspondence, Despatches and Other Papers of Viscount Castlereagh*, ed. C. W. Vane (John Murray, London, 1853).
Churchill, W. S. *The Second World War* (Cassell, London, 1948).
—— *Churchill and Roosevelt: The Complete Correspondence*, ed. W. Kimball (Princeton University Press, 1984).
Clarendon, G. W. F. *The Life and Letters of George William Frederick, Earl of Clarendon*, ed. H. Maxwell (Edward Arnold, London, 1913).
Dayan, M. *The Story of My Life* (Weidenfeld and Nicolson, London, 1976).
Gladstone, W. E. *The Political Correspondence of Mr Gladstone and Lord Granville, 1868–1876*, ed. H. Maxwell (Royal Historical Society. London, 1952).

Goebbels, J. *The Goebbels Diaries, 1939–1941*, ed. F. Taylor (Hamish Hamilton, London, 1982).

Gromyko, A. *The Memoirs of Andre Gromyko* (Hutchinson, London, 1989).

Hardinge, C., Baron Hardinge of Penshurst. *Old Diplomacy* (John Murray, London, 1947).

Hull, C. *The Memoirs of Cordell Hull* (Hodder and Stoughton, London, 1948).

Jebb, Hubert Miles Gladwyn, Baron Gladwyn. *The Memoirs of Lord Gladwyn* (Weidenfeld and Nicolson, London, 1972).

Kennan, G. *Memoirs 1925–1950* (Hutchinson, London, 1968).

Khrushchev, N. *Khrushchev Remembers*, trans. S. Talbott (Little Brown, New York, 1971).

Leahy, W. *I Was There* (Gollancz, London, 1950).

Lloyd George, D. *The Truth about the Peace Treaties* (Gollancz, London, 1938).

Metternich, K. *Memoirs of Prince Metternich*, ed. Prince R. Metternich, trans. Mrs Alexander Napier (Charles Scribners' Sons, New York, 1880–1).

Moran, C. M. W., first Baron. *Winston Churchill: The Struggle for Survival* (Constable, London, 1966).

Morgan, J. H. *Assize of Arms, being the Story of Germany and her Rearmament* (Methuen, London, 1944).

Morgenthau, H. *From the Morgenthau Diaries, Years of War 1941–1945*, ed. J. M. Blum (Houghton, Boston, 1967).

Morley, J. *Early Life and Letters of John Morley*, ed. F. W. Hirst (Macmillan, London, 1927).

Murphy, R. *Diplomat among Warriors* (Greenwood Press, Connecticut, 1964).

Napoleon, *Lettres inédites de Napoleon I*, ed. L. de Brotonne (Champion, Paris, 1897).

—— *Correspondance de Napoleon 1er publiée par Ordre de l'Emperor Napoléon III* (32 vols, Plon, Paris, 1858–70).

—— *Correspondance militaire de Napoléon 1er* (Plon, Paris, 1870s).

—— *Lettres inédites de Napoléon I*, ed. L. Lecestre (Plon, Paris, 1897).

Roddie, S. *Peace Patrol* (Chistophers, London, 1932).

Russell, J. *The Later Correspondence of Lord John Russell*, ed. G. P. Gooch (Longman Green, London, 1925).

St Paul, *Colonel St Paul of Ewart, Soldier and Diplomat*, ed. G. G. Butler (St Catherine Press, London, 1911).

Shigemitzu, M. *Japan and her Destiny: My Struggle for Peace* (Hutchinson, London, 1958).

Simon, J. A., first Viscount. *Retrospect* (Hutchinson, London, 1952).

Stimson, H. L. *On Active Service in Peace and War* (Harper, New York, 1948).

Strang, W., first Baron. *Home and Abroad* (André Deutsch, London, 1956).

Tardieu, A. *The Truth about the Treaty* (Hodder and Stoughton, London, 1921).

Truman, H. S. *The Memoirs of Harry S. Truman: Year of Decision, 1945* (Hodder and Stoughton, London, 1955).

SECONDARY SOURCES

Ahmann, R., Birke, A. M., and Howard, M. E. *The Quest for Stability* (Oxford University Press, 1993).

Armstrong, H. F. *Chronology of Failure: The Last Days of the French Republic* (Macmillan, New York, 1940).

Baumgart, W. *The Peace of Paris, 1856* (ABC-Clio, Santa Barbara, Calif., 1981).

Bessel, R. *Germany after the First World War* (Clarendon Press, Oxford, 1993).

Bialer, U. *The Shadow of the Bomber* (Royal Historical Society, London, 1980).

Black, J. *The Rise of the European Powers 1679–1793* (Edward Arnold, London, 1990).

Blainey, J. *The Causes of War* (Sun Books, Melbourne, 1973).

Block, P. J. *History of the People of the Netherlands* (Putnam, London, 1912).

Bond, B. and Roy, I. (eds), *War and Society* (Croom Helm, London, 1975).

Borg, D. and Okamoto, S. (eds), *Pearl Harbor as History* (Columbia University Press, New York, 1973).

Botting, D. *In the Ruins of the Reich* (Allen and Unwin, London, 1985).

Bradbury, J. *The Medieval Siege* (Boydell Press, Woodbridge, 1992).

Buhite, R. *The Dynamics of World Power* (Chelsea House, New York, 1973).

Bullock, M. *Austria 1918–1939: A Study in Failure* (Macmillan, London, 1939).

Burkman, T. W. *The Occupation of Japan: The International Context* (MacArthur Memorial, Norfolk, Va., 1984).

Cabantous, A. *Histoire de Dunkerque* (Editions Privat, Toulouse, 1983).

Carsten, F. L. *The Reichswehr and Politics, 1918–1933* (Clarendon Press, Oxford, 1966).

Carter, A. C. *The Dutch Republic in the Seven Years War* (Macmillan, London, 1971).

Caven, B. *The Punic Wars* (Weidenfeld and Nicolson, London, 1980).

Chandler, D. *The Campaigns of Napoleon* (Weidenfeld and Nicolson, London, 1967).

Charmley, J. *Lord Lloyd* (Weidenfeld and Nicolson, London, 1987).

Clough, R. N. *Embattled Korea* (Westview Press, Boulder, Colo., 1987).

Cobban, A. *A History of Modern France* (Penguin, Harmondsworth, 1962).

Cooper, D. *Talleyrand* (Jonathan Cape, London, 1964).

Corbett, J. *Some Principles of Maritime Strategy* (Brassey's, London, 1988).

—— *England in the Seven Years War* (Longmans Green, London, 1907).

Craig, G. A. *The Politics of the Prussian Army* (Clarendon Press, Oxford, 1955).

—— *Germany 1866–1945* (Clarendon Press, Oxford, 1978).

Davies, N. *God's Playground: A History of Poland* (Clarendon Press, Oxford, 1981).

Donald, R. *The Tragedy of Trianon* (Thornton Butterworth, London, 1928).

Dorey, T. A. and Dudley, D. R. *Rome against Carthage* (Secker and Warburg, London, 1971).

Duffy, C. *Fire and Stone: The Science of Fortress Warfare, 1660–1860* (David and Charles, Newton Abbot, 1975).

—— *The Fortress in the Age of Vauban and Frederick the Great, 1660–1789* (Routledge, London, 1985).

Dunn, F. S. *Peace-Making and the Settlement with Japan* (Princeton University Press, 1960).

Dyck, H. L. *Weimar Germany and Soviet Russia 1926–1933: A Study in Diplomatic Instability* (Chatto and Windus, London, 1966).

Dyson, S. L. *The Creation of the Roman Frontier* (Princeton University Press, 1985).

Edwards, S. *The Paris Commune* (Eyre and Spottiswoode, London, 1971).

Emmerson, J. K. *Arms Yen and Power: The Japanese Dilemma* (Dunellen, New York, 1971).

Feis, H. *Churchill, Roosevelt, Stalin* (Princeton University Press, 1957).

—— *From Trust to Terror: The Onset of the Cold War* (Anthony Blond, London, 1970).

Ferrero, G. *The Reconstruction of Europe: Talleyrand and the Congress of Vienna, 1814–1815* (Putnam, New York, 1941).

Fischer, D. *Towards 1995: Prospects for Ending the Proliferation of Nuclear Weapons* (UNIDIR and Dartmouth, Aldershot, 1993).

Fischer, F. *Germany's Aims in the First World War* (Chatto and Windus, London, 1967).

Gatzke, H. W. *Stresemann and the Rearmament of Germany* (Johns Hopkins Press, Baltimore, Md., 1954).

Geike, R. and Montgomery, E. *The Dutch Barrier 1705–1719* (Cambridge University Press, 1930).

Gilbert, M. *Churchill: A Life* (Heinemann, London, 1991).

Griffith, P. *Military Thought in the French Army, 1815–1851* (Manchester University Press, 1989).

Ha, Y.-S. *Nuclear Proliferation World Order and Korea* (Seoul National University, 1983).

Hamilton, C. D. *Sparta's Bitter Victories* (Cornell University Press, Ithaca, 1979).

Harries, M. and Harries, S. *Sheathing the Sword: The Demilitarisation of Japan* (Heinemann, London, 1987).

Hebbert, F. J. and Rothrock, G. A. *Soldier of France: Sebastien Le Prestre Vauban* (Peter London, New York, 1989).

Henderson, E. F. *Blucher and the Uprising of Prussia against Napoleon* (G. F. Putnam, New York and London, 1911).

Hoensch, J. K. *A History of Modern Hungary* (Longman, London, 1988).

Holland, Rose J. *William Pitt and the Great War* (G. Bell, London, 1911).

Howard, M. E. *The Franco-Prussian War* (Dorset Press, New York, 1990).

Ike, N. *Japanese Politics* (Eyre and Spottiswoode, London, 1958).

Jaffe, L. S. *The Decision to Disarm Germany: British Policy Towards Postwar German Disarmament 1914–1919* (Allen and Unwin, London, 1985).

Jelavich, B. *The Ottoman Empire: The Great Powers and the Straits Question, 1870–1887* (Indiana University Press, Bloomington, 1973).

Kagan, D. *The Fall of the Athenian Empire* (Cornell University Press, Ithaca, 1987),.

Kann, R. A. *A History of the Habsburg Empire 1576–1918* (University of California Press, Berkeley, 1974).

Kawai, K. *Japan's American Interlude* (University of Chicago Press, 1960).

Kihl, Y. W. *Politics and Policies in Divided Korea* (Westview Press, Boulder, Colo., 1984).

King, J. C. *Foch versus Clemenceau* (Harvard University Press, Cambridge, Mass., 1960).

Kiraly, B. K., Pastor, P., and Sanders, I. *War and Society in East Central Europe: Total War and Peacemaking, A Case Study of Trianon* (Brooklyn College Press, New York, 1982).

Kissinger, H. *A World Restored* (Gollancz, London, 1973).

Kitchen, M. *A History of Germany from the 18th Century* (Weidenfeld and Nicolson, London, 1975).

Lane-Poole, S. *Turkey* (Fisher Unwin, London, 1914).
—— *The Life of the Right Honourable Stratford Canning* (Longman Green, London, 1888).
Lawrence, A. W. *Greek Aims in Fortification* (Clarendon Press, Oxford, 1979).
Layhe, E. *The History of Berwickshire's Towns and Villages* (Entire Productions, Paxton, Berwickshire, 1994).
Lazenby, J. F. *Hannibal's War* (Arris and Phillips, Warminster, 1978).
Lefebvre, G. *Napoleon from Tilsit to Waterloo* (Routledge and Kegan Paul, London, 1969).
Lettrich, J. *History of Modern Slovakia* (Atlantic Press, London, 1956).
Livy. *The War with Hannibal*, trans. A. de Selincourt (Penguin, London, 1974).
Longford, E. *Wellington: The Years of the Sword* (Weidenfeld and Nicolson, London, 1992).
Lorenz, K. *On Aggression*, trans. Marjorie Latzke (Methuen, London, 1966).
Lucas, R. *George II and his Ministers* (A. L. Humphrey, London, 1910).
Luttwak, E. N. *Strategy: The Logic of War and Peace* (Belknap Press, Cambridge, Mass., 1987).
Macartney, A. A. *The Habsburg Empire 1790–1918* (Weidenfeld and Nicolson, London, 1968).
Madelin, L. *Histoire du Consulat et de l'Empire* (Hachette, Paris, 1945).
Mahan, A. T. *The Influence of Seapower upon European History 1660–1783* (Methuen, London, 1965).
Mann, G. *Secretary of Europe: The Life of Frederich Gentz, Enemy of Napoleon* (Archon, Hamden, Conn., 1970).
Massie, R. K. *Peter the Great: His Life and World* (Gollancz, London, 1981).
Michael, W. *England under George I* (Macmillan, London, 1939).
Mitchell, A. *Victors and Vanquished: The German Influence on Army and Church in France after 1870* (University of North Carolina Press, Chapel Hill and London, 1984).
Morgan, C. *Reflections in a Mirror* (Macmillan, London, 1945).
Mosse, W. E. *The Rise and Fall of the Crimean System: 1855–71* (Macmillan, London, 1963).
Napier, W. F. P. *History of the War in the Peninsula and in the South of France* (Constable, London, 1992).
Nicolson, H. *The Congress of Vienna: A Study in Allied Unity, 1812–22* (Constable, London, 1946).
Oman, C. A. *A History of the Art of War in the Middle Ages* (Greenhill Books, London, 1991).
Orieux, J. *Talleyrand, the Art of Survival* (Secker and Warburg, London, 1974).

Padour, S. K. *The Revolutionary Emperor: Joseph II of Austria* (Eyre and Spottiswoode, London, 1967).

Palmer, A. *The Lands Between* (Weidenfeld and Nicolson, London, 1970).

Parker, W. H. *An Historical Geography of Russia* (University of London Press, 1968).

Paxton, R. D. *Parades and Politics at Vichy: The French Officer Corps under Marshal Pétain* (Princeton University Press, 1966).

Peterson, E. *The American Occupation of Germany: Retreat to Victory* (Wayne University Press, Detroit, 1977).

Porch, D. *Army and Revolution in France 1815–1848* (Routledge and Kegan Paul, London, 1974).

Preston, A. *General Staffs and Diplomacy before the Second World War* (Croom Helm, London, 1978).

Pritchett, W. K. *The Greek State at War* (University of California Press, Berkeley, 1991).

Pronay, N. and Wilson, K. *The Political Reeducation of Germany and her Allies after World War Two* (Croom Helm, London, 1985).

Pujo, B. *Vauban* (Albin Michel, Paris, 1991).

Puryear, V. J. *England, Russia and the Straits Question, 1844–1856* (University of California Press, Berkeley, 1931).

Roskill, S. W. *Naval Policy Between the Wars* (Collins, London, 1968–76).

Quinn, D. B. and Ryan, A. N. *England's Sea Empire* (Allen and Unwin, London, 1983).

Ranelagh, J. *The Agency: The Rise and Decline of the CIA* (Sceptre, Cambridge, 1987).

Riker, T. W. *Henry Fox First Lord Holland* (Clarendon Press, Oxford, 1911).

Rothenberg, G. E. *Napoleon's Great Adversaries: The Archduke Charles and the Austrian Army 1792–1814* (B. T. Batsford, London, 1982).

Russell, J. G. *Peacemaking in the Renaissance* (Duckworth, London, 1986).

Schaller, M. *The American Occupation of Japan* (Oxford University Press, New York, 1985).

Schonberger, H. B. *Aftermath of War: Americans and the Remaking of Japan, 1945–1952* (Kent University Press, Ohio, 1989).

Schroeder, P. W. *The Transformation of European Politics, 1763–1848* (Clarendon Press, Oxford, 1994).

Scott, H. M. *British Foreign Policy in the Age of the American Revolution* (Clarendon Press, Oxford, 1990).

Seton-Watson, H. *The East European Revolution* (Methuen, London, 1961.

Shanahan, W. O. *Prussian Military Reforms, 1786–1813* (Columbia University Press, New York, 1945).

Shaw, S. *History of the Ottoman Empire and Modern Turkey* (Cambridge University Press, 1976).

Simon, W. M. *The Failure of the Prussian Reform Movement, 1807–1819* (Cornell University Press, Ithaca, 1955).

Sked, A. *Europe's Balance of Power 1815–1848* (Barnes and Noble, New York, 1979).

Sorel, A. *L'Europe et la Révolution française* (Plon, Paris, 1903).

Temperley, H. *A History of the Peace Conference of Paris* (Henry Frowde, Hodder and Stoughton, London, 1920).

Terraine, J. *A Time for Courage: The RAF in the European War* (Macmillan, New York, 1985).

Thomas, D. H. *The Guarantee of Belgian Independence and Neutrality in European Diplomacy, 1830s–1930s* (D. H. Thomas, Kingston, Rhode Island, 1983).

Thomas, H. *Armed Truce* (Atheneum, New York, 1986).

Thompson, M. W. *The Decline of the Castle* (Cambridge University Press, 1988).

Towle, P. *Arms Control and East-West Relations* (Croom Helm, London, 1983).

Trevor-Roper, H. *Hitler's Table-Talk* (Oxford University Press, 1988).

Umiastowski, R. *Poland, Russia and Great Britain 1941–1945* (Hollis and Carter, London, 1946).

Vagts, A. *A History of Militarism* (Hollis and Carter, London, 1959).

Vansittart, R. G., Lord. *Lessons of My Life* (Hutchinson, London, n.d.).

Veve, T. D. *The Duke of Wellington and the British Army of Occupation in France, 1815–1818* (Greenwood Press, Westport, Conn., 1992).

Werner, M. *The Military Strength of the Powers* (Gollancz, London, 1939).

Webster, C. K. *The Foreign Policy of Castlereagh* (Bell, London, 1934).

—— *The Congress of Vienna, 1814–1815* (Thames and Hudson, London, 1963).

Wellesley, V. *Diplomacy in Fetters* (Hutchinson, London, n.d.).

Wheeler-Bennett, J. W. *Brest-Litovsk: The Forgotten Peace March 1918* (Macmillan, London, 1938).

Williamson, D. G. *The British in Germany 1918–1930: The Reluctant Occupiers* (Berg, New York, 1991).

Zayas, A. M. de *Nemesis at Potsdam* (Routledge & Kegan Paul, London, 1979).

Zink, H. *The United States in Germany 1944–1955* (Van Nostrand, Princeton, 1957).

Index